BURNING

DOWN

"THE SHACK"

How the "Christian" Bestseller

Is Deceiving Millions

JAMES B. DE YOUNG

WND Books

D1416593

BURNING DOWN THE SHACK

WND Books

Published by WorldNetDaily
Washington D.C.

Written by James B. De Young
Jacket design by Mark Karis
Interior design by Maria Fernandez, Neuwirth & Associates, Inc.

WND Books are distributed to the trade by:
Midpoint Trade Books
27 West 20th Street, Suite 1102
New York, NY 10011

WND Books are available at special discounts for bulk purchases. WND Books, Inc.
also publishes books in electronic formats. For more information call (541-474-1776) or
visit www.wndbooks.com.

First Edition

ISBN: 978-1-935071-84-6

Library of Congress information available

Printed in the United States of America

10 9 8 7 6 5 4 3 2 1

I dedicate this book to my companion in marriage and life, my beloved wife, Patricia Ann. Her character and love for me and faithfulness to God have inspired me for these forty-five years that our gracious Lord has given us together.

CONTENTS

The Story behind the Story

How *The Shack* was Built

"The first aspect of God is never that of the absolute Master, the Almighty. It is that of the God who puts himself on our human level and limits himself."
—William P. Young, *The Shack*, 88

"When we three spoke ourself into human existence as the Son of God, we became fully human" (ibid., 99).

"Although Jesus is fully God, he has *never* drawn upon his nature as God to do anything" (ibid., 99–100).

"God *cannot* act apart from love" (ibid., 102).

The Father, the Spirit, and Jesus were together at the cross and together were crucified (ibid., 95–96, 102, 222).

God says: "I am not who you think I am." (ibid., 120)

"I don't need to punish people for sin. Sin is its own punishment, devouring you from the inside. It's not my purpose to punish it; it's my joy to cure it" (ibid., 120).

In a "circle of relationship" involving God and people there is no authority and no submission (ibid., 122–124).

God cannot send any of his children to an eternity of hell just because they sin against him (ibid., 162).

"Your understanding of God is wrong." I'm not one who will "condemn most to an eternity of torment" (ibid., 162–164).

God loves all his children the same, equally, and "perfectly," but "differently." (ibid., 154–163)

"Mercy triumphs over justice because of love" (ibid., 164).

"Judgment is not about destruction but about setting things right" (ibid., 169).

"Every human institution is the matrix, a diabolical scheme" (ibid., 122–124).

"I don't create institutions—never have, never will." The institutions of the church, government and marriage are the "man-created trinity of terrors that ravages the earth and deceives those I care about. . . . It's all false" (ibid., 179).

About all people Jesus says: "I have no desire to make them Christians" (ibid., 182).

"I am now fully reconciled to the world. . . . It's not the nature of love to force a relationship but it is the nature of love to open the way" (ibid., 192).

God has opened "a path of reconciliation" (ibid., 222).

The Holy Spirit says: "I have a great fondness for uncertainty" (ibid., 203).

"For you to forgive this man [the murderer] is for you to release him to me and allow me to redeem him. . . . He too is my son. I want to redeem him" (ibid., 224).

"In Jesus, I have forgiven all humans for their sins against me, but only some choose relationship" (ibid., 225).

Dear reader,

It is my pleasure to greet you among the many readers of *The Shack*—and some who may not yet have read it. I know that many of you have been deeply affected by the reading of this novel by William P. Young. Its record-breaking sales show that it is resonating with many people who feel that they are alienated from God and want a way back. Many of you have not found help in local churches and/or by reading the Bible. *The Shack* has touched a nerve that many have not known before. You believe that you are now finding a relationship with God deeper than you've ever experienced. *The Shack* has affected many of your lives, and the catalyst for the author's writing it deeply changed him—*in ways that few people know.*

But the quotes and statements above are just some of the many troubling claims found in *The Shack*. They go to the heart of many important doctrines, including the nature of God himself; the meaning of the incarnation and the crucifixion of Christ, sin and judgment, hell, the church; and many more. Some reviewers have pointed to the portrayal of God the Father as a black woman and the Holy Spirit as an Asian woman as violations of the Ten Commandments. Many who read the Bible have charged that the book contains bad doctrine, even heresy. Is there a basis for this charge? Because of my personal acquaintance with the author, I will bring new light to this question.

Paul Young's Shack Experience

Since January 2008, when I first read *The Shack*, I have been concerned that people are generally uninformed about the background behind the writing of *The Shack* so that they do not read the novel with the carefulness that they should. But Paul Young's (he prefers to go by his middle name) vigorous and repeated denials that he is a universalist, his assertions that he is fully transparent, his claims that his life was dramatically changed several years ago, his peculiar beliefs expressed in interviews, and his aggressive marketing of himself and his book all force the issue—someone must address the book with knowledge of its background.

In scores of meetings in churches and in the media, Paul Young has acknowledged that *The Shack* is partly biographical. Like Mack in his novel, Paul has openly acknowledged his immoral past. But, unlike Mack in his novel, he has not revealed the doctrinal wanderings of his pilgrimage. From my vantage point I am convinced that a major part of Paul Young's real "shack experience" was where he embraced universal reconciliation. It is this doctrine that changed his life and his beliefs (as he himself has claimed) and originally was the main thrust of his novel.

My Acquaintanceship with Paul Young

For more than a dozen years, I have known Paul Young. We have lived within a half dozen miles of each other outside of Portland, Oregon. He lived in Boring; I live in Damascus. Our kids attended and graduated from the same Christian school. Much of our socializing was centered around our kids participating in high school basketball and volleyball. He was an assistant coach at the school. Paul and his kids have helped me put up hay and plant Christmas trees on my small farm. On one occasion, we golfed together. My kids and his have gone camping together. Paul Young and his family never attended my church, but he did his own church—which is reflected in the anti-institutional statements found in *The Shack*.

M3 Forum

One of the most rewarding experiences for me personally and professionally was the time in 1997 when Paul Young and I co-founded a Christian think tank that met monthly during the school year in Portland, Oregon. M3 Forum (named after the approach of the third millennium) allowed an outlet for our group of eight to twelve or more people to discuss and to probe any and all Christian topics and doctrines or problems from the Bible in an open and nonthreatening atmosphere. At times we discussed especially significant issues, such as the date of the creation, the nature of the Flood, the role of government, the emergent church, the nature of Scripture, speaking in tongues, the role of women in ministry, and how science and Scripture complement each other. Some presented book reviews. Near the beginning we had a presentation from a world-renowned British scientist seeking to correlate science and faith. We had only two principles for M3 Forum: the Bible was our ultimate authority, and love was our controlling ethic.

For almost seven years Paul and I drove together to almost every meeting—a trip of about thirty minutes. We would share our latest thinking about a host of things. It now appears that some of the ideas found in *The Shack* took seed during those discussions. But none of the presentations at M3 Forum ever rose to the level of heresy as the evangelical church defines the term—not till 2004, that is.

The Unacknowledged Background to *The Shack*: Paul's Embrace of Universal Reconciliation

In April of that year, in a 103-page, single-spaced paper, Paul surprisingly presented his embrace of universal reconciliation. It is the Christian form of universalism, not the pagan form. It is crucial to understand this distinction. The pagan form, also called general universalism, claims that there are many ways to God and that Jesus Christ is only one of the many ways to God. This is rightly rejected in *The Shack*.

So-called Christian universalism, which Paul Young did embrace, insists that all must come to God through Jesus Christ either before they die or after they die. If people do not believe in Jesus before they die, God will use the fires of hell to purge away (not punish) the unbelief of all, even that of the devil and fallen angels, so that hell is finally emptied of all beings and all go to heaven. In other words, after people die, they have a second chance to repent of their sins—actually not just a chance to repent but a certainty that they will. The point is that in the end hell ceases to exist. There is no eternal judgment. This is the form of universalism embedded in *The Shack*. In the appendix section of this book, I outline the points of universal reconciliation.

Why Do People Embrace Universal Reconciliation?

Why do people embrace universal reconciliation? They are persuaded by one overriding thought—How can a loving God allow people to suffer eternally for their sins? God's love is so powerful that it supersedes his holiness and justice, and he will draw to himself all beings, humans and angels, including the devil. If God is almighty, and almighty in love, then nothing and no one can thwart his love. This is an emotive argument, not a biblical one.

However, the *chief defect of universalism arises from its central belief.* If God's love trumps his justice at any cost, then even the cost of the death of Christ is unnecessary. And if God is unrestricted or unlimited love, then why did he allow hell in the first place? Why did he allow Adam and Eve to fall into sin? Why did he send Jesus Christ to die innocently a horrible death? Indeed, why does sin bother God?

The quotes and citations at the beginning of this introduction are just some of the examples of the theology as found in *The Shack*. In the following pages, I seek to show that they all can be traced back to one core error, and that is universal reconciliation.

Every Christian should be concerned whether universal reconciliation is biblical. This concern is so critical because every person's eternal destiny is at stake. If there is no eternal hell, then the gospel is redefined as a proclamation of God's love and not also as a proclamation that all are sinners and unless people repent and believe the good news about Jesus Christ before they die, they will spend an eternity separated from God.

I am not speaking here about slight variations of doctrine, or about my interpretations of the Bible on some secondary issues that differ from Paul Young's. What is at stake is the very heart and soul of the gospel, the good news. It is about the meaning of the death of Christ on the cross, how people find forgiveness and eternal life, and find peace (relationship) with God. More importantly, it is about how God in the person of Jesus Christ became a human being in the incarnation, about the nature of the Trinity—the nature of God the Father, Jesus Christ the Son, and the Holy Spirit. It is about the reality of heaven and hell, and who will spend eternity where. And universalism has been an antagonist to the Church since the third century.

To Continue the Story behind the Novel: Paul's Life Changed by His Embrace of Universal Reconciliation

Part of Paul Young's extensive defense of universal reconciliation included his personal testimony about how much this new doctrine had impacted his life. He wrote that it had made him a more loving person toward God and toward people. He claimed that universalism had changed his total perspective on life and his beliefs about God, about the church, evangelism, eschatology, and other matters. He deliberately stated that he was putting aside his earlier "evangelical paradigm." He was not just considering a new belief; he had committed to it. Paul Young's paper surprised and saddened me.

In his rejection of an orthodox view of judgment and hell, Paul Young made statements about God the Father and our Savior Jesus Christ that, in my opinion, were slanderous and pushed the envelope of fairness and good taste (see below).

My Response in 2004

In the next month of 2004, I gave a written response to Paul Young's paper before the M3 Forum. I addressed every one of Paul's many points that he had made to defend his new theology—points based in Scripture, history, and logic and emotion. I noted that Christians had come to identify universal reconciliation as heresy in the sixth century. I did not attack Paul Young as a person.

When I concluded reading my paper, Paul, according to my recollection, asked just one question. "Jim," he said, "do you think that I am a Christian?" I answered: "Paul, the only thing that a person must do to become a Christian is to put personal faith in Jesus Christ as one's Savior from sin." Paul said nothing else about this issue.[1] After this meeting, he never came back to M3, even though I pursued his return with several phone calls. Later that year (2004), because of his embrace of universal reconciliation, Paul lost his position as assistant coach in our Christian day school. The doctrinal position of Damascus Community Church and school affirms the eternal suffering of the lost.

Examples from Paul's Defense of Universal Reconciliation

Paul Young's views are common to universalists, and I wrote my paper to answer not just Paul's views but also the position of Christian universalism in general. Here are some examples of Paul's attack on evangelical belief that he wrote in 2004, which I addressed.[2]

1. Jesus is a lamb who would never harm or torment. His "desire is entirely redemptive" (p. 3).
2. Those who commit the unpardonable sin will be pardoned in the coming age, that a "way opens up for even forgiving such a sinner as this" (20).
3. The judgment of the wrath of God (in Rom. 2:5–9) is only remedial and temporary.
4. Jesus "is fundamentally involved" in the torture of billions of people. "In one hour, in a hot searing hell, our Lord will inflict more pain and agony on each person than Satan inflicted on that person during

his entire life." Paul went on to affirm that his own compassion "seems greater than God's." He asserted that "God in the end is grossly unjust"; and that in comparison to Pharaoh, Nero, and Hitler, "The doctrine of eternal torture makes Jesus *a million times* [italics his] more vicious and vindictive than these three put together" (5).

5. "Either those who teach eternal torture are extremely and brutally calloused or *they do not truly believe what they teach*" (italics his) (5).

6. Eternal judgment is "unreasonable, illogical . . . wicked and unjust" for a temporal sin committed within time. Eternal judgment is "sadist humbug."

7. A sinner commits a "crime which is inherent in his own nature." Paul went on to affirm that people have "no choice but to sin," that they are "slaves" to sin, that Adam "already made the choice for each person" (6).

8. The church is to be faulted for creating a way for infants to be saved (6).

9. The traditional view of the death of Christ cannot maintain that Christ ever atoned for sin because he never suffered eternal torment (his comments on Rom. 6:23) (6). Thus, Paul concluded that by evangelical logic, Christ is not the Savior from sins; he died "a failure and in vain and never saved anyone"; and thus "he is not even a good man but a liar, a rogue, and a deceiving rascal." Calvary is a "farce, a travesty, and a sham. Salvation is a mere myth."

10. Paul Young struggled with the nature of God and the command that Jesus gives us, that we should love our enemies, while God himself, in the traditional view, refuses mercy to his enemies and tortures them forever in hell. "Are we required to be more loving than God?" he asked (7).

11. Paul questioned whether physical death fixes our eternal destiny. He claimed that there is not one text in Scripture that limits God's grace to physical life. It would mean that God has "no will and no power" to save a spirit without a body. He concluded that "there is more love and compassion in the natural world than there is in the spirit world." He affirmed that "God will not inflict punishment on men who have not had ultimate knowledge" of the way of salvation (8).

12. Paul asserted that universalism was the view of the church for the first five centuries before Augustine corrupted the theology.[3]

13. Paul asserted that "forever" means only "for an age." One must recognize the limited nature of hell, gehenna, the "smoke that rises forever," and the "lake of fire and second death" (10). None of these are eternal or everlasting.

14. "God's judgment is not vindictive punishment"; rather, it is restorative. Hell and the lake of fire are not final but places of cleansing from which all of "God's people," including Satan and his angels, will be restored to God. All will finally be restored to fellowship with God that he may be all in all (10).

15. The churches "too often cared nothing for [the lost], and cares next to nothing for them today" (37).

There are perhaps millions of ardent supporters of *The Shack*. But reflection on these beliefs, especially numbers 4, 6, 9, and 14, should deeply concern everyone who reads the novel.

Events from 2004 to *The Shack*

Within the next two years after his presentation at M3 Forum, Paul Young completed writing his novel for his children for Christmas. When he sent the manuscript to some friends, they were highly impressed that it had great possibilities. However, these people were opposed to the universalism embedded in it and acknowledge publicly that they spent over a year trying to remove it.[4] The novel was rejected by many mainline Christian publishers, and so Paul and his three friends started their own publishing company. And the rest is history. Several millions of copies have been sold, and a movie is in the making. The point to note here is that *The Shack* was birthed in universal reconciliation.

Subsequent Events Following the Release of *The Shack*

When I met Paul Young in a church in June 2007, he protested my opposing his views and reminded me that he followed universal reconciliation, not universalism. When I carefully read *The Shack* in January 2008, I was dismayed to find universalism still embedded, deeply and subtly, in it. In February 2008, I wrote an extensive review of *The Shack* and set up a Web site to make it and other critical reviews available.[5]

Later in February 2008, I invited Paul and several M3 Forum people and my pastor to come to my home and to hear Paul's concerns about my opposition to his writing. He professed to be no longer a "universalist" but refused to say what he believed. He claimed that he was a person in process, that he was a person in flux. He said: "I am not today where I was yesterday." He did say that he hoped that the lost would not spend an eternity in hell.[6] In response to his request, I agreed to stop circulating his paper from 2004. Yet I did not say that I would remain silent about his history nor about my paper of 2004 that responded to and quoted from his paper.[7]

Now the above history raises serious concerns about Paul Young's theology. There are clear distortions on several core doctrinal issues that go to the heart of Christian faith. On other points Paul is ambiguous.[8] It is not surprising that in *The Shack*, Paul Young has the Holy Spirit (named Sarayu) say that she delights in uncertainty.

The chief points of this account are these. The author of *The Shack* embraced universal reconciliation at some time before April 2004 and wrote in defense of it. He wrote his novel with universal reconciliation in it. The team of four rewrote the novel to attempt to remove its universalism. In 2007, after publishing *The Shack*, Paul clarified that he believed in universal reconciliation, not general universalism. More recently, in 2008, he claimed that he has moved away from this position by stating that he does not want to be pinned down, that he is a person in flux, that he is not "a universalist" (I presume he means that he does not embrace general or pagan universalism).

Now the crucial issue is this. In the end, it does not matter what the author now personally believes. This is not the issue. It is what is in the book that counts and what influenced its contents. The doctrine represented in *The Shack* is the issue.

In the coming pages I show that many of the beliefs of universal reconciliation remain in the novel. This theology is the focal point of what strikes many people as being unbiblical and liberal.[9]

Why I've Related This Personal History with Paul Young

Now some will question the relevance of my dealing with Paul Young's background and writing. But this history lays the groundwork for the plausibility of uncovering universalism and other errors in the book.[10] It is often said that one can understand a book better by knowing the author; we even say this about knowing the Author of the Bible. This applies also to *The Shack*.

Consider some analogies. If we find a polluted stream, we must examine the spring from which it comes to see how it became contaminated. We understand a child by knowing his or her parents. We know what is in the leaves of a tree by what feeds its roots. A computer virus must be traced back to the hacker. So it is with *The Shack*. We can understand its contents by knowing what informs it.

By knowing the author and his beliefs, we are able to avoid

misunderstanding. Other recent books that evaluate *The Shack* lack knowledge of Paul Young's personal background and beliefs, and this ignorance distorts the reviewers' understanding of the novel. For example, Roger Olson makes several judgments about what he thinks Paul Young believes—and he is greatly off base. As a result, he fails to deal critically enough with the doctrinal distortions. Since he does not know Paul's past writings, he prefers to give him the benefit of the doubt—thinking that he could not be a universalist.[11] This same author makes other wrong assumptions: that Paul is theologically trained and a seminary graduate; that he experienced a terribly evil event like that in the novel that brought to him a "great sadness"; that the author experienced a special intervention from God that brought him to a "new awareness of God's character and God's ways"; that the book "rings true" because of (Olson's) own experience; and other uninformed, even gratuitous judgments.[12] People misread *The Shack* because they do not know what the author has embraced in the past that was the catalyst for his writing the novel.

Why I've Written This Book

I'm writing this book for a twofold reason. First, I seek to uncover the embedded errors in *The Shack*, those mostly belonging to universalism, and to show from Scripture why they are so serious—how they strike a dagger into the heart of the gospel.[13] From my personal acquaintance with Paul Young's writing, I bring insight to the reading of Paul's novel that other reviewers lack.

The more positive goal for my writing is to show how there are wonderful stories and instruction in Scripture that would have helped Paul's fictional character, Mack, find the forgiveness and restoration that Mack so desperately sought but was not offered. I will introduce these stories and teaching as Mack enters each step of his conflict with God that is beyond his resolution. I'm convinced that the Bible provides just the right message for his and everyone's crisis. My hope is that those who appreciate *The Shack* will find even greater help and encouragement from the Bible and its ever-relevant message and story for us today. There is no suffering so great that God cannot heal through the Bible.

My other great hope is that people will return to the institutional church to find for their support a community of faith that is both local and international. While the church needs renewal and revival, we need to remember that Jesus laid the foundation for the church by loving it and dying for it (Eph. 5:25). He promised that it would prosper against all assaults (Matt. 16, 18). His apostles expanded on the importance of the church—it is the key to relationships and spiritual growth (for example, in 1 Cor. 12–14; Eph. 2:19–22; 4:4, 11–16; 5:8–19; Col. 2:18–19; 3:12ff.; James 2; Heb. 10:25; 13:17; 1 Pet. 5:1ff.; and much of the books of 1 Timothy, 2 Timothy, and Titus). These texts refer to both the visible, institutional church and the invisible church.

Another concern compels me to write. As an instructor in the New Testament and a life-long teacher in a local church, I have a responsibility to teach the truth of the Bible and to expose error—to declare the "whole counsel of God" (Acts 20:26-27). I am to teach and live out the gospel correctly (Jam. 3:1; Heb. 13:7; 1 Tim. 4:6), to be trustworthy of the gospel (1 Cor. 4:1-2; Gal. 2:14; 2 Tim. 2:15), to feed the sheep (John 21:17).[14]

The Chief Error of *The Shack*

How does *The Shack* approach the teaching of the Bible? A familiar pattern is to give one aspect of a theological issue while ignoring another equally important aspect that qualifies or limits the first one. It is a deceptive maneuver. As Christians, we should be deeply concerned that the theology of *The Shack* (and the theology of any novel) should match *all* that the Bible says.

People can prove almost anything from the Bible, by citing a verse here and there, and out of context. But it is the full context of the Bible that must be the final determiner of what we believe.

Excuses Made for *The Shack*'s Distortions

I know that some will say, "Well, Mack was incapable of hearing what the Bible or other Christians in churches might have said to help him." But why does the author ignore these sources of help when he continues the story years later after Mack is healed, forgiven, and restored to God? How is Mack to grow in relationship with God and with others apart from these? The author deprives his readers of this growth by giving little attention in his novel to the Bible and by subverting the local church.

Other readers will say, "Well, *The Shack* is only fiction." Even the author in public meetings makes this claim to fend off charges of universalism. Yet in a recent publication, the author has said the opposite, that the book is true, that it is mainly his story.[15] If this is so, then he really believes the doctrine in the book. He sought to teach his children what he conceived of as the truth—universal reconciliation (see other excuses in the appendix.)

Clearly, the author wrote the novel to teach theology. The novel serves the theology; the theology does not serve the story. The book belongs to the genre of theological fiction. Universalism has long employed fiction to forward its goals of distorting doctrine.

In addition, reviewers see the book as a serious attempt to teach liberal, even radical, theology. Beal applauds it for bringing the "liberal and radical academic theological discourse from the 1970s and 80s" into more conservative evangelicalism. Jeffrey indicts the book as "post-biblical" and "heretical" and not a new *Pilgrim's Progress.*[16]

My Procedure, both Positive and Negative

In the following pages, I will treat *The Shack* chapter by chapter. In each chapter I will first summarize the main theological content in the context of the story. I will begin my evaluation first by showing the positive features of the chapter's teaching. Then I will raise concerns in each chapter by asking just two or three main questions for reflection, that go to the heart of the doctrine the novel is actually teaching. Then I lead you, the reader, to several great stories and texts of the Bible—those from the Old Testament and from Jesus Christ and his apostles—that provide corrective and helpful understanding of Christian suffering and the love and holiness of God. In a way my response represents a mini-catechism of Christian belief. Sometimes on rare occasions I will share some of my own background and experiences, just as the author has interwoven some of his past into his novel.

Bringing the History and the Novel up to Date

What do we learn about the doctrine in *The Shack* from Paul Young's recent public statements? Now several years later after writing the novel, the author continues to make public statements that reinforce the serious errors that are embedded in the book. While the author has denied in public appearances and interviews that he is a general universalist, he has not, to my knowledge, denied that he follows universal reconciliation. He continues to affirm that God the Father was crucified with Christ; and he denies that we can say that anyone is presently in hell for rejecting Christ.[17] He also has asserted that he does not believe in penal substitution—the evangelical view of the death of Christ.[18] As noted above, he has also said that he "hopes" that the wicked will not suffer eternal punishment. These statements would strongly lead most people to conclude that he follows some form of universal reconciliation—"another gospel" that wanders far from the gospel revealed by Jesus Christ and his apostles. In Galatians 1, Paul the apostle warns that following "another gospel" leads to eternal judgment. The doctrines of *The Shack* distort major beliefs that Christians have agreed on for the past two thousand years. They are not a matter of individual interpretation.

Clarifying Some Issues

In many public meetings and interviews, the author of *The Shack* has affirmed that his own personal shack is no more. No longer is he bound by guilt. He is totally open; he has nothing to hide; he has become fully transparent; he is fully honest. He openly confesses the struggles and conflicts of his childhood: molestation from the natives of New Guinea; his becoming a predator of boys; his anger at being verbally abused by his father; his distance from his mother. He confesses his mixed-up adulthood during which he committed adultery while married. His marriage was about to fall apart. The author has voluntarily made all these things a matter of public record. Then something happened that changed him.

In a probing interview in late 2008, the author attributes his change to "intense therapy." The result was, to cite the words of the interviewer, "a new understanding of God. Instead of a distant, judgmental God, Young says he came to experience God as intimate and loving."[19]

Now everyone of us can rejoice with the author in his turn around. But in 2004 the author wrote that the doctrinal basis for this change was his rejection of the traditional paradigm of evangelical faith and his embrace of universal reconciliation. It is this that changed his beliefs about God and accomplished the personal changes in his life, even before he decided on its validity! Thus the author acknowledges his moral failings but not his past embrace of universal reconciliation. If now he has come full circle and no longer believes in universal reconciliation, to what does he now attribute his doctrinal and personal changes?

The Appendices Have Vital Information

At the end of the book, I devote appendices to (1) questions that I would like to ask Mack and (2) questions that readers of *The Shack* would most likely want to ask me regarding my opposition to *The Shack*. Another appendix (3) cites the several creeds of universalism as published over the last two hundred years. Another appendix (4) shows why evangelical faith is safer than universalism; and why hell, just from the standpoint of logic, must be forever and why people cannot change once they are there. Another appendix (5) addresses the shame that pastors who endorse *The Shack* should feel for their uninformed endorsement of the novel. The final appendix (6) is a discussion guide to this book for use in homes and churches.

Truth and Love

In the following pages I may make misjudgments in what I write. I do not claim to be perfect. But I seek to bring everything in the novel to the touchstone of the Bible to see if it stacks up. I'm not seeking personal vindication or gratification; indeed, it is a painful exercise to expose the doctrinal deviations of a friend. My concentration is on the beliefs found in *The Shack*, not its author. But in the following pages I seek the truth that has been secured by the triumph of the crucified One. My final allegiance is to Jesus Christ.

The greatest challenge to every Christian is to balance love and truth (cf. Phil. 1:9). I have kept this in mind as I've written. My hope is that we together will grow in love and truth toward greater appreciation of the greatness of our Savior and his love for us, and the truth he came to reveal, which alone is able to save us from judgment and to set us free (John 8:32; 17:17). The fiction of universal reconciliation, as represented by *The Shack*, is just that—a fiction.

My hope is that some will come to faith as a result of concentrating on what the Bible truly teaches. Perhaps *Burning Down "The Shack"* will be a tool that helps some find God in the ashes.

Exposing the Foundation of The Shack

WHAT IS IT ALL ABOUT?

Everyone is looking for answers to the questions, "Why do I suffer? Where is God in my suffering? How can God be good if he brings suffering into my life?"

In the first several chapters of *The Shack*, Paul Young builds the background for why Mack came to rebel against God. Readers come to sympathize with Mack and his suffering. They learn why he has entered his "great sadness." These chapters tell why Mack's encounter with God is necessary and why it is so fulfilling and remedial. The following is a summary of the first five chapters.

Summary of Mack's Estrangement from God

As Willie the storyteller recounts it, the story is about Mack, who grew up in the Midwest on a farm. His father, a strict church elder, and an alcoholic, was abusive toward his wife and children. After one particularly awful beating from his dad, Mack put poison in his dad's whiskey and left home for good at the age of thirteen. He spent time overseas, probably fought in a war, and attended a seminary in Australia in his early twenties. After he "had his fill of theology and philosophy," he returned to the States and moved to Oregon where he married his wife, Nan. Apparently his marriage was tumultuous at first, but it had endured for thirty-three years. To Mack and Nan were born five children (three boys, two girls), with two of the boys grown up by the time of the events related in the novel. The youngest child was named Melissa (affectionately known as Missy).

Willie notes that about seven years before, a great tragedy happened to this family. It brought "The Great Sadness" to Mack's life. It resulted in Mack's becoming angry at God. Yet about three and a half years later, something dramatic happened in Mack's life that took away forever the sadness and anger. The novel is Willie's reporting of what Mack told him about the event that caused the sadness and how it was removed for good by a very special encounter with God himself. This encounter took place at the shack.

The story opens with Mack discovering a mysterious note in his mailbox one winter day outside his home in Oregon. It is signed as coming from "Papa" (Nan's name for God). It invites Mack to visit him, if he wishes, at the shack where he will be that weekend. The shack represents the great tragedy that has brought sadness to Mack and his family. Mack decides, however irrational it seems, to return to the shack in the wilderness. This opening event allows the storyteller to go back and relate the tragedy that found its consummation at the shack, and what happened on Mack's apparent return to the shack to meet God.

Mack's "Cloud of Darkness"

On a Labor Day camping trip to the Wallowa Mountains in northeast Oregon, Mack finds himself enjoying the outdoors at Wallowa Lake with his three children and some friends he had made in the campground. Nan, a nurse, is taking a class in Seattle, Washington. On the morning of the last day of the vacation, Mack rescues his son and older daughter from the lake when their canoe overturns.

While he is doing this heroic deed, some unknown person kidnaps his youngest, Missy, and disappears with her into the forests. The FBI and others comb the woods in the search for Missy. It turns out that the kidnapper is already known to the authorities from previous kidnappings and murders and has left his calling card, a piece of jewelry in the form of a ladybug. This has led the authorities to identify him as the "Little Ladykiller." By the end of the next day, the FBI and Forest Service personnel discover a shack deep in the forests, and in it is Missy's bloody, red dress. Like other victims of the killer, Missy's body is never found. It is this tragedy that leads Mack to become "sick of God and God's religion, sick of all the little religious social clubs" that don't make any difference in the world.

Biblical Tales of Tragedy: Jacob and Joseph

Mack's tragedy and its consequences have significant parallels in the Bible. I think of Jacob and his sons in Genesis; of Job in the book by his name; and the example of Jesus Christ himself. These stories have all the earmarks of real-life suffering and tragedy. They involve sibling rivalry and jealousy, parental abuse and deception, youthful rebellion, the loss and death of a favorite son, the death of a beloved wife, economic deprivation, exile—and miraculous reversal—including the special visitation of God. The parallels with the story of Mack are quite unremarkable—because they characterize all of our living experiences.

Joseph was the eleventh child of Jacob and born to Jacob's favorite wife (among two wives and two concubines). Jacob had fallen in love with Rachel while working for his cousin Laban among his other relatives in the land of Haran to the north of Israel. Jacob's (and Joseph's) story began many years before in the story of Abraham.

Abraham, the Father of a New People

Abraham is the forebear of a new people on the face of the earth. He represents the beginning of a new thing in the history of mankind.

He and his descendants are the people through whom God began to rescue the whole of mankind from its sin. In this line, Jesus Christ himself would eventually come to provide salvation from sin and death.

Abraham, Jacob's grandfather, had left his idolatrous background in Ur of Chaldea (modern Iraq) and in obedience to the true God, Yahweh, had traveled west by way of Haran and then into Canaan—following an ancient trade route through the fertile crescent. God told Abraham that he wanted to make from Abraham a great nation of descendants through whom all the world would be blessed (Gen. 12:1–3). It was here in Canaan (modern Israel) that Abraham exercised personal faith in God and was declared to be righteous on the basis of his trust in God (Gen. 15:6; cf. Rom. 4). By faith alone he persevered through many trials until God's promise of a true, special son was accomplished, when he was a hundred and Sarah, his wife, was ninety! Isaac's birth was truly miraculous.

Later, when Isaac was about twenty years old, Abraham proved his faith once again by being willing to offer Isaac as a sacrifice in obedience to God. He still believed that God would keep his promise of a line of descendents that would eventually become a nation (Gen. 22). At the last possible moment, God intervened and stopped Abraham's slaughter of Isaac. God had tested Abraham's faith (Gen. 22:1), and Abraham had come through the test. Hebrews 11 gives the commentary on this event. It points toward Christ and his death at the hands of his Father in heaven.

Later again, Abraham's son Isaac had twin sons, Esau and Jacob, who vied for the blessing of promise passed on from Abraham. Indeed, Jacob deceitfully stole the birthright's blessing from the older twin, Esau. The situation became so conflicted that Jacob, at the urging of his mother, Rebekah, left Canaan and traveled north to Haran (also known as Padan Aram) of northwest Mesopotamia with a special intent: to find a wife and escape from

Esau's revenge. With this background we can return to the story of Jacob in Haran.

Jacob's Great Love and Loss

Jacob worked a total of fourteen years to pay the bride price for Rachel and another seven years to acquire his flocks. Along the way Laban tricked Jacob into marrying Leah, Rachel's sister. Each sister was accompanied by a concubine who also bore children for Jacob. While in Haran, eleven sons were born to Jacob, with Joseph being his last son and the first one from Rachel.

While returning to Canaan after an absence of twenty-one years, Jacob renewed his worship of the true God (Gen. 35). Consequently God changed Jacob's name to Israel ("prince with God"). Shortly thereafter, Jacob had another son from Rachel, who died while giving birth to him—to Benjamin (Gen. 35:16–20). So great a loss was Rachel that Jacob erected a special memorial that lasted for many generations. Jacob could hardly live without her. His favorite wife was his companion no more.

Joseph: From Tragedy to Triumph

Jacob hallowed Rachel's memory by making Joseph, her firstborn, his favorite son. He made for Joseph "a richly ornamented robe" (popularly translated, "a coat of many colors," Gen. 37:3). While Joseph enjoyed such favoritism and even had dreams to reinforce it, his brothers hated him and eventually plotted to kill him. Through the intervention of an older brother, Joseph was spared from death but was sold to traders, who took him south to Egypt, where he was sold as a slave to a high official of Pharaoh.

Now imagine what Joseph must have felt. He had gone from favoritism to slavery, from prominence to rejection, from enjoying life to suffering. All this happened when he was seventeen.

When Jacob saw Joseph's bloodied robe, he concluded that Joseph must have been killed by a wild animal. Like Mack, he entered his own "deep sadness," refusing to be comforted and swearing that he would rather die and join his son in the grave (Gen. 37:34–35). Imagine losing one's favorite, beloved wife and one's favorite son, both within a few years.

Joseph was ill-treated by his brothers, then by Potiphar, the official to Pharaoh. When approached by Potiphar's wife, who wanted to have sex with him, Joseph refused and consequently was falsely accused, removed from his position, and imprisoned. Through this all, Joseph maintained his faith in God and refused to compromise his faith and his fidelity to the moral standards of his God (Gen. 39).

You, reader, know the rest of the story. God had purposes to fulfill unknown to Joseph at the time. One day Joseph was released from prison and exalted to be the highest official of Egypt, second only to Pharaoh. Because of Joseph's dreams, the whole land of Egypt was saved from the ravages of a plague that lasted for seven years. And this salvation reached Jacob and his sons and daughters living in Canaan. Pharaoh invited them to come to live in Egypt to escape the famine. There they prospered. Over the next four hundred years, the Israelites multiplied and became a numerous people, a great nation.

The Significance of the Story of Jacob and Joseph: Perseverance by Faith

Notice the parallels between the stories of Jacob and Joseph and that of Mack in *The Shack*. All experienced great loss, and in Joseph's and Mack's case, in their youth. Even a bloodied garment ties the stories together. They experience special visits from God.

Yet the point I wish to make is that in the biblical accounts there is not a hint that Jacob or Joseph questioned God's promise and his ultimate goodness. It appears that Jacob did enter a state of some bitterness (note Gen. 42:36–38). Years later he was still suffering from grief (43:14) and never got over his loss (44:29–34) until he learned that Joseph was alive. It was then that his spirit revived (45:27). Still the memory of Rachel was never forgotten (48:7). He may have even questioned how God could ever keep his promise to bless all nations through Abraham and his descendants.

But after going to Egypt and living there for seventeen years, he recounted how God had earlier passed on to him the promise made with Abraham (Gen. 48:4). He affirmed his conviction that God was going to keep his word. He made his son Joseph swear that after his death Joseph would take his body back to Canaan to have it buried there (47:29–31), in the land of God's promise.

Not long before he died, Jacob blessed Joseph and his sons and began with an affirmation of his own faith: "May the God before whom my fathers Abraham and Isaac walked, the God who has been my shepherd all my life to this day, the Angel who has delivered me from all harm, may he bless these boys . . ." (48:15–16). Jacob also promised Joseph that God would take Joseph back to the land of his fathers (48:21). Thus Jacob believed that God was good and had preserved him all his long life.

And after Jacob's death, Joseph assured his brothers that he was not in the place of God to take vengeance. Rather, with a keen perception that unites divine sovereignty with human responsibility, he said: "Don't be afraid. Am I in the place of God? You intended to harm me, but God intended it for good to accomplish what is now being done, to the saving of many lives" (Gen. 50:19–20). Earlier Joseph repeatedly invoked God's intervention to explain how he came to be second ruler of Egypt (Gen. 45:5–9). In Joseph's great act of forgiving his brothers he is a type of Christ, who called out from the cross: "Father, forgive them, for they know not what they are doing" (Luke 23:34).

Now my point in relating this story of Jacob and Joseph is to show that there is biblical precedent for the believer's severe suffering. But whereas Paul Young brings Mack out of his great sadness by redefining the nature of God as a God of love who does not express wrath or vengeance, there is no such questioning of the nature of God in the biblical story. Mack faults God for his past suffering and the loss of his daughter, but Jacob and Joseph praise

God that, even though they do not understand his ways, their suffering is not reason enough to redefine and defy God.

While the end of the story is the same for Jacob and Mack—both are restored and come to affirm their trust in God—the manner in which they get there is vastly different. Jacob held on to God's word, his promise, and continued to believe and trust God, but Mack questioned the character of God and redefined him and never invoked the promises of Scripture. Yet it is to these promises that God must be true. It is these promises that carry believers through their trials. *The Shack* mostly ignores the promises of the Bible.

The Story of Job

Now another story needs recounting. That is the story of Job and his wife. It is especially pertinent, lest some think it is wrong to question God. The book of Job has much questioning of God, particularly from Job's wife rather than from Job.

You remember this story. It is one of the great ones in the Bible. God allowed Satan to work havoc in this couple's lives in order to test their fidelity to him. Satan accused Job of believing and following God only because God was good to him. To rebut this charge, God permitted Satan to withdraw all kinds of supports from Job. Job was exceedingly wealthy, with many possessions, a very large household, and had seven sons and three daughters. He is described as "the greatest of all the people of the East" (1:4). More significantly, after the very first mention of his name (1:1), he is said to be "blameless and upright, and one who feared God and shunned evil" (1:1, 8). One proof of this is his regular offering of sacrifices for his children to atone for any sins they may have committed (1:5). Job was a righteous and good man.

The story of Job begins with Satan's (literally "the opponent") claiming that Job is a righteous person who obeys God only because of the personal benefits that come to him. So God permitted Satan to use various means to withdraw his material wealth and kill all his children. What a great loss Job suffered!

Yet after all of this Job "blessed the name of the LORD"; he "did not sin nor charge God with wrong" (1:21–22).

Again, God defended Job to Satan as one who was "blameless and upright, who fears God and shuns evil" (2:3). Job held fast to "his integrity" in spite of the afflictions God brought into his life (2:3). Once again, Satan challenged Job's integrity by asking that he be able to inflict great suffering on Job, believing that suffering would lead Job to curse God. This too God granted but did not allow Satan to take Job's life (2:6). In the midst of his suffering, Job's wife advised him to give up his integrity and "curse God and die" (2:9). With these words Job's wife failed the test of fidelity to God. But Job passed the test.

What made the difference? His wife's lack of faith turned the test into a temptation to rebel against God, to which she yielded. Job identified the counsel of his wife as foolish, and the biblical writer identifies it as sin (2:10).

It is not wrong for a person to question "why" as Job did repeatedly (Job 3), and as Mack in *The Shack* also does. But it is wrong to turn these questions into accusations against God.

Because Job and his friends did not know of Satan's challenge to God in Chapter 1, Job's friends speak a lot of bad theology and wrongly applied truth. Only we the readers know the satanic impulse behind all of Job's suffering. The book refutes Satan's challenge that prosperity is a sign of one's goodness and that one's suffering is a sign of one's sin. This is the same idea that impelled the apostles regarding the reason for the blind man's blindness (in John 9), which Jesus corrected. But the book's chief point is to show that God is totally free and sovereign to do as he pleases, yet he is also truly good. The only correct response to the sovereign, omnipotent God is that of submission and trust.

Job's Counselors Compared to Mack's Counselors

Now Job had three friends who first came to comfort him. They clearly misunderstood the cause for Job's suffering. They did their best to help him by accusing him of sin and needing to repent—even though Job's suffering was not caused by sin. The three misread Job's condition and gave him erroneous advice. They invoked a lot of theology but it was wrong nevertheless. At the end of the story God corrects the three friends of their false beliefs, of not speaking "what is right" (38:1–39:30; 42:7–8). They find acceptance with God only through Job's intervention and prayer (42:8–10).

It seems to me that these three "friends" correspond to Paul Young's three divine "characters"—Papa, Jesus, and Sarayu. Each of them is a character in Paul's (and Mack's) mind, a figment of his imagination, and through them Paul gives advice—wrong advice—to Mack. They indulge in all kinds of theological reflection and make many assertions, but they are often wrong.

There is a lesson here. It is possible to write a story about God and develop much theology, but it can be bad theology.

It is Job's fourth friend, the younger Eliphaz, who gives counsel nearer to the truth. And it is Job himself who is theologically closer to the truth. Young's novel lacks a fourth friend, a fourth counselor; and Mack is no Job. In *The Shack* there is a resolution for Mack's suffering, but it comes via the "bad theology" and "wrongly applied truth" of Mack's three counselors.

The Major Difference

One thing more needs to be pointed out. When one examines the end of these stories—that of Job and that of Mack—there is a clamorous difference. Job repents at the end, as does Mack, but Job does not confess sin but confesses that he went so far in his questioning of God. He realized that God is free to do as he pleases, which agrees with his nature as God. Job repents of his lack of understanding who God is (42:2–60).

There is no such confession at the end of *The Shack*. Whereas Paul Young brings God down to us and redefines him in our image, Job lifts us up to God to help us become like him.

The Story of Jesus

There is no one in the Bible and in all of history who has suffered as Jesus Christ did. He is a favorite, unique son. He was once beloved by everyone but came to experience rejection by almost everyone, including his own disciples. He died a horrible death, innocently. Yet there was total reversal—he came alive out of the grave and remains alive (as all the Gospels and 1 Cor. 15 show).

It is Jesus' story that is the greatest story ever told. His self-less death was in place of everyone else's, opening the way for all to come into a relationship with God. He died not just as an example but also as a sacrifice for sin. On him God laid the sin of all humanity—for which he paid the eternal penalty for the brief time he hung between heaven and earth on the cross. His being raised from the dead is God's confirmation that his work was perfect and finished. It is really this story about Jesus Christ that the rest of this book is all about. It will take the chapters that follow to fill it in completely.

It is up against Jesus' story and his teachings that Mack's story, and all our stories, must be compared. And it is just here that Young's story about Mack falls significantly short.

In the coming chapters, I will return to biblical stories for further insight into resolving the suffering of those who believe in God. I will also show how other saints who question God—such as David in the Psalms—nevertheless relied on biblical truth and theology to get them through. Contrary to *The Shack*, they did not rewrite theology so as to remove its unpleasant and challenging features. I will also cite the story of Jesus Christ our Lord and his teaching. He is the greatest example for us to follow.

The Nature of God
and the Death of Christ

WHAT IS GOD LIKE?
WHY DID JESUS CHRIST DIE?

Three and a half years after Missy's death, Mack finds the note in his mailbox and irrationally decides to accept the invitation of the note and to return to the shack, the scene of the killing. What he discovers there goes far beyond what he could have imagined. Winter changes to spring. He encounters God—all the persons of the Godhead. The Father or Papa appears as a large, African American woman, Jesus as a Jewish handyman and carpenter, and the Holy Spirit as a small Asian woman called Sarayu. Papa is fun-loving, cooks great meals, and likes contemporary and all other kinds of music. Jesus becomes Mack's companion during the next two days. Sarayu is almost ethereal and grows gardens where both chaos and order rule together. It is a fractal incorporating chaos and order at the same time.

The last two-thirds of the book are discussions between Mack and the persons of the Godhead around various topics. The chapters are appropriately labeled and address particular theological issues. I take up each of these chapters in greater detail.

"God Cannot Act Apart from Love"

Chapter 6, "A Piece of π," has many positive statements about what Christians have historically believed as derived from the Bible. The chapter attempts to introduce God as the triune being that he is and uses three metaphors or persons to display his triune being. The chapter also deals with the nature of God as wholly other and as love, and how freedom is experienced in relationship with this God. It also deals with the meaning of the incarnation and the crucifixion and its impact on the Trinity.

Here are the main points of the chapter. Mack learns that God may appear, at his or her pleasure, as several metaphors, and Mack has to deal with his stereotypes of God. Because men are more needy than women are, God usually presents himself as a male figure, but in truth he is neither male nor female. He is without sex. He appears as an African American woman to Mack because this is what best jolts Mack's stereotype and meets his need. Because of Mack's own estrangement from his father, God could not appear as a man to Mack without significant obstacles to overcome. Mack also learns that humans are free (94–95); what the meaning of freedom is; that the Truth—Jesus—is the only one able to set humans free (95); that freedom "is a process that happens inside a relationship with him" (95); that Papa bears the marks of crucifixion in his or her wrists just as Jesus does; that the crucifixion cost them—the Three—dearly (96); for humans to live unloved is a limitation (97); that God is "holy, and wholly other" than Mack (98); that God became incarnate and chose in the person of Jesus to be limited; that Jesus, while fully divine, did all of his miracles as a human being fully trusting God, not as divine (100); that love and relationship among humans is only possible because they exist within the Trinity, who love and relate among themselves; that love defines God, and yet his loving is not "limited by his nature" since then he "could possibly act without love" (102); that God "cannot act apart from love" (102); that Jesus died for all, not just

Mack. Yet Jesus would have died for just Mack if he had been the only one on earth, but he wasn't (103).

This chapter declares some basic theological truths that every Christian should embrace. Young's mention of freedom and its source in Jesus Christ is absolutely right on. In our sex-crazed culture and its obsession with absolute freedom, this message of *The Shack* is refreshing indeed. Jesus promised that if he, the Son, makes a person free, he or she will be truly free (John 8:12). This is one of the greatest truths of the Bible's revelation of God.

It is also correct, in the minds of most evangelicals, to affirm that a deeply personal relationship with God is essential. It is the heart of the gospel (cf. Rom. 10:9–10). Young is also straight on with the Bible to declare that God is holy and wholly other or different from any human and that he is also love. This description may otherwise be called God's transcendence. In contrast, God's attribute of love and relationship speak of God's immanence and his relationship with his creation. God's transcendence refers to his existing above all of his creation, removed and distinct from it.

The immanence of God speaks of his presence among humanity. This is what Christmas is all about. In the words of one of the wise men in the film, *The Nativity Story* (2006), when he discovered Mary and Joseph and the Christ child in the manger, "God is made flesh." In this brief sentence, he captured both the transcendence and immanence of God. Affirming both of these attributes of God (his transcendence and immanence) keeps our understanding of God balanced and complete.

Unfortunately, Young says many things about how God's holiness or justice relates to his love that seriously undermine evangelical faith. These issues are expanded several times in later chapters, and it is there that I will deal with them again.

Serious Concerns

But there are also some serious concerns in this chapter. As I promised in the introduction, I have narrowed my concerns in each chapter to two or three major questions. Here they are for this chapter. (1) Does the depiction of God as an African American woman violate the Second Commandment? (2) The second question is twofold, since it concerns the meaning of the incarnation and death of Christ. What does Paul Young intend by having "Papa" (representing God) identify himself with the marks of crucifixion when only Jesus was crucified? At the same time, what are the consequences of the claim that Jesus did all of his miracles and teachings as a human being without drawing on his divine nature? (3) How does the treatment of love as God's most important attribute distort the biblical presentation of God's nature, of who he is?

(1) The Personification of the Trinity

In regard to the first question, many reviewers of *The Shack* are upset about the metaphors that Paul uses to picture the Trinity—in particular the large black woman to represent God the Father. What does the Bible say about such metaphors?

The Bible employs many metaphors, including a whole host of personifications that put the truth about God in human terms and descriptions. A personification ascribes to God human traits or functions. For example, every statement in the Bible about God's speaking, listening, seeing, walking, or even thinking is an accommodation of God to humans in order to communicate something that corresponds to what people do.

Remember how Genesis 3 tells us that God walked with Adam and Eve in the Garden of Eden? This is a personification. God does not have feet. And Jesus himself declared to the woman of Samaria that God is a Spirit (note John 4:24). This means that he has no physical body with various organs (a mouth, ears, eyes, brain, hands and feet, etc.) to carry out the very different functions of speaking, hearing, seeing, thinking, holding, walking, and so on. God is able to do all these things and more without the need of physical organs or a physical body. What does this tell us about God? He is supremely greater that any human being. He is infinite; people are finite. One of the implications is that God is not limited by space and time as all of us humans are.

The Meaning of the Second Commandment

There is another emphasis in Scripture that refers to the metaphors or personifications of God. Some readers of *The Shack* are concerned that the depicting of God as an African American woman and the Holy Spirit as an Asian woman may violate the Second Commandment, which reads:

> You shall not make for yourself an idol in the form of anything in heaven above or on the earth beneath or in the waters below. You shall not bow down to them or worship them; for I, the LORD your God, am a jealous God, punishing the children for the sin of the fathers to the third and fourth generation of those who hate me, but showing love to thousands who love me and keep my commandments (Exod. 20:4).

The details reinforcing this commandment are in length second only to that of the Fourth Commandment, which commands remembrance of the Sabbath day. There is also an implicit universal nature to the command, for the mention of three realms (heaven, earth, waters below) recalls the mention of three categories elsewhere to reinforce universalism (cf. in the New Testament: the several trilogies of Rev. 4:8–9, 11). In other words, this commandment is for all peoples for all times everywhere. Its seriousness is also underscored by the fact that no other commandment carries with it such a warning for disobedience—punishing those who hate God. In addition, there is an extension of the punishment to the successive generations of those who commit idolatry. By way of contrast, those who love God and do not commit idolatry are recipients of God's love to "thousands" of generations. No other commandment carries such a serious weight and consequence.

Now in light of this commandment, does Paul Young's depiction of God as an African American woman, and later as an old, white man with white hair (in chap. 16), violate the commandment? It seems that the core of the seriousness of the commandment is the purpose for which one makes an image of something—to make it an "idol"—to claim that it is a deity, a god to be worshipped in the place of the one true God himself. It seems that the commandment is prohibiting the making of an image for the purpose of worshipping it—prohibiting idolatry.

The commandment also seems to prohibit the making of an image of the one and only true God. For in trying to depict the one and only true God, one must decide on some physical object in the present world to use to depict God. And there is nothing in the universe that is adequate to depict God, for everything is created by him. And it is obvious that the created thing could never correspond adequately and fully with the Creator of it (note this principle in Heb. 3:3–4). Every attempt to picture or model God the Father will fail to do so adequately, and therefore slander him—fail to give him the glory he is worthy of.

The Potential Confusion

A person may claim to be worshiping the true God behind the image, not worshipping the wood or metal or paper object itself as God. Yet how can one separate the two acts? If one makes a replica of God and declares that it is God, the implicit if not explicit implication is that it is to be worshipped. At least it seems that one's adoration may slip from the God so depicted to the worship of the object itself. An image of God will probably end up being worshipped as God. After all, this is what all the other peoples and religions of the world, except for Judaism, Christianity, and Islam, do—they worship images as their gods.

All idols of other gods are inherently limited by virtue of

being physical objects and belonging to the creation that the Creator has made. To try to depict the true God this way is to limit him; to make him one with his creation; to make him finite, decaying, and limited. Yet God is not this. He is transcendent and distinct from his creation; he is infinite; he is unchanging and immutable; he is unlimited. Many modern religions make God finite and limited, including such religions as idolatrous Hinduism, and such nontranscendent religions as Buddhism and Mormonism.

The Unique Place of Jesus Christ

Another thing should be observed. In the New Testament, John warns believers about idolatry in the very last words of his letter (1 John 5:21). In light of the context, this prohibition probably means to think of Jesus Christ in any way less than the visible, divinely incarnate, only true Son of God. John is also the same author who says several times that "no one has ever seen God" (John 1:18; 1 John 4:12, 20). The unique Son, the one and only Son of God, Jesus Christ, has "interpreted" or "revealed" God to us (John 1:18). The Son of God came, among other reasons, to "give us understanding, so that we may know him who is true" (1 John 5:20). Just prior to his death, Jesus told his disciples that in knowing him they know the Father and have seen the Father (John 14:7–9). To the disciple Philip's request to be shown the Father, Jesus replied: "Don't you know me, Philip, even after I have been among you such a long time? Anyone who has seen me has seen the Father. How can you say, 'Show us the Father'?"

It seems from these texts that there is only one who can adequately and fully reveal God in another being, and that is Jesus Christ, one of the three-in-one Being. Where *The Shack* goes wrong, it seems, is on the larger issue of the Trinity. Once one attempts to represent the Trinity as three separate persons without also portraying or representing at the same time that the Three are one in nature or essence, a person gets into trouble. To the degree that God is separately portrayed or visualized apart from Jesus Christ, the more a writer goes astray, it seems.

In the future state, the Father and the Son are both described as the temple of the New Jerusalem, and its light (Rev. 21:22–23), and both sit on one throne. This suggests that people will view God only by viewing the glorified Jesus Christ (Rev. 22:1–4).

What does all this mean as far as *The Shack* is concerned? The error is not that Paul calls for the explicit worship of God as a black woman (he does not do this), but that some may take it that way. In many Christian homes there is a portrait of Jesus Christ, and in some circles even icons of him. At Christmas and at Easter we celebrate by using various forms of Christ, as a baby and as a crucified Savior. We do not err when we do this, for Jesus Christ is the one among the Trinity who became human and revealed God. We should celebrate his humanity and his deity.

But we should never try to depict God the Father this way. It seems that if someone should try to make figurines of the Three based on *The Shack* that this would violate the Second Commandment because it may lead to the thinking that two of them do depict God the Father and the Spirit when this is impossible and may lead to confusion in understanding the divine Persons behind them. It is blasphemous to do this.

In addition, the emphasis in *The Shack* is clearly on "Papa" (representing God the Father) rather than on Jesus Christ or the Holy Spirit, and this violates the New Testament and the centrality of Jesus Christ. He, Jesus, is "the true God and eternal life" (1 John 5:20). He is the one "who is over all, the eternally blessed God. Amen" (Rom. 9:5).

In the history of universalism, universalists complain that we evangelicals pay too much attention to Jesus Christ and neglect the Father and his love.

My response is that we can never overly adore or worship Jesus, for in so doing we bring glory to the Father. To glorify Christ is to glorify the Father. The more we glorify Jesus Christ, the more we glorify the Father. It is Jesus' prayer that he be glorified so that he may glorify the Father (note John 17:1–5, 10, 22, 24; cf. 14:13).

Finally, Paul's depiction of God as either a black woman or a white man continues to fuel stereotypes of God that in the end only confuse for many what God is like, who he is. The best procedure is to stay as close as possible to the boundaries of the Bible to avoid unforeseen consequences of trying to make God relevant or contemporary.

So what does all this mean in regard to our first question? I'm not sure that *The Shack* violates the Second Commandment, for it does not call for making figures or objects to worship. In the context of the idolatry of the ancient Near East, this commandment means that God alone is the only true God (cf. Ps. 96:4–5). The commandment forbids the making of a physical or mental image to depict him as an object of worship, in contrast to the universal habits of all other peoples and their many deities. In the New Testament the Apostle Paul makes the observation that people turn to idolatry when they reject the true Maker of the heavens and the earth (Rom. 1:18ff.).

But from Paul Young's "Trinity" some may get the idea that the Trinity is embodied in three separate persons and so to worship them—and this would be idolatrous. This would be an unforeseen consequence of portraying the Trinity this way. It is inappropriate to ever portray God the Father in some form derived from his creation or our imagination. In his depiction of the greatness of God, the Prophet Isaiah twice has God ask: "To whom then will you liken God? Or what likeness will you compare with him? 'To whom then will you liken me that I should be equal?' says the Holy One" (40:18, 25). The answer is: "There is none."

In public, Paul Young has defended his depiction of the Father and the Spirit by his metaphors by appealing to the personification used in the Bible (God "speaks," "hears," "walks," and more). Yet these are partial forms representing actions of God. Never does the bible portray God as an entire human being in an extended story and assign a name to the person – no doubt because none is adequate to do so and because this detracts from the glory of who God is in his person and nature. Then all the special attributes of God (omnipresence, omniscience, and omnipotence) cease. All such portrayals redefine God to be like us when, as Isaiah said implicitly he is not. Like us when he is not. Yet Young wants to change our idea of God (see ch. 4).

Further, the people who are pushing a metaphorical theology are radical liberals who have little respect for the authority and uniqueness of God and his word. Finally, Young ends up portraying the Trinity not as Three-in-One, but as Three-in-One-in-Three! This is idolatry, and does violate the Second Commandment.

(2) The Question of the Nature of Christ

There are other issues as we address the second major question concerning the nature of the incarnation and the crucifixion of Christ. This matter is one of the most crucial for all Christians and has been discussed for all of the church age. The orthodox view of the church is that Jesus Christ is truly God and truly human, as the totality of Scripture makes clear. Many texts touch upon both of the natures of Christ (John 1:1, 14, 18; John 10:30; 1 John 2:22–23; 4:1–6; 5:1–5, 20; Col. 1:15–20; 2:9; Rom. 9:5; Heb. 1:1–3). These and several other texts emphasize both his deity and his humanity. Jesus Christ is the one person who uniquely has two natures and two wills.

a. The Incarnation of Christ

For people today, the deity of Christ is more difficult truth to believe than his humanity. Virtually the whole world accepts the fact that Jesus was human; but few, only Christians, believe that he is also deity. But in the past, shortly after Jesus ascended to heaven and the gospel first spread to new territory, it was the humanity of Christ that was challenged in many circles. The rise of Gnosticism that championed superior knowledge as the means of salvation became a challenge to Christianity. Gnosticism comes from *gnosis*, which in the Greek means "knowledge." This heresy considered the physical to be evil and the spiritual to be good. Since matter was considered evil, the god who created all that exists is different from the God of the rest of the Bible. Gnosticism was willing to embrace the deity of Christ, but rejected the true humanity of Christ. This teaching asserted that the Christ from heaven only seemed to appear as a human (much as a phantom would); or alternatively, that the divine Christ came on the human Jesus at his baptism and left just before the crucifixion. In Gnosticism, which is seeing a resurgence, there could not be a true, everlasting union of the human and divine natures in Jesus Christ.

In modern times the challenges to true belief have reversed so that people now challenge Jesus' divinity. But Scripture makes it quite clear that Jesus Christ is both God and human (cf. also 1 Tim. 2:4: "There is one mediator between God and human beings, Jesus Christ, himself human."). But there remains the question of how the two natures of Jesus Christ related while he was upon the earth, especially during his earthly ministry of about three and half years, when he taught as no one else before him and did many signs and wonders (miracles). It is an important question, and *The Shack* directly addresses it (96–102).

When Jesus became man, did he lay aside all the exercises of his nature as God without laying aside his deity? This is the most obvious conclusion from the great passage on the humility of Christ that Paul gives us (Phil. 2:6–8):

> Who being in very nature God, did not consider equality
> with God something to be grasped, but emptied himself
> (or, made himself nothing), taking the very nature of a
> servant, being made in human likeness, and being found
> in appearance as a man he humbled himself and became
> obedient to death—even death on a cross!

The key words are "emptied himself," which the New International Version (NIV) renders, "made himself nothing." It is clear that this cannot mean, in light of other texts from the Apostle Paul and from other authors in the New Testament (such as Rom. 9:5 and Col. 2:9 and others cited above), that he ceased to be God. This is never stated anywhere. So most Christians understand the words of Philippians 2 to mean that Jesus Christ laid aside for a while the exercise of his divine attributes—especially those of his omniscience, omnipresence, and omnipotence. Perhaps it is even better to say that he laid aside the independent exercise of these attributes. This qualification allows one to say that on rare occasions Jesus exercised these divine attributes but did so as a man wholly dependent on and committed to God.

Did Jesus Ever Draw on His Deity?

Now it seems that all of Jesus' miracles were exercised, or could be explained as being exercised, by his being a human totally committed to and dependent on God his Father, without his invoking his deity to exercise divine powers. But it seems that there must be at least one exception or qualification of this. The one sure exception must be his death on the cross. For in order to carry the sins of the whole world upon himself, he must have died not only a human death but a death having the weight of the eternal judgment of the sins of the world upon himself. No mere man was able to provide for the reconciliation of the whole world to God and provide adequate payment for the redemption of all. Not even a perfect man could do this. Jesus Christ became sin for us (2 Cor. 5:21), the just for the unjust, to provide atonement for all sins (Rom. 3:25). Christ was made unto us "wisdom and righteousness and holiness and redemption" (1 Cor. 1:30).

It seems that *The Shack* overstates the case, then, by claiming that Jesus did all his work as a human only and not also as God, that he "never" drew on his divine nature "to do anything" (99–100). Jesus' atoning work on the cross must have involved his dying as both human and divine.

In addition, there are several statements in the Gospels that make it clear that Jesus was aware of his deity. He was self-consciously aware that he was God. One of the more well-known statements is that of John 10:30: "I and the Father are one [one in essence or nature]." The Jews understood this assertion to be a claim of equality with God, and they took up stones to kill him for blasphemy (v. 33). He also identified his Father to be God (not Joseph); he claimed to have existed previously before he was born; and he claimed that his works were the works of God, his Father. Jesus forgave sins—which only God can do (Mark 2:1ff.). Finally, at his trial, Jesus' claim to be the fulfillment of the "Son of Man" as seen in vision by Daniel (Dan. 7:13) was considered by the high priest to be a blasphemous claim to be the divine Son of God (Matt. 26:63-65).

b. Was the Father Crucified with Jesus?

This first question leads directly to the next issue concerning the relationship of the Father with the Son. When Jesus died, did he die alone, or did the Father die with him? *The Shack* asserts that Papa (as God the Father) also died with Jesus, and that the scars of the crucifixion are visible on the hands of the Father as they are also on the hands of Jesus (although this latter idea is assumed and not actually said) (95, 102). The novel wants the reader to see the great suffering of the entire Trinity for the sins of the world.

Now it is possible that Paul Young simply wants to relate the fact that the entire Trinity is compassionate, and therefore somehow involved in the suffering of Jesus on the cross. But this could well have been stated without going so far as to have Papa bear the scars of crucifixion. This seems to distort Scripture.

The Father Was Separated from Christ While He Was on the Cross

What Scripture am I thinking about? First of all, the great passages of Isaiah 53 speak to this. Christians have always interpreted this prophecy as predicting the coming of Jesus as the Messiah of Israel. This understanding is what Philip stated to the eunuch from Ethiopia in Acts 8:32–35. Philip spoke of Jesus as fulfilling Isaiah 53:7–8.

In Isaiah 53 several texts show that the Father is the one who brought Christ to suffering, to the cross. The texts read :

> Surely he took up our infirmities and carried our sorrows, yet we considered him stricken by God, smitten by him, and afflicted. But he was pierced [by God] for our transgressions, he was crushed for our iniquities, the punishment that brought us peace was upon him, and by his wounds we are healed. . . . and the LORD has laid on him the iniquity of us all. . . . For he was cut off from the land of the living, for the transgression of my people he was stricken. . . . Yet it was the LORD'S will to crush him and cause him to suffer, and though the LORD makes his life a guilt offering, he will see his offspring and prolong his days and the will of the LORD will prosper in his hand (Isa. 53:4–6, 8, 10).

The role of the Father as the inflictor of suffering rather than the receiver of suffering could hardly be clearer. It is entirely inappropriate to depict "Papa" as co-crucified. If one does this, then it may be asked: Who was the inflictor of suffering? The Romans? The Jews? The Gentiles? The biblical answer is that these people were the intermediate or indirect inflictors of suffering. The direct cause was God the Father. That the Son came into the world to be an offering for sin completes the picture of the suffering, innocent lamb belonging to the Day of Atonement to be offered annually for all the sins of the people, as commanded in the Old Testament (Lev. 16).

Then there are many New Testament texts that explicitly say that Jesus, and not also the Father, died for our sins. Like the Old Testament, the New Testament shows that the Father's role is to plan for Jesus to be the sacrifice, the atonement for sins, and that

Jesus obediently fulfilled this will of the Father. Many texts assert or assume this (Phil. 2:8: "obedient to death"; Col. 1:19–20: "For God was pleased to have all his fullness dwell in him, and through him to reconcile to himself all things . . . by making peace through his blood, shed on the cross"; 2 Cor. 5:18, 21: "God, who reconciled us to himself through Christ and gave us the ministry of reconciliation . . . God was reconciling the world to himself in Christ . . . God made him who had no sin to be sin for us, so that in him we might become the righteousness of God"). Finally, Hebrews 10:9–10 records Christ as saying: "Then he said, 'Here I am, I have come to do your will.' He sets aside the first [covenant] to establish the second. And by that will we have been made holy through the sacrifice of the body of Jesus Christ once for all."

God the Father could not have been crucified for us because he has no body and he is not human. Only a special human sacrifice could deal with human sin. For *The Shack* to create the marks of crucifixion in Papa's hands is a serious betrayal of the gospel message. The church has pronounced this interpretation to be heresy—patripassianism—that the Father suffered equally with the Son in his suffering for sin.

Also, there are serious consequences regarding the nature and scope of Jesus' death.[20] If the Father becomes so much identified with Jesus so as to confuse the two persons as just one person, another error results. This idea reflects the heresy of modalism, that God is a monadic or singular being who reveals himself in three different modes, rather than as a Triune being, a Trinity of three persons-in-one.[21] Paul Young's portrayal of God also runs counter to the Bible, which attests that at the cross Jesus died alone, forsaken by the Father.[22] This separation was recognized by Christ himself when he cried from the cross (Mark 15:34): "My God, my God, why have you forsaken me?" He quoted these words from the Psalter (22:1). Twice more the Psalmist implores God not to be far from him and to hear his cry for help (vv. 11, 19). He asserts that God had brought him down to the dust of death (v. 15). Yet the Psalmist asserts that the Lord will hear him and deliver him—which was fulfilled in deliverance from death by resurrection (vv. 21–24). The Father was not crucified with the Son. While Paul Young discusses this matter of the forsaking of Christ (96), he seems to overstate the case by having God the Father bear the marks of crucifixion (95, 102).

Also, if the Father was crucified with Christ, did he then also die? Did he also spend three days in the grave, and then did he also rise from the grave? With what body was he raised? And who raised him? And how could this happen if he is the one who raised the Son from the grave in resurrection? See Colossians 2:13–15; 3:1; and many other texts (e.g., Rom. 6:1–11).

In public comments about this matter, Paul Young has said that Jesus was never forsaken by the Father at the cross because Jesus acknowledges that the Father is present just before he dies. He says: "Father, into your hands I commit my spirit." But these words come at the very end, after a period of darkness that lasted three hours. It is this darkness that led to Jesus' cry about being forsaken. It is during the darkness that Jesus is separated from the Father because he became sin for us (2 Cor. 5:21). After this experience of sin-bearing, Jesus acknowledges the return of the Father's presence.

Another story confirms the reality that God offered his only Son, that he did not suffer with him. It is the story of Abraham's offering of Isaac in obedience to God's command (Gen. 22). The New Testament tells us that this act typifies the divine act of God offering up his only or unique Son (Heb. 11:17–19). Clearly, Abraham typifies God the Father, and Abraham's own unique son, Isaac, typifies the Son of God, Jesus Christ. Abraham was not a co-sufferer with Isaac.

Finally, Young has an anti-institutional bias throughout *The Shack*. The first signs of it occur here, when Mack reflects that "none of his old seminary training was helping in the least" (91). I will say more about this bias in the pages to come.

(3) The Relation of Love to Holiness or Justice: An Occasion for Distortion

The third major question concerns the most significant issue that *The Shack* raises. While some imprecision could be granted Paul for his treatment of the co-crucifixion of the Father with Christ, his understanding of how the love of God relates to the justice and holiness of God, and the implications of this, is a far more serious matter. This chapter lays the foundation for affirming that love is the supreme attribute of God above all others and that it is intended to be such for people as well. It also shows that love is the basis for all that God wills, and asserts that God "cannot act apart from love" (102). Yet these assertions give rise to distorting who God is.

This exaltation of the attribute of the love of God above all other attributes of God is very similar to what universal reconciliation affirms about the love of God. Universalism affirms that because God is love he cannot act in holiness to punish or judge anyone in the future who rejects him now. There is no judgment now or in the future but only a corrective affliction of pain in hell to bring about repentance and restoration to fellowship with God.

In *The Shack,* Paul Young does not overtly embrace universal reconciliation. He did in his first draft of the novel. But he clearly exalts love as the supreme attribute of God. And in a later chapter (8) he has Papa assert that she as God does not "need to punish people for sin. Sin is its own punishment. . . . It's not my purpose to punish it; it's my joy to cure it" (120). And later Young has Papa assert: "He chose the way of the cross where mercy triumphs over justice because of love" (164). This statement comes closest to that of universalism, where justice is made subordinate to love. While the statement seems to be a quote of Scripture (Jam. 3:13), it is hugely distorted from what James asserts. I will deal with Paul's views in depth on this as I discuss the crucial Chapter 11.

Above I dealt with the Second Commandment that prohibits idolatry. Part of the wording of this commandment may seem to support universalism by appearing to say that the love or mercy of God trumps his holiness or justice. This idea may appear to find support in the words of the commandment that contrast God's acting in judgment "to the third and fourth generation" with his showing mercy "to thousands." But the idea of universalism is foreign here. Whereas universalism would subject one attribute to another, to qualify and limit justice by love, or to conquer justice by love, the commandment simply means that God's mercy is greater than his judgment. Judgment is not subjected to love; it is not redefined by love; it does not assert that "mercy triumph[s] over justice because of love" (in the words of *The Shack*, 164). The different attributes of God (such as his love and justice or holiness) are never put in tension with one another. They are always in full and perfect balance. They are part of God's nature and he cannot change.

By my reckoning, Young mentions the holiness of God and his being "wholly other" only once or twice (p. 98), and yet constantly and repeatedly he deals with God's attribute of love. This emphasis on love is commendable, we may think, but when we look at the author of Scripture who most often affirms the love of God, namely John the apostle, he affirms the justice or judgment or holiness of God in close tandem with God's love.

Love and Holiness Together Define God

John 3:16–18 is a prime example of this. While this text begins with the love of God ("God in this way loved the world: he gave his one and only Son . . ."), it immediately continues with words reflecting God's holiness, such as "perish" and "condemn" for those "who do not believe." Indeed, verse 19 begins: "Now this is the basis for judging. . . ." Universalists characteristically downplay or ignore John 3:16—a text especially dear to Christians.

Allow me to remind the reader of several statements regarding the love and holiness of God as given within a few stories from the Bible. In the story of Abraham there is the event of Abraham's offering up his special, unique son (already referred to above, from Gen. 22). In obedience to God Abraham began his act; but he never for a moment lacked love for his son.

The Parable of Ezekiel 16

There is hardly a more touching story, or allegory, than that of Ezekiel 16. Here God portrays his love for his people Israel as that of a stranger who took in and cared for a newly born baby abandoned by her mother and left in a ditch along the road. Yet the baby became a beautiful young woman who grew to despise her savior and went after other lovers. The great act of love was rejected. Consequently, God delivered Israel over to her false lovers to punish her and bring her back to him.

The Prodigal Son (or Daughter)

Jesus' story of the Prodigal Son (Luke 15:11ff.) is memorable for the patient love of the father for his wayward son. Yet the son experienced much suffering before he came back. While the son wavered in his devotion to his father, the father never wavered in his love for his son. It is the son who confesses that he had sinned against both God and his father. There is nothing in the story that has the son redefining who God is and what he is like, or his father. The son returns to confess allegiance to the same God and the same father he had known before.

What is distorted in the statements about love in *The Shack*? It is a very difficult matter to address, for while we do not want to diminish the love of God in any way, we must also affirm equally the holiness of God. We do this because Jesus did this. No one affirms the reality of hell and judgment as much as Jesus Christ does. The parables of the sheep and the goats and the rich man and Lazarus affirm this emphasis on judgment and punishment. These parables contain some of the strongest statements in all of Scripture about the punishment of hell for those who disobey, who disbelieve. And they come from our Lord Jesus.

The Parable of the Sheep and the Goats

In the parable of the sheep and the goats (Matt. 25:31–46) Jesus gives warning to his disciples (note the context of chaps. 24–25) about the future and his return as Shepherd, King, and Judge (roles inspired by the Old Testament, from Ezek. 36; Zech. 14; and Dan. 7). At the end of the age, Jesus, having the power of the final judge, will determine the destiny of all people. Those who are unbelievers, and thus who treat poorly Jesus' followers (the believers), will "go away into everlasting punishment" (the word *kolasis* is a strong term). The righteous (v. 37), who have believed on him, will "depart into everlasting life" (v. 46). The destiny of all is limited to one or the other, and it is eternal. The righteous (depicted by the sheep) are also designated as in the state of perpetual blessing by the Father and are inheritors of a kingdom prepared and locked in place for them from the beginning of the creation of the world (v. 34). In contrast, the wicked (depicted by the goats) are described as being perpetually accursed (the opposite of the sheep being blessed or loved by the Father) and depart to a state of "eternal fire perpetually prepared for the devil and his angels" (v. 41).

The parable could hardly be clearer. There are only two destinies, one characterized by blessing from God and eternal life, the other characterized by being accursed, eternal fire and eternal punishment. It is Jesus who draws this stark contrast for his disciples. For anyone to downplay one destiny below another, or to exalt one to the neglect of the other, is to distort the message of Jesus for the future of humanity. The proclamation of the gospel must contain both destinies. It is a prostituting of the gospel to downplay either destiny.

The Parable of the Rich Man and Lazarus

Similarly, in the parable of the rich man and Lazarus (Luke 16:19–31), Jesus makes it clear that after death there are only two destinies, and each is determined by what one believes while alive.

There is a destiny in the presence of Abraham where tranquility, peace, relief, and abundance—blessing—reside. This destiny comes to those who hear and obey the revelation God has given them through Moses and the prophets (v. 29). The other destiny is that of hell where one suffers pain (v. 24) and "torment" (v. 28; here *basanos* is the strong term) for disregarding the revelation from God. The principle is that if one rejects the revelation of Scripture, nothing will convince one to fear and believe God, even if a miracle of one returning from the dead to warn the living would occur (vv. 30–31).

Once again, Jesus' words are both encouraging and foreboding. None can change one's destiny after death (v. 26); and one's destiny is fixed by what one believes and does while living (v. 25). And the principle I just gave in the preceding paragraph means that there is nothing that could compel people to repent in hell if they have rejected the gospel while alive. Nothing!

Any understanding of the love of God must take into consideration these two great texts from Jesus himself. These texts are the greatest obstacles to the falsehood of universal reconciliation. However, what they teach goes unmentioned and unappreciated in *The Shack*.

The Parable of the Wicked Tenants

In his last and most explicit parable, Jesus told about his own mission in coming to the people of Israel. In the parable of the wicked tenants (Luke 20:9ff.; see the parallels in the Gospels of Mark and Matthew), Jesus compares Israel to a vineyard that had been rented by a farmer (who is God) to tenants (Israel's leaders, the scribes and Pharisees). Instead of giving part of the first fruits of the harvest to a servant sent to collect it, the tenants beat three servants sent in succession. Then the farmer sends his own "beloved son" (clearly Christ), thinking that the tenants would surely respect him and pay the first fruits. But the wicked tenants kill the son. Jesus then asked what the owner of the vineyard would do. Jesus provides the answer by saying that the owner would come and kill the tenants and give the vineyard to others (probably believing Gentiles). As proof of this action, Jesus cites Psalm 118:22, which prophesies that builders would reject a stone as initially unsuitable but it would turn out that this stone would become the capstone—the most important one. The scribes and chief priests knew that Jesus had indicted them as the wicked tenants, and thus they sought an opportunity to arrest him.

Now how is this parable significant for our purposes? It shows that Jesus could speak in one and the same parable of the grace and goodness of God (he gave out a vineyard to tenants) and also of his judgment (he would kill the wicked tenants) that comes upon those who do evil. The parable teaches that it is thoroughly appropriate and necessary to speak of God as both demonstrating love and holiness expressed in justice. God will judge wicked people for their wicked acts. But *The Shack* would deny God's judgment of wicked people.

The validity of my statements here about the shortcomings of how Young treats the relationship of the holiness of God to the love of God will be reinforced when we consider his Chapter 12, the chapter on judgment.

The Principle Derived from the Story of Sodom and Gomorrah

Scripture affirms both—that God is loving and just. One of the great principles of the Bible is found in Genesis 18:25. As God is about to judge Sodom and Gomorrah for their great iniquity (see Gen. 13:13), Abraham appeals to the justice of God, that he cannot destroy the righteous with the unrighteous. Abraham asks rhetorically: "Will not God the Judge of all the earth do right?" It is rhetorical because it is equivalent to the assertion that "God the Judge of all the earth must do right." As a result God rescued "righteous Lot" (2 Pet. 2:7) and his family from the destruction that came on Sodom because of its great evil including homosexuality (Gen. 19).

But note that Abraham did not appeal to the love of God as the basis for why God should rescue Lot. Even though God was not bound by promise to rescue Lot, he was bound by his nature to do both the just and the loving thing. For Young and universalists to say that God cannot act apart from love is a lie if it is meant that the ultimate and overriding consideration is love to the exclusion of his justice.

Before I leave my interaction with this basic chapter (6) of *The Shack*, I wish to underscore how crucial this chapter is. It subtly lays the foundation for much of what will follow in understanding how God as a God of love will solve Mack's problem. God as a righteous and holy God barely receives notice. Certain traits of God's holiness are denied. This distorts the biblical picture of God. Papa may say to Mack that "this weekend is about relationship" (102), and Young may defend his lack of mentioning God's holiness by saying that his novel is about relationship, but this will not do. I will show in the next chapters that his treatment of love repeatedly compromises who the God of love is, as presented in the Bible.

· 3 ·

God Is Holy and Love

HOW DOES THE HOLINESS OF GOD
RELATE TO HIS LOVE?

C hapter 7 of *The Shack*, "God on the Dock," presents Jesus'
and Mack's conversation while lying on their backs at night
on the dock of a lake and looking at the stars that Jesus has made.
Even Jesus, now as a man, is enthralled by what he did as God. But
the chapter begins with Mack's enjoying a meal with the Three
and observing the love that they each have for the others. Power
is denounced as contrary to relationship; hence "one way to avoid
the will to power is to choose to limit oneself—to serve." This love
is "simple, warm, intimate, genuine; this was holy" (107). Mack
observed that this holiness was not the cold or sterile concept he
thought it to be.

After Mack joins Jesus in drying the dishes, they spend some
time on the dock. While gazing at the heavens, Jesus tells Mack
that Sarayu is the Holy Spirit, that she is Creativity, Action, the
Breathing of Life (110). Her name is from one of the human lan-
guages and means "wind." She is Jesus' Spirit. Papa is also known
as Elousia, meaning that she is the Creator God who is, who is

truly real and the ground of all being. Mack also learns that he and the whole human race are in the center of God's love and purpose (111). Jesus defends his Jewish ethnicity and big nose. Yet Mack is told that appearances don't matter, for "being always transcends appearance—that which only seems to be" (112). By Mack's real living or indwelling in Jesus and Jesus' dwelling in Mack, the Spirit restores the union that God originally intended for humanity. In this way Mack came to the end of his first day with God.

This chapter presents a creative way to portray the persons and works of the Trinity. It is commendable, and doctrinally correct, for Paul Young to affirm that Jesus Christ is the one who created the universe. Scripture makes this clear in John 1:6, Colossians 1:15–17, and Hebrews 1:3. Many Christians are unaware that while God planned the universe, he brought it into existence through the agency of Jesus Christ. Indeed, Paul the apostle affirms that all things—the entire universe of rational, irrational, and inanimate creatures and things—were "created through him . . . and exist as created by means of him and for him"—the last words meaning that he is the goal or end of all creation (Col. 1:15–17). One cannot overestimate the role of Jesus Christ in the creative activity of God.

(1) Is Power Opposed to Relationship?

However, the statement that power is a hindrance to, or contrary to, relationship raises one of the two questions I find in this chapter. While it is commendable to speak of servanthood as the way to avoid the "will to power," is it not going too far to say that power is contrary to relationship? There is no doubt that the relationship within the Godhead belongs to a depth of love, purity, holiness, and genuineness such that no mortal relationship could ever experience. But there is also the exercise of power, or at least the exercise of authority, within the Trinity such that the Father "sent the Son" (stated twice in 1 John 4:9–10) to be the Savior of the world; the Son did not send the Father. In addition, both the Father and the

Son send the Holy Spirit to be another Comforter; the Spirit does not and did not send the Son or the Father.

In other words, there are roles exercised within the Godhead that assume power and authority over the other. Such authority is never ill-motivated or corrupted or unjust, for this would violate the nature of God as love and holy (1 John 4:8, 16).

It is interesting that power is associated with Christ in numerous places in the Bible. For example, he bears all things—the universe—by "his powerful word" (Heb. 1:3). I mention this here because later Paul Young will speak of a "circle of relationship" in which God and humans participate perfectly and equally, and where, according to Paul, any exercise of power by any participant breaks the "circle of relationship." I will deal with this concept again in the appropriate chapter, but for Paul to assert here that power is opposed to relationship is overstatement if not misstatement. For was there not a perfect relationship among the Trinity even while power or authority was being exercised by the Son when he created, and, even more to the point, when the Father sent the Son to be the Savior?

Also, the words that disparage authority as antithetical to relationship reflect something that Paul writes later in his novel—an antipathy to authority, including that of the institutional church, state, and marriage. In the church there is the exercise of authority by elders and deacons, and this violates Paul's model of relationships. Yet does not the very fact that Christ is the "head of the church" mean that he is ultimately in the position of prominence and authority? Again, I will return to Paul's opposition to the local church in the appropriate chapter, but it is significant that in this early chapter Paul expresses seeds of what later will appear as a full flower.

(2) Is Not Holiness Love?

Finally, to say that the love within the Trinity is "simple, warm, intimate, genuine; this was holy" (107) raises the second question.

One wonders why the opposite is not true for Paul as well, namely, that what is holy is loving. John the apostle declares that God is love (1 John 4:8, 16); he also declares in the same letter that God is light (1 John 1:5). The latter probably refers to purity and holiness in the light of the context of chapter 1, which emphasizes truth and sin. Thus both love and holiness are equally God's attributes. Young's statement makes love superior to holiness; he defines love as holiness. To define love as holy seeks to elevate one attribute over another and depreciates the attribute of holiness as distinctive in its own right. Without affirming and demonstrating the reverse, that holiness is love, Young projects an imbalance in the character or nature of God. And this can never be. But it is what all universalists maintain.

When we consider the larger context of Scripture, we find direct assertions of the holiness and justice of God. Under the covenant of the Law, Moses recorded God's self-disclosure: "I am holy" (Lev. 19:1). Under the present era of the new covenant, Paul the apostle asserts that "God is just" (Rom. 3:25), that God pursues "righteous judgment" (2 Thess. 1:5), that his retribution is "righteous" (1:6), and that Jesus takes "vengeance" on those who do not know God nor obey the gospel (1:8). In light of these texts, it is absolutely certain that holiness and justice are equally attributes of the Trinity, and that there is no contradiction between the love of God and the justice of God. How could the apostles write of both attributes if there were a contradiction or imbalance between them?

In the perfection of God, all attributes must be equally significant. If God's attributes are not altogether equally perfect and complete, then there is imperfection in God. One or more of his attributes is in danger of compromise. This imperfection would contaminate others. Thus no one attribute can exist, perfect and complete, without the others.

One may respond to me by saying that I'm arguing on the basis of silence, that Paul Young may truly believe that holiness is equally God's attribute but just does not affirm it with equal emphasis because it did not fit his novel. Mack needs love; he has already heard much of God's holiness. Yet the coming chapters of evaluation will leave little doubt that Paul Young shirks the holiness of God.

I think, therefore, that in the "gospel according to Paul Young" there is an imbalance such that the nature of God is distorted and misrepresented. And anything short of a full disclosure of all God's attributes on an equal basis amounts to limiting the glory of God as God truly is. This early, distorted emphasis on the love of God will have significant consequences for how Young will later treat the judgment and wrath of God in the next and following chapters. If an overemphasis or improper emphasis on the judgment of God can lead to unbiblical understanding of God's nature and character, so can a distorted emphasis or improper emphasis on the love of God. We should always strive for a complete and balanced understanding of God's nature. If this were not so, then God would be unworthy of our trust.

This chapter provides the foundation for the next chapter where the love of God comes into seeming conflict with the anger of God. While I've written briefly in this chapter, it lays the foundation for the longer chapters that follow.

· 4 ·

The Judgment of God and the Children of God

DOES GOD PUNISH SIN?

Chapter 8 of *The Shack* is titled, "A Breakfast of Champions." It leads much deeper into Paul's special concepts of God and his relationship to sin and punishment. It is one of the most provocative and problematic chapters in the book and deserves extended treatment.

I divide this chapter into three sections, following the chapter's own order. Each section concerns one major issue, which raises a major question regarding the error of each section. The first concerns very old issues: what is the anger of God and who are God's children? The second is: what does it mean to be in an intimate relationship with God? The final is: What is the meaning and significance of institutions?

Each of these three questions is so significant that each deserves a separate chapter devoted to it. Thus, in this and the next two chapters I take up these three questions in an attempt to deal adequately with them all.

But first, what is commendable in this chapter? There are several profitable points.

God's Children and an Angry God

This chapter begins with Mack's falling asleep and having a beautiful dream of soaring over lands and oceans. But his dream turns ugly when he dreams of Missy calling for him out of her distress. He suddenly awakens to his second day with God.

At a breakfast cooked and served by Papa, Mack discovers that she has no favorites among people but is "especially fond" of everyone and by nature has not found any she is "not especially fond of" (119–120). Indeed, while Papa gets angry at some of her/his children, such anger is "an expression of love all the same. I love," Papa says, "the ones I am angry with just as much as those I'm not."

To Mack's query as to whether Papa is the one who spills out "great bowls of wrath" and throws people "into a burning lake of fire," Papa tells Mack that God is not who Mack thinks God is, that he doesn't need "to punish people for sin. Sin is its own punishment, devouring you from the inside. It's not my purpose to punish it; it's my joy to cure it" (120). When Mack protests that he doesn't understand, Papa replies only that Mack is right, he doesn't understand. But she will tell him more in the near future.

This first section raises two issues: Who are the children of God? And what is the wrath of God? The two questions are related since God's wrath is commonly thought to be directed toward those who have rejected God's provision of salvation in Christ. So who are God's children, and what does God's anger with people mean?

This first section seeks, it seems, to extend the understanding of the nature of God presented in the previous chapter as supremely loving above all other attributes. It is significant for people who have either manufactured or inherited an unhealthy understanding of God as cruel and vindictive to realize that there is no one who is as compassionate and loving as God in Christ is. To the extent that this chapter assures all people that God is a God of love and compassion, its message is a wonderful thing. Unfortunately, this positive message is only part of the story of both the Old Testament and the New Testament.

The Powerful Promises of God's Love and Holiness in Exodus 34

Of all the great texts of the Old Testament, the one quoted or alluded to most frequently in the Old Testament is that of Exodus 34:6–7. Its proclamation of the love of God comes in the midst of a powerful section on judgment.

The story is one of the great ones from the time of Moses. It records the very time that Moses was on Mount Sinai receiving from God the Ten Commandments on stone and the other commandments and regulations for the building and services of the tabernacle to give to the people of Israel (Exod. 24–31). The Israelites below the mount became impatient during the forty days and yielded to the temptation of immorality and idolatry (chap. 32). In response God became angry and determined to destroy the people and make from Moses a great people who would obey him (32:7–10). In his angry jealousy for God, Moses broke the tablets of the Ten Commandments (32:19)

But Moses interceded on behalf of the people. He reminded God that God had made an everlasting promise to Abraham to make of his descendants a great nation (vv. 11–13). Moses also made atonement for their sins (32:30). In response, God relented and turned from his purpose to destroy the people.

Nevertheless, Israel's disobedience called for judgment. Moses gave the people an opportunity to choose the Lord's side, and the tribe of Levi did. They became God's instrument to purge the wicked from among the Israelites, and God sent plagues among them (32:25–35). The people repented, and God renewed his promise to bring them into the land of promise and to accompany them with his presence. God also began a special relationship with Moses (33:1–23). Then God commanded Moses to ascend again Mount Sinai to make duplicates on stone of the original Ten Commandments (34:1–4).

It is in this context of judgment and grace that God makes his great self-disclosure as recorded in 34:6–7:

And the LORD passed before him and proclaimed, "The LORD, the LORD God, merciful and gracious, longsuffering, and abounding in goodness and truth, keeping mercy for thousands, forgiving iniquity and transgression and sin, by no means clearing the guilty, visiting the iniquity of the fathers upon the children and the children's children to the third and the fourth generation."

God's powerful self-disclosure immediately evoked a powerful response from Moses. It is no wonder that Moses' response to this greatest act of compassion should be that he worshipped and confessed: "If now I have found grace in your sight, O Lord, let my Lord, I pray, go among us, even though we are a stiff-necked people; and pardon our iniquity and our sin, and take us as your inheritance."

The Persuasive Promises of Psalm 145

This event evoked ongoing response throughout the Old Testament and into the New Testament. In the Old Testament the text of Psalm 145 is typical. In this alphabetic psalm David praises God first for his majesty (vv. 1–7), then for his compassion (vv. 8–9), then again for his majesty (vv. 10–13), then again for his graciousness (vv. 14–21). It is interesting that David weaves together in back-to-back statements praise of God's goodness and righteousness (v.7); his graciousness and compassion and mercies (vv. 8–9); his transcendence, his power, over all for all time (vv. 10–13); and his immanence, his "nearness to all who call upon him" (v. 18). In one sentence David says that God is both "righteous in all his ways, and gracious in all his works." For David there was no friction between God's grace and righteousness.

Furthermore, David beautifully balances truth and love. He asserts that God is near to those who "call upon him in truth" (v. 18) and will "preserve all who love him" (v. 20). Finally, he saw no contradiction to speak of the preservation of God's saints (v. 10) who love him (v. 20) and the destruction of God's enemies, the wicked (v. 20). It is fitting to quote the last verses (vv. 17–21):

> The LORD is righteous in all his ways, gracious in all his works. The LORD is near to all who call upon him, to all who call upon him in truth. He will fulfill the desire of those who fear him; he will also hear their cry and save them. The LORD preserves all who love him, but all the wicked he will destroy. My mouth shall speak the praise of the LORD, and all flesh shall bless his holy name forever and ever.

Appropriately, David begins with general names and titles for God ("God," "King"; v. 1), but from then on employs the intimate name of the "LORD" (Yahweh), and this name he "will praise forever and ever" (v. 2).

There can be little doubt that David is reflecting on the great passage of Exodus 34. It is the big lie of liberal theology to assert that the God of the Old Testament is a God of wrath and judgment, but that the Jesus of the New Testament is the loving Savior. As I will show, God is the same in the Old Testament and in the New Testament, and Jesus is similarly the God man who espouses judgment and grace and/or love.

And it is this thought that brings me back to *The Shack*. Young comes close to reinforcing this misrepresentation in the Old Testament and in the New Testament. Yet the promises of Exodus 34 and Psalm 145 make it clear that God loves all those who call on him. And it is this text that extols God's attribute of love and compassion that is most frequently repeated in the Old Testament. It is love set in the context of judgment, but it is the aspect of love, not judgment, that predominates.

Note how there is emphasis on God's graciousness in Exodus 34:6–7 itself. The character of God as "merciful and gracious, longsuffering, and abounding in goodness and truth, keeping mercy for thousands, forgiving iniquity and transgression and sin" is reinforced and made emphatic by the abundance of terms (seven of them) employed, by the use of the word, "abounding," by using three terms to reinforce what is forgiven, and by affirming that God extends "mercy for thousands," perhaps meaning "thousands of generations."

In contrast, the promise of judgment is real, but it is brief. The attribute of holiness will be expressed, but it is summarily defined: "by no means clearing the guilty, visiting the iniquity of the fathers upon the children and the children's children to the third and the fourth generation."

But who would the guilty be? Clearly from the passage it is those who do not seek or want forgiveness. They reject the offer of forgiveness and prove it by their choice of idolatry. Hence they do not receive mercy but judgment. It is implicit that judgment comes because guilt still exists, because iniquity has not been confessed and repented of. Such a judgment for sin extends to additional generations. By their own example parents leave a terrible heritage for their children and influence them toward their evil ways.

The Rebellion at Kadesh

The pattern of what happened at Mount Sinai was soon, sadly, repeated at the event when Israel was given the opportunity to enter the Promised Land and receive all that God had promised as their inheritance. Numbers 13–14 records that Israel because of disbelief disobeyed God and refused to go into Canaan at Kadesh. They heeded the evil report of the ten spies, leaders of the people, rather than follow the report of Caleb and Joshua, men of faith. They even chose rather to die in the wilderness than to enter Canaan!

For all the generation that came out of Egypt, this rebellion became their turning point. For every day that the twelve spies took to spy out the land (forty days) the Israelites were condemned to wandering in the desert for a year (forty years)—and get their wish to die there. Only their children would ever see what the fulfillment of God's promise meant for them. The ten spies who brought the "evil report" immediately died by plague "before the LORD" (14:37).

The Israelites then repented, and attempted to go into the land, but it was too late. Their presumption to go without the LORD's being present with them was a new disobedience (14:43–44), and they were defeated by the inhabitants.

As at the rebellion at Mount Sinai described in Exodus 34, this rebellion at Kadesh provoked God to anger. Again, God determined to destroy Israel and cast them off as his special people and make from Moses a great nation. Again, Moses interceded and reminded God that he could not do so without violating his oath of promise (14:16) given to Abraham and the patriarchs to bring them into the land. And once again, God relented and forgave the people.

It is at this point that Moses records the nature of God as both gracious and punishing, using terms that clearly refer back to the earlier incident at Mount Sinai. He wrote (14:17–19):

> Now may the Lord's strength be displayed, just as you have declared: "The LORD is slow to anger, abounding in love and forgiving sin and rebellion. Yet he does not leave the guilty unpunished; he punishes the children for the sin of the fathers to the third and fourth generation." In accordance with your great love, forgive the sin of these people, just as you have pardoned them from the time they left Egypt until now.

Clearly Moses saw this rebellion as paralleling the occasion at Mount Sinai and saw the response of God to be parallel to that at Sinai.

The Pattern of Grace and Judgment as an Interpretative Grid

This pattern of God's self-disclosure as the God of grace and judgment becomes the most frequently cited of all Old Testament texts. But it also serves another purpose. It is a theological under-pinning for understanding other texts that challenge human comprehension.

For example, when Israel did finally enter the Promised Land, the people under Joshua were told to destroy all the inhabitants, including their children (see Gen. 14:13–20; Josh. 8–11). This annihilation of the inhabitants of Canaan has been an ongoing stumbling block for Christians and non-Christians through the ages. How can a loving God command such a thing?

At least one biblical response is this. The inhabitants of Canaan were exceedingly evil in their practices. They engaged in idol-atry, polytheism, child sacrifice, human sacrifice, self-emulation, drinking blood, cannibalism, bestiality, homosexuality, and many more vices (see the lists in Lev. 18 and 20). If they had been allowed to exist side-by-side with Israel, they would have soon contaminated Israel and led to its falling into idolatry and eventual extermina-tion by punishment for such sins, perhaps in the form of sexually transmitted diseases. The text of Exodus 34 then is to be read as a backdrop to such commands. God is exceedingly gracious, but he is also holy and will most assuredly exercise judgment, both upon his own people and upon those who are not his people.

So Also the Destruction of Sodom and Gomorrah

This paradigm is reflected in one of the great warning passages of the Old Testament: the destruction of Sodom and Gomorrah. These two cities had become exceedingly evil—an identification made early on in Genesis (13:13) and assumed elsewhere (14:21–23). Their chief sin was homosexual behavior. It had taken over the men so much so that it had become their core identity (see Gen. 19:1–29). When their destruction finally arrived, it set a pattern for God's future dealings with evil societies and is memorialized in the rest of Scripture (Isa. 1; Ezek. 16), including the words of Jesus (Matt. 10:15; Luke 17:28–29). However, the judgment was also accompanied by grace. For in spite of Abraham's intercession that God not destroy the righteous with the wicked if there were but ten people there, God did not do this with just four people there. He delivered the four righteous people from destruction that came on the wicked.

God was true to one of the greatest principles of Scripture that Abraham used in his intercession with God (18:25). Abraham asked: "Far be it from you to do such a thing—to kill the righteous with the wicked, treating the righteous and the wicked alike. Far be it from you! Will not the Judge of all the earth do right?"

It is this principle, that God must be true to every aspect of his own character, that lies at the foundation of the great texts of Exodus 34 and Numbers 14, and the rest of the Bible, including the book of Revelation. And it is the principle that universal reconciliation rejects.

In the New Testament, we have many applications of the principle that God will be gracious to his people but will also judge them for sin. At the trial of Christ, just prior to his crucifixion, the Jews chose Barabbas to be set free and Jesus to be crucified. They cried out that Jesus' blood should be on their own heads—that they should be held accountable for their choice that Jesus should die and Barabbas should live (Matt. 27:25). And so it was. Within one generation the nation was militarily conquered by the Romans and Jerusalem destroyed (AD 70), just as Jesus had warned (Matt. 24–25; Luke 21). In less than another hundred years Rome would crush another rebellion (about AD 145) by the Jews—the Bar Kochba revolt—and Rome would end Jewish occupation of the land of Israel for the next eighteen hundred years till 1948. Once again, Israel would be punished horribly during the Holocaust under Hitler, during which time six million Jews would be slain.

But through all this suffering, God has not abandoned his people. He has punished the Jews for a crime, a sin, greater than any in the Old Testament: they have rejected Jesus Christ as their promised Messiah and Redeemer, the true descendant of Abraham. But he has not abandoned Israel but will one day bring them, his "natural people," to repentance and redemption in Christ and back to himself (as Paul the apostle writes in Rom. 11). God is still gracious in his exercise of judgment.

The Need to Balance Divine Sovereignty and Human Responsibility

It needs to be emphatically pointed out that both the texts of Exodus 34 and Psalm 145 speak of both divine sovereignty and human responsibility. While all the earth is the Lord's and his kingdom and dominion are everlasting (Ps. 145:13), he brings blessing to those who seek him (vv. 15), who desire him (v. 16), who call on him (twice said, v. 18), who desire and fear him, who cry to him (v. 19), and who love him (v. 20) and praise him (v. 21). It is clear that the rest who do not do all these things are wicked and will be destroyed by God (v. 20b). Those who fail to do what the righteous do are held accountable for their disbelief, rejection, and independence. It is their decision that brings them under God's judgment.

In the New Testament this same balance of God's attributes is seen first in the teaching and practice of Jesus. As shown above from the parables of the sheep and the goats, the rich man and Lazarus, and the wicked tenants, Jesus distinguished and affirmed his love for the righteous but his judgment for the wicked who reject him.

In the early church, the story of Ananias and Sapphira (Acts 5) illustrates that during the powerful days of the beginning of Christianity, the Holy Spirit could bring physical death to those who knowingly and deceitfully lied to the early believers.

John 3:16–19

Probably the most favorite verse of Christians through the ages is John 3:16, with its wonderful promise to those who believe (I briefly touched upon this text in the previous chapter). But verse 16 is followed by verses 17–19 with their warnings about judgment for those who refuse to believe. These verses cap the great discussion between Jesus and Nicodemus and the need to be born again, to be born spiritually, that is, to enter the kingdom of God.

It is not difficult to think that Jesus, and the Apostle John, have Exodus 36 in mind in the wording of 3:16–19. The parallels are quite clear, with the stress on the graciousness of God followed by the judgment of God. Even the parallels with the sovereignty of God and the responsibility of people are embedded here. This wonderful promise of life for some and sober warning of judgment to come for others reads:

> For God so loved the world that he gave his one and only Son, that whoever believes in him should not perish but have everlasting life. For God did not send his Son into the world to condemn the world, but [he sent him so] that the world through him might be saved. He who believes in him is not condemned, but he who does not believe is condemned already, because he has not believed in the name of the one and only Son of God. And this is the condemnation, that the light has come into the world, and men loved darkness rather than light, because their deeds were evil (John 3:16–19).

The Wrath of God

In a caricature unworthy of a novel that seeks to bring people to a proper understanding of the nature of God, Paul Young makes Mack confess that he thought God was a God who "spills out great bowls of wrath" and who "throws people into a lake of fire." These words are an obvious attempt to use terminology derived for the most part from the book of Revelation (see chaps. 19–22). But everyone, including Young, should acknowledge that this book is one of symbolism. The terminology is stark and strong to make people take stock of their destiny. For Young to have Papa deny that this represents her/him is regrettable. For while symbolism is employed, John is referring to a reality behind the symbolism that is, no doubt, even worse than the symbols suggest. In light of the texts dealt with above from both the Old Testament and the New Testament, Young has failed to do justice to the witness of Scripture. Yet the promises of redemption and salvation in the Revelation are equally strong (3:10; ch. 7).

There are other features of the portrait of God's wrath that need to be filled in. Paul Young makes no mention of those with whom God is perpetually angry—his enemies (cf. Ps. 2:3, 12; 9:15-20; and countless other texts from Genesis to Revelation). In 2 Thessalonians 1:5-2:14 the apostle Paul gives a sustained treatment of how Jesus at his return will "punish with everlasting destruction" those who reject the gospel but rescue those who believe, who are "loved by the Lord." The Bible never calls unbelievers the "beloved of God" (cf. Rom. 1:7; Col. 3:12), nor does it place them within the church, his body. It also does not call them the "bride of Christ." These terms are reserved for believers. It is these who will live in heaven, identified in Revelation 20–22 as the new Jerusalem. Outside its walls exist all the wicked who continue to live wickedly, who have refused to repent (Rev. 21:8; 22:15). Clearly they are outside the blessing and care of God and Christ. In these ways, at least, Scripture distinguishes between those who are loved by God and those who are not.

In addition, Young says virtually nothing about human accountability to believe in order to avoid going to judgment. The closest he comes to saying something about believing, in a later chapter, is immediately put down.

Finally, Young fails from these great texts of the Bible to emphasize God's compassion over his judgment. Instead, Young has Papa go to the extreme of denying altogether that he/she is a God of wrath or judgment and grace. The above texts from the Old Testament and the New Testament show together that God is both.

Are All People God's Children? Yes and No

The other grave error of this section is to have Papa as God affirm that he "loves all his children perfectly," even when he is angry with them. This assertion is deliberately clarified to mean that all the people of the earth are loved equally.

In contrast to Young's assertion placed in the mouth of Papa as God, God does have enemies among the people of earth who will experience his wrath and judgment. Again, the above Old Testament and New Testament texts make this clear. It is entirely without biblical support to maintain that God equally loves "all his children," that he is "especially fond" of everyone.

A whole group of Psalms are known as the imprecatory Psalms. They ask God to bring judgment on the Psalmist's enemies because they are also God's enemies. In the New Testament, when the Apostle Paul discusses Pharaoh's refusal to allow the Jews to leave Egypt (Rom. 9), he says that God further hardened Pharaoh after he first began hardening his own heart. It is hardly possible to say that God was loving Pharaoh at that point. When Israel disobeyed God during the Exodus, God sent plagues on them and kept them from entering into Canaan (Heb. 3:7-19). And it is not conceivable that God loves the devil; yet Young has Papa say that she is "especially fond" of "every being ever created" (118–119). Young violates the biblical and historical evidence. But this is a basic premise of univeralism.

Another text will clarify the fact that there are two ways to understand the meaning of the "children of God." It helps to show that the answer to the question, "Are all people God's children," is both yes and no.

In one of the great texts of the Bible (Acts 17) that clarifies the nature of God, Paul the apostle gave a short oration on how the God of the Jews and Christians differs from the gods of paganism and idolatry. It is here that the apostle distinguishes the two meanings of the "children of God."

While on his second missionary journey, Paul the apostle preached in Thessalonica and Berea, and then stopped over in Athens. There, deeply moved by the idolatry of the famous city, Paul sought to distinguish clearly the God of the Bible from the multiple deities of the Athenians. Being invited to clarify "the new doctrine" and "strange things" of which he had been speaking in the city, Paul was invited to speak in the meeting before the Epicurean and Stoic philosophers (vv. 18–21). After speaking of God's attributes of transcendence (vv. 22–26), he spoke of God's immanence (vv. 27–31). He said:

> People should seek the Lord, in the hope that they might grope for him and find him, though he is not far from each one of us, for in him we live and move and have our being, as also some of your own poets have said, "For we are also his offspring." Therefore, since we are the offspring of God, we ought not to think that the Divine Nature is like gold or silver or stone, something shaped by art, and man's devising. Truly, these times of ignorance God overlooked, but now commands all men everywhere to repent, because he has appointed a day on which he will judge the world in righteousness by the Man whom he has ordained. He has given proof of this to all by raising him from the dead.

The response to the apostle's message was threefold. Most of the philosophers scoffed at Paul's mentioning of the resurrection of Christ (cf. v. 18) and refused to hear any more (v. 32). But some wanted to hear more some time (v. 32). And a few, including a woman, Damaris, believed (v. 34), apparently after further discussion with Paul (v. 33). This threefold response occurs whenever the gospel is preached.

Note how clearly Paul the apostle distinguishes the general offspring of God, as recognized by even pagan poets (Epimenidies and Aratus), from those who truly know God because they place faith in the resurrected Jesus Christ. It is clear that being in the general category of the "offspring of God" does not place one in the position of being a true son of God. Even the "offspring of God" have to repent and believe the gospel. In agreement with the Old Testament and New Testament texts cited above, only believers are the sons of God who have forgiveness and will experience eternal life. The rest do not.

But Young makes no such distinction. He thinks and writes of only one sense of the "children of God," and it is these words and such a concept that put him in league with universalism. It is the clearest demonstration yet that "the gospel according to Paul" is more in line with universalists than it is with Jesus and the Bible. Universalists cannot tolerate any beyond the pale of God's love.

The Nature of God and the Nature of Sin

Once we have discovered the nature of God, we immediately become aware of what violates God's nature and will so that it calls forth an understanding of God as both gracious and angry. God's forgiveness assumes that he is upset with sin and all its forms and cannot tolerate its presence. He would not have to be forgiving if there were no sin to be forgiven. In addition, he is angry toward sinners only because they refuse to repent of sin and believe the gospel. Forgiveness and eternal life may be received by all. God offers them freely, as a gift, to all simply as a result of having faith in Jesus Christ (Gal. 2:16; Eph. 2:8–9).

This close connection between the nature of God and that which violates God's nature is strongly and correctly recognized in Paul Young's novel. When Mack wonders if God is not the one who pours out bowls of wrath, Papa replies that he/she as God "is not who Mack thinks he/she is." Notice that the words focus on who God *is*, what his nature *is*. This discussion leads in the very next words to a discussion of the nature of sin.

But note the point. Young is in the process of redefining the nature of God. When *The Shack* has God say, "I am not who you think I am," Young is seeking to have Mack (and all the readers of *The Shack*) question his understanding of God, to "change the way we think about God forever." Young himself questions everything.

The words, "I am not who you think I am," is Young's challenge to the Bible's declaration in Exodus 3 of, "I am who I am," and Jesus' declarations of "I am." This redefinition of God recalls the Tempter's first subtle question (to Adam and Eve in Genesis 3): "Is God who you think he is?" Young's words put in the mouth of God may well be the summation of the whole thesis or purpose of *The Shack*—to challenge our understanding of God.

The Nature of Sin

So what is sin? In the text of Exodus 34 discussed above several terms were used, including "trespass," "sin," "iniquity," and others in other passages. Each of these has its particular twist or emphasis. "Trespass" and "transgression" assume that a standard, such as God's law, has been violated. "Sin" assumes that a standard of perfection has been unrealized; people "miss the mark" or fall short of God's absolute holiness. "Iniquity" assumes a nature that is opposed to God. Other terms suggest other nuances.

When I was a student in seminary, I did a study of the terms for sin and sin offerings in the Old Testament.[23] It was a revealing study, for it showed how multicolored and complex the understanding of sin and evil is in the Old Testament. And this diversity is carried over to the New Testament, where all the same terms occur. I also discovered that no other religion and no other literature in all the world had so many terms and such variety to characterize what is in conflict with the nature of God and his will. In a special sort of way, this variety of terminology validates the God of the Bible and the message of the Bible as the only true religion or faith. The multifaceted nature of sin emphasizes the depth of the holiness of God and what it means to violate it.

Does God Not Punish Sin?

In this section of Chapter 8 of *The Shack*, Young has Papa assert that he/she as God does not need "to punish people for sin. Sin is its own punishment, devouring you from the inside. It's not my purpose to punish it; it's my joy to cure it" (120). Since these words come right after Mack's assertion that he thought God cast people into a lake of fire to punish them, it is assumed that people are being punished for their sin. But Papa seeks to correct Mack's understanding of both punishment and sin, and who God is.

Implicitly, then, Young is denying that there is eternal punishment for sin in the lake of fire, which the Bible calls the "second death." It is a death that comes after a physical death, hence it must be an everlasting death—a dying or separation from God that never ends.

Among other texts, the book of Revelation makes all this clear. After unbelievers die, they spend some time in hell (Rev. 20:5). Then at a future great judgment before God's white throne, the wicked are resurrected to come before God and be assigned their just place and just degree of punishment in the "lake of fire" (Rev. 20:11–15). The Bible presents this as the final destiny of those who do not have their names in the "book of life," who have refused to believe and so be delivered from such a destiny (see Rev. 14:6–7).

Thus when Young has Papa say what he/she does say about sin he projects a somewhat cavalier attitude toward sin. When he defines punishment for sin by saying that "sin is its own punishment," he is giving only a partial truth. It is also blatantly false to say that God does not punish sin.

There is one passage that has particular bearing on Young's words, and it is in Romans 1. At one point Paul the apostle warns that as part of God's judgment God gives people over to the inevitable consequences that come with unbridled sin—idolatry and immorality. Three times he says that God gives people over to pursue their sinful desires once they have turned away from God. He gives people over to uncleanness, lusts, and to bodily corruption (v. 24). Second, God gives people over to the "vile passions" of lesbianism and homosexuality (v. 26). Such people "receive in themselves the penalty of the error that was due them." This probably points to various kinds of sexual deviancy, sadism and masochism, illness, even premature death. Finally, God gives such people over to debased thinking because they have rejected God in their thinking. Consequently, they indulge in all kinds of sinful behavior. The list that follows (vv. 29–31) is the longest list of sins in the New Testament.

Now Papa's declaration that sin is its own punishment agrees with such passages as verse 26 above ("they receive the penalty of the error due them") and verse 27 above. Turning from the light that God is (so 1 John 1:5) and has given to people (John 1:6–9) leaves a vacuum that darkness rushes in to fill—in various forms of sinful behavior.

Half the Truth

But Papa's declaration is only half of the truth; and for Papa to go further and say that he/she does not punish sin is directly contrary to the truth. That God punishes sin is one of the most obvious truths in the Bible, as we discovered even in the texts of the Old Testament and the New Testament discussed above.

God's judgment of sin permeates the first chapters of Romans. Even in the chapter that supports the idea that sin does carry its own punishment (Rom. 1:24, 26, 28), there is the greater message that God punishes sin. Verse 18 affirms that the "wrath of God is being revealed [note the present tense] from heaven against all ungodliness and unrighteousness of people" (v. 18). In addition, the last verse (v. 32) concludes that evil people know "God's righteous decree that those who do such things are worthy of death." This death must be eternal death in light of the context (Rom. 6:23: "the wages of sin is death"). And note that it is "God's righteous decree"!

Just an overview of Romans 2–3 quite clearly reveals, in line with the rest of Scripture, that God judges sin. We find such statements as the following: "The judgment of God is according to truth against those who practice such things" (2:2). "Do you think that you will escape the judgment of God (2:3)?" "In accordance with your hardness and your impenitent heart you are treasuring up for yourselves wrath in the day of wrath and revelation of the righteous judgment of God who will render to each one according to his deeds" (2:5–6). "To those who are self-seeking and do not obey the truth, but obey unrighteousness—indignation and wrath, tribulation and anguish, on every soul of man who does evil" (2:8–9). There is a day "when God will judge the secrets of men by Jesus Christ, according to my gospel" (2:16). "How will God judge the world?" (3:6).

These are just a few of the multitude of passages that teach that God judges, even condemns, people who reject him (cf. Rom. 8:1). Even the wonderful text of John 3:16–19 refers to the condemnation that comes to those who believe not.

How God relates to judgment is not a matter of what Mack thinks but what Scripture teaches. The scene closes with Papa denying that he/she punishes sin. To have Papa say that she/he "cures" sin rather than "punishes" it (120) is standard terminology that universalists use. They deny that the fires of hell are punitive but say they are restorative, corrective, and purgatorial. There is absolutely no support for this idea of punishment. It is an illusion, a figment of the imagination born of a mind having a distorted idea of the love of God.

God Is Always Involved in Judgment

Finally, Young's statement about sin being its own punishment, not God's, is a glaring oversight. Just because on occasion sin is said to be its own punishment does not mean that God is not involved. After all, from where does the principle that sin is its own punishment come? It will not do to appeal to an impersonal law of retribution. Is not God omnipotent and immanent (present, near)? If God has made the universe a moral universe, and he has, then he cannot be exempted from responsibility when sin gives rise to its punishment.[24] Has not God built this principle, this law, into his universe, much like the law, "As a man sows so shall he reap"?

Thus God is responsible for all that happens, directly or indirectly, when it comes to the consequences of sin. God directly causes much; he also permits sin to occur to forward his plans. He is involved even when "sin is its own punishment."

Compare God's Providence

As an illustration on the more positive side, consider the providence of God. In the Sermon on the Mount, Jesus exhorts his listeners to trust God and not to worry (Matt. 6:25–34). As an illustration, he points to "the birds of the air that neither sow or reap or store away in barns, and yet your heavenly Father feeds them" (v. 26). Next, he points to the lilies of the field that "do not labor or spin," yet God dresses them in greater splendor than Solomon had (vv. 28–29). Jesus' portrayal of the providence of God attributes to God what the non-theist would attribute to "laws of nature" and "survival of the fittest," and so on. Yet the theist sees behind even the bird lover's providing of seed in a bird feeder the hand of God.

Why Bad Things Happen

On the more negative side, the Gospel of Luke records how Jesus explained divine involvement in human disaster. Some people reported to Jesus that Pilate had killed Galileans, apparently while they were sacrificing at the Temple in Jerusalem (Luke 13:1ff.). What was Jesus' reply? It was not to utter compassion and support for them but to issue a warning to correct a human misunderstanding of why people suffer. They suffered not because they were worse sinners. He said:

> Do you think these Galileans were worse sinners than all the other Galileans, because they suffered these things? No, I tell you! But unless you repent, you will all perish as well! Or those eighteen who were killed when the tower in Siloam fell on them, do you think they were worse offenders than all the others who live in Jerusalem? No, I tell you! But unless you repent you will all perish as well!

What is Jesus' point? What the people thought of as human and "natural" disasters Jesus linked immediately with the work of God in the world. He is involved in these events, in everything that happens, since all are at least allowed to happen in his plan. He is sovereign over all. Among other possible reasons that could be suggested, these calamities are all meant at least to cause people to think about future judgment—their perishing—and how repentance for sin will stave off judgment.

Thus Young's attempt to distance God from the punishment of sin is a vain attempt, and fails to understand the wrath of God and how people are reconciled. The wrath of God is the obverse of the love of God; it is not something that flows from his love. We are not forced "to choose between a God of wrath and a God who loves."[25] He is equally, eternally both.

Another aspect of this is to consider what the enmity of God is about. There is an obstacle that prevents God from being at peace with humanity, and that obstacle is sin. The Bible teaches that people are at enmity toward God (Col. 1:21–22), and that God is at enmity with people (Rom. 5:9–11; see also the many references to the "wrath of God" cited above). But significantly, reconciliation has been achieved. God and man have been reconciled at the cross because Jesus paid the penalty that our sin demanded and removed the obstacle that brought enmity between God and people.

Reconciliation

This discussion brings us to the whole matter of what reconciliation means. Is it true, as universalists of all kinds assert, that reconciliation has been accomplished for all—for everything in the universe? This is indeed universal reconciliation. But then how can Scripture say that God displays wrath toward some? And what is the role of faith?

In Chapter 12 of *The Shack,* Paul Young directly addresses these matters. He makes what I think are totally distorted statements of the meaning of reconciliation and the role of faith. But

I am putting off addressing these questions until we arrive at that chapter. Over two chapters I will give extensive discussion to the marvelous doctrine of reconciliation.

God Judges His Own People

One more matter needs to be addressed. God judges his own people as well as his enemies. This is true in the Old Testament, as seen in a multitude of examples where God judged his own people, the Israelites. They spent forty years in the desert for their disobedience after the Exodus. They spent seventy years in terrible captivity and exile in the land of Babylon because of their idolatry.

But it is also true in the New Testament. Taking just one book, 1 Corinthians, there are multiple statements in the first few chapters that show God judges those who are truly his children. Paul the apostle affirms that believers will be judged on the basis of their works (3:12–15). The Lord judges the Apostle Paul (4:4) and will judge all (4:5). Indeed, believers are exhorted to "judge those within the church" in order to discern immorality and sin within the church" (5:12), while "God judges those outside" (5:13).

The implications are clear. To say that God doesn't judge sin is to contradict what these verses affirm. And if God judges his own people, he will certainly judge those who are not. Indeed, in the verses just cited believers are encouraged to judge others, and in so doing they act in the place of God. Thus to assert that Christians should not judge others is only partially true.

It is now necessary to address the second question raised in this chapter, and I devote a whole new chapter to that question.

· 5 ·

Relationship and Obedience

HOW DOES A PERSON RELATE TO GOD?

The second matter of Chapter 8 of *The Shack* ("A Breakfast of Champions") concerns what it means to have an intimate relationship with God. Every Christian wants to develop such a relationship as deeply as possible. Yet how one does this is crucial. It concerns both the nature of God and what Jesus says about this. If anyone can tell us what such a relationship looks like, Jesus certainly can. So the second major question, the concern, of this chapter is this: What does it mean to have a relationship with God?

Chapter 8 asserts a definite view of what a relationship with God looks like. Mack observes that there seems to be equality in the relationship among the Trinity, with no hint of subordination. The Three affirm a "circle of relationship" and deny a "chain of command" (122). There is no power over the other, no hierarchy. The latter is the problem of humans and their institutions, including politics, business, marriage, and the church, which use power to enforce rules and regulations, thereby destroying relationships. A full discussion of the meaning of institutions becomes the focus of the next chapter.

This chapter asserts that it is in this "circle of relationship" that believers are to participate. There is to be no hierarchy, no authority figure, no exercise of power over others, but full equality. The Three within the Trinity are fully submissive to each other and to humans.

The Shortcoming of Such a View of Relationship

Now while there is a certain beauty to describing the relationship within the Trinity as a "circle of relationship" without a hierarchy or exercise of power of one over the other, there is a serious error. For while the Three-in-one in the Trinity are by nature all equal, there are various responsibilities or exercises of power appropriate to different ones in the Trinity. Theologians call this the economic understanding of the Trinity.

For example, God the Father planned the making of creation, but it is Jesus Christ who actually did the creating (John 1:6; Col. 1:16; Heb. 1:3), while the Holy Spirit was in attendance, perhaps overseeing it or guiding it (Gen. 1:3). The Son was the agent of God acting on his behalf. In the work of redemption, God the Father "sent his unique and only Son into the world" (1 John 4:9); he "sent his Son to be the propitiation for our sins" (v. 10); he "sent the Son as Savior of the world" (v. 14). Similarly God determined "by him to reconcile all things to himself" and "made peace through the blood of his cross" (Col. 1:19–20).

It is said of the Son of God that when he entered into the world he delighted to do God the Father's will (Heb. 10:8–10). Prior to his death, he prayed in Gethsemane that the Father's will, not his will, be done (Matt. 26:39, 42, 44), praying this three times. In response to his obedience to the Father in going to the cross, the Father highly exalts Christ in the most supreme way, giving him "the name which is above every name" (the name Yahweh) (Phil. 2:11).

In addition, the Son of God promised to send another Comforter, the Holy Spirit, after his death and return to the Father (John 15:26; 16:7). Earlier he said that the Father would send the Spirit in response to his request to the Father to do so (John 14:16–17, 26). Further, the Spirit "will not speak on his own authority but will speak whatever he hears" (16:13). The Spirit will "glorify" Christ, for "he will receive" from Christ what is his and will tell it to the apostles (16:15). In a real sense, the Spirit is the presence of Christ in the world today.

Thus the Spirit is subordinate to both the Father and the Son, and the Son is subordinate to the Father. There is not a mutual reciprocity on this matter, for the Spirit is never said to send the Son, nor is the Father or the Son subordinate to the Spirit. Finally, Jesus affirms that the "Father is greater than I am" (John 14:28).

At the end of the age, when all creatures are brought into subordination to the Son, Paul says that then even the Son will be subject to the Father so that he "hands over the kingdom to the Father" so that he may be "all in all" (1 Cor. 15:24–28). These and many more statements demonstrate that there are different roles in the Trinity, and an authoritative subordination of one to the other.

It is a dangerous distortion for Paul Young to say that there is not subordination in the "circle of relationship." Much is lost when this distortion is made. It is a distortion of the relationships within the Trinity and in the relationship that Christians have with the Triune God.

Obedience Is the Key to Relationship

In fact, there is subordination of believers to the Trinity within a biblical "circle of relationship." Subordination exemplified by obedience is the key to prayer, and the proof that one is a Christian, a follower of Jesus. Obedience brings answers to prayer, for Christians are "to ask God in the name of Jesus whatever they desire" and it "will be granted to them" (John 14:13–14; 16:24), if they obey. Obedience identifies who is a true follower of Christ, for obedience to the commands of Christ is proof that one loves Christ (John 14:15: "if you love me, you will obey my commandments"). The idea that obedience to commands proves who truly loves Jesus and the Father is repeatedly made (note in John's writings: John 14:15, 21—it is the basis for Jesus' response of love; v. 23—it is the basis for the Father's love of the Christian; v. 24—the person who doesn't love doesn't obey; 15:12, 17—the disciples are commanded to love).

Even more significant is the fact that Jesus obeyed the commands of the Father to prove that he loved the Father (John 14:31), and this fact is given as an example of what will happen when the disciples obey the Father—they will be loved by the Father (15:10). Such obedience and its consequence of love will bring joy (15:11; 16:24). Obedience to the command of Christ means to be a "friend" of Christ (15:14). Having eternal life comes by knowing God and Jesus Christ sent by the Father (17:2, 8, 18, 21, 25: being "sent" by the Father is repeatedly said). Jesus glorified God because he completed the work God gave him to do (17:4)

Most of these references suggesting some form of subordination come from the apostle who most frequently writes about love—John the apostle. The apostles never conceived of the idea that somehow love and subordination were inconsistent with each other.

In summary, the existence of hierarchy in the Godhead, of subordination of one to another, calls for our obedience to commands as it called for Jesus' obedience. This subordination is proof of love, the key to answered prayer and joy, the entitlement to being called a "friend of God" and having eternal life, and is the means of glorifying God. Rather than being a hindrance to relationship, obedience to a command proves we are in relationship and love another—whether this be said of our relationship to God or to other believers.

Scripture opposes such a thing as a "circle of relationship" if this is defined as having no subordination or the exercise of authority and power. It also makes Paul Young's claim to love God in this kind of a "circle of relationship" to be without biblical support, to be false.

The Church

The beauty of a biblical "circle of relationship" is that intimacy can only be known within the exercise of obedience to commands. In the church, believers are to be in an intimate relationship with one another. This is the divinely designed place of intimacy such as cannot be found outside the church. But this same church with its leaders, such as pastors, elders, and deacons, is a place where authority and power are exercised, and people are to be in submission to the leaders and to one another (note 1 Tim. 3; Eph. 5:21; Heb. 13:17). The chief point that makes it different from the structure of the world is that those who exercise authority are to do it as shepherds and servants of the flock, following Jesus' example (1 Pet. 5:1–11). They love the flock.

My discussion of a "circle of relationship" is not yet complete, for *The Shack* takes up the topic again in Chapter 11, and things are said there that need to be addressed.

But the preceding discussion has raised the issue of institutions, particularly the institutional church, where relationships should develop the best and the deepest among people who confess Christ. But the attitude of *The Shack* is that institutions are an obstacle to relationships, a hindrance, not a vehicle for relationships. The novel construes the institutional church as "diabolical." What does the Bible say about this?

This leads us to the third and final section of Chapter 8 of *The Shack,* as we explained above in my Chapter 4. I now take up this issue and devote a whole chapter to the important matter of the church.

· 6 ·

The Essential Place of Institutions

ARE INSTITUTIONS FROM GOD OR FROM THE DEVIL?

The third and final section of Chapter 8 of *The Shack* is an extended discussion of institutions. This topic flows right out of the preceding discussion of intimacy in relationships.

Sarayu comments that authority is usually an "excuse the strong use to make others conform to what they want" (123). Systems (such as institutions) represent struggles for power, the "will to power and independence"; they form a "matrix, a diabolical scheme" in which humans are entrapped (124). Thus Young attributes virtually all institutions to the devil. But this is contrary to the witness of Scripture that asserts that God, not Satan, has established government (Rom. 13:1–7) and marriage (Gen. 2), and that Jesus has established the church (Matt. 16:18). Paul wrongly attributes to the devil what Scripture attributes to God and Christ!

Sarayu goes on to assert that when humans protect themselves with power they yield to the matrix, not to God. God desires people to join him/her in "a circle of love" to change this (124). Yet God will use every human choice, or free will, for power, and rights and evil, for the "ultimate good and the most loving outcome" (125).

Note here the lack of mentioning a just or right outcome. But Paul the apostle speaks of government accomplishing a just outcome (Rom. 13:1–7).

People need to trust God as good; his goodness covers all the means, the ends, and all the processes of individual lives. Speaking as God, Papa claims that s/he is not a "bully, not some self-centered demanding little deity insisting on my own way. I am good, and I desire only what is best for you. You cannot find that through guilt or condemnation or coercion, only through a relationship of love" (126).

Imperfect Institutions

Now all of us have experienced institutions that act diabolically and/or abuse their power. These may be churches, governments, and even marriages and families. The story of history includes the abuse of totalitarian governments; and Scripture (the Old Testament) clearly faults empires such as Egypt, Assyria, Babylon, Greece, and Rome. These powers persecuted and sent the Jewish people into exile. It was under the abuse of power by the Romans that Jesus was crucified and that the apostles were persecuted and even martyred. The book of Revelation forecasts a coming abuse of governmental power under the Antichrist, and God's judgment on it.

Currently there is a movement in American Christianity in which many Christians are virtually fed up with the institutional church. For them Sarayu's evaluation above rings true and finds much sympathy. Some of these have formed "emerging churches," gatherings of Christians that have come to view the usual Christian or Evangelical church with suspicion and discontent. Brian McLaren and others with him proudly embrace the "Emergent Church" to redefine what Christianity is and what a Christian is. They have carefully delineated different characteristics of their brand of church and have made specific attempts to distance themselves from evangelical churches.[26]

Some seminary graduates are starting churches (or perhaps it is better to use another term) that gather in people's homes and that never anticipate having their own church building. Others have started churches in places that on Monday through Saturday serve as bars or nightclubs. Others gather in places specifically designed to reach the homeless, street people, the disadvantaged, the jobless, and others who would not normally "make it to church."

These efforts of outreach are innovative and commendable. There is nothing wrong in seeking to redefine ecclesiology as long as biblical doctrines regarding God, Jesus Christ, the Holy Spirit, the Trinity, and other crucial matters are not also redefined.

So there seems to be significant discontent about institutions, whether the government, the church, or even marriage. But much of this discontent represents opposition to abuses by these institutions. It is possible to have institutions represent the legitimate exercise of power for which God designed them, including governments (see Rom. 13:1–7; 1 Pet. 2:13–17). After all, God designed them. To these governments Jesus himself and the apostles exhort submission and obedience (see the same references and the pivotal text, Matt. 22:22ff.). They exhort us to pray that God will accomplish his plan through institutions that lead to the salvation of people (1 Tim. 2:1–2).

But Sarayu in this chapter condemns all institutions out of hand. The question for Paul Young is this: Would Jesus exhort submission to "Caesar" (in Matt. 22:22ff.) if the institution itself was diabolical (even though a specific leader may be)?

Similarly, there may be churches where leaders abuse power and authority. But the remedy is not to stop attending church but to reform the church. During the Middle Ages, the Roman Catholic Church abused power by becoming a state as well as a church—the Holy Roman Empire. Yet the Reformation came, not to destroy the church as an institution, but to purify it and reform it. And this was a great success!

Subversion of Institutions

Paul Young's position of opposition to virtually all institutions makes him subversive and leads to anarchy. If he opposes the institutional church, then he encourages its demise; yet Jesus designed it to serve his purposes. If he subverts legitimate governments, then chaos and anarchy result, and worse governments arise, such as despotism and dictatorships. If he subverts marriage, then everyone will decide how to define marriage and the family.

The Essential Place of Institutions

In fact, on the last issue, Paul's opposition to marriage as an institution places him in league with the most blatant subverters of marriage today, the gay rights community. This group is seeking to redefine marriage in revolutionary ways. Should they succeed, the traditional model or paradigm will be destroyed.

This is the point that David Blankenhorn has made in his recent book, *The Future of Marriage.*[27] He writes not as a Christian but as a concerned sociologist. The destruction of the traditional model of marriage will lead, he asserts, to a collapse of our other institutions, such as the government and the church. Rather than being a hindrance to the community, institutions such as marriage save the community and society.

What is a social institution? Blankenhorn defines it as a "relatively stable pattern of rules and structures intended to meet basic social needs."[28] He points out that an institution "is bigger than an organization or a process."[29] Thus social institutions create and maintain rules, including "rules for who is, and is not, a part of the institution."[30] In addition, social institutions create "authoritative public meaning." A "social institution builds and expresses shared agreements about what is important and what is to be valued."[31] Finally, and most importantly, "Social institutions exist in order to solve basic problems and meet core needs."[32] With much of this Paul Young would find fault, but he is wrong. Strangely, he demonizes the institutional church and institutions such as seminaries. But he is not averse to speaking engagements and selling his novel in churches and institutions.

What will happen if Young's version of universalism is achieved? By opposing marriage and other institutions as institutions, he is changing the definition of them and they cease to exist. That's right. If marriage, government, and the church cease to be institutions, the result is that there is no marriage, no government, and no church. In their place come sexual promiscuity, anarchy, and irreligion and idolatry, with its moral chaos.

Instead of forecasting a brave new world of openness, freedom, and relationships centered on love, there will be enslavement, corruption, bondage, and the ensuing destruction of culture and civilization. It is not a better future; it is a reversion to what existed before five thousand years ago when people first began breaking from the mold of their long heritage of anarchy to form social institutions. Blankenhorn gives compelling evidence for the development of social institutions from the ancient Egyptians and Sumerians.[33]

How and Why Institutions Arose

The biblical record is that God redefined the institutions of the cultures surrounding Israel, giving new rules and regulations for marriage, the state, and the church. With the coming of Jesus Christ, these institutions received greater clarity and definition. Jesus spoke about each of these institutions in such a profound way that his followers, the church, have influenced marriage, the state, and the church around the world for two thousand years. In a way the Jews bequeathed the heritage of their institutions to the rest of the world.

The church, like government and marriage, involves both personal relationships and institutions.[34] To limit any one of them to a matter of personal definition or relationship alone destroys the existence of marriage, government, and the church itself. It is not surprising that Young and other universalists oppose the rules and beliefs, the creeds, that churches embrace as detrimental to the achievement of universal goals. Particular beliefs lead to particular creeds and churches, and to social ordering.

Blankenhorn gives similar definitions that reinforce this understanding of institutions and their roles. Douglas C. North describes institutions as "the humanly devised constraints that structure human interaction. They are made up of formal constraints (e.g., rules, laws, constitutions), informal constraints (e.g., norms of behavior, conventions, self-imposed codes of conduct), and their enforcement characteristics."[35] For North institutions primarily concern what one may not do.

A. R. Radcliff-Brown defines social institutions as "the ordering by society of the interactions of persons in social relationships." The conduct of people is controlled by "norms, rules, or patterns." A person "knows that he is expected to behave according to these norms and that other persons should do the same."[36]

Social institutions carry public meaning. It is this that makes them objective and authoritative—and opposed by universalism. Without "specific rules and agreed-upon public purposes" the social institutions cease.[37] If institutions are only relationships to be defined privately, there is no need for these to exist. "The clear logic of deinstitutionalization is not transformation or even redefinition, but extinction."[38]

Thus it is just the opposite of the truth for Young and most universalists to assert that rules and creeds of beliefs affirmed by institutions oppose the freedom to be found in relationship. Their idea of relationship will end the existence of the church, marriage, and government.

Young and other universalists oppose institutions, as though there are no benefits but only obstacles. But Blankenhorn describes the amazing benefits and pluses to institutions. He writes:

A social institution is a pattern of rules and structures intended to meet basic social needs. Institutions are fundamental enablers of human sociality. They give humans the gift of knowing what to expect of others and what others expect of us. By reducing the burden of choice and permitting us to take some things for granted, institutions are essential pathways to higher and more complex forms of human creativity, deliberation, and cooperation. Finally, institutions guide behavior in specified pro-social directions. They wield authority in two ways. The first is when institutions provide meaning and aspiration that we experience as both natural and desirable. The second is when institutions pressure and coerce us.[39]

Institutions Promote Freedom

Institutions actually promote freedom for the common good and hinder autocratic despotism within or without the church. Rules are beneficial, not harmful. Young and other universalists sound like spoiled children casting off the restraint that actually produces a greater good and the freedom to do the good. As shown above, Jesus defined love as obedience to commandments—to rules. His words anticipate what history and sociology have discovered.

Recall from above that Young describes what he calls a "circle of relationship" in which there is mutual parity among humans and the Trinity. There is no subordination of anyone to anyone else; otherwise relationship would cease, he maintains.

Pure Relationships Are Subversive

But is this the case? Interestingly, Blankenhorn takes up the issue of "pure relationships," which is virtually what Young affirms. Blankenhorn finds fault with the idea that one should prefer a "pure relationship" without the institution. He writes, in part quoting Anthony Giddens, as follows:

A pure relationship is just us, for us, made by us, and without the encumbrances of socially defined meanings, forms, and purposes. A pure relationship, says Giddens, "is one in which external criteria have become dissolved." It is "entered into for its own sake, for what can be derived by each person from a sustained association with the other. Its central motif is the search for emotional intimacy." Two of its primary traits are instability and impermanence: "It is a feature of the pure relationship that it can be terminated, more or less at will, by either party at any particular point." Giddens reports, not surprisingly, that enshrining the pure relationship as our primary model of intimacy not only seriously undermines marriage as an institution, but also is likely to prove "a subversive influence on modern institutions as a whole."[40]

Blankenhorn and Giddens could hardly speak more convincingly of the danger that Young's view of intimacy poses for our culture. Young's "circle of relationship" is damaging, not helpful. It is self-centered, not caring for the wider community of faith and of the world.

Giddens foresees the far-reaching effects that opposing the institution of marriage will have on other institutions. But I think the priority lies with the church. In refusing to be bound by rules, creeds, and institutions, Paul Young and other universalists embrace a scenario for their relationship with God that is similar to what Giddens has traced for marriage.

I maintain that the undermining of the institution of the church, which sanctions government and marriage, will have even more severe consequences for society. I would argue that the very undermining of the institution of marriage presently going on by the gay community is a result of the undermining of the church that preceded it. After all, it is the church that defines what is moral and sin, and homosexual behavior is condemned in Scripture. Yet many churches are embracing certain forms of same-sex behavior. It is these churches that are to blame for the erosion of the institution of marriage. If the institution of the church is undermined, as it is in *The Shack* and in some emergent churches, then the consequences are grave.

A "Circle of Relationship" Is No Circle At All

Young and universalists have a faulty view not only of relationships but also of the role of social institutions in society. By making a mutual relationship with God in a "circle of relationships" the supreme value and goal, they distort truth and violate Scripture with its recognition of the role of laws, rules, and regulations for the common good.

Universalists are the anarchists of our day in league with others who seek to destroy institutions, including those terrorists who seek to overthrow governments and the gay community. Since the "circle of relationships" is self-centered, none can count on the other to be there when most needed. This "circle" is not a circle at all but a broken series of individual arcs sloppily arranged for selfish interests.

Universalists could learn much from social scientists. But then again, universalists oppose institutions—including schools of higher learning—and the wisdom they could impart. So they languish in self-deluded understanding of their own making! The Bible has something to say about this form of pride (see 1 Cor. 1–2; Col. 2:16–23).

One of the most powerful statements comes from the Apostle Paul in his last letter to Christians. He warns: "But evil people and charlatans will go from bad to worse, deceiving others and being deceived themselves" (2 Tim. 3:13). The corrective is the knowledge of Scripture, as Paul writes in the very next verses (14–17).

It is unfortunate that the author of *The Shack* juxtaposes or places in opposition relationship and authority, and faults implicitly the church as a "diabolical" institution. This can hardly be the case if Jesus designed it—which he did, contrary to Young's claim that Jesus never did and never will institute an institution.

An Institution That Loves!

Let me illustrate how important and loving the institution of government is. In the spring of 2009, I attended the memorial service for a man from my community in Damascus, Oregon, who retired from the local fire department after serving it for forty-six years. I was impressed by this and other acts of community service that this gentleman did over his life of almost eighty-two years. I was also impressed that over seventy fire-fighters from the surrounding communities attended the service. At its conclusion the honor color guard from the state took the flag from his casket and carefully folded it—a process that took at least five minutes! I later learned that every one of the specific thirteen folds has a special meaning.

During this time I reflected on how this ceremony reflected the high level of dignity the firefighters esteemed for the deceased. It also reflected the discipline that the fire department exhibits in its daily duties. I remarked about this to a friend afterward, and he responded: "Of course! Can you imagine a fire department without exacting rules and tight regulations? It is these that make them successful. They are in the business of protecting and saving lives and preserving their own in the process!"

It strikes me that the institution of government, including fire and police departments, is essential to the livelihood of a society. In light of fallen human nature, how gracious it is for God to have given us this institution! For Young and others to assert that they are diabolical and a barrier to relationship because of their rules and lines of authority is absurd. There are different kinds of relationship, and I for one am glad to be involved in a "circle of relationship" with firemen who are characterized, in the end, by a love for their

neighbors that can hardly be surpassed by any other occupation—
that the rest of us rarely, if ever, engage in. Didn't the Apostle Paul
mean this when he said that "very rarely will anyone dare to die for a
righteous man, though for a good man someone might possibly dare
to die" (Rom. 5:7)? It is only Christianity, and the Judeo-Christian
ethic, that has influenced government so much that such love, voluntarily given, even to strangers, has become "institutionalized" in
fire and police departments. For some such as Young to fault such
institutions and want pure relationships—whatever this means!—is
itself diabolical. For the enemy of our souls promotes chaos and
destruction. The love that firemen have comes from God; it is not
from Satan, who is incapable of love. Opposition to institutions puts
one in league with the devil and his work among nations.

Also, what would Young say to those individual Christians who
serve in these institutions as firemen or policemen, who routinely lay
down their lives for others? Are they servants of the devil? With the
Apostle Paul, I believe that they are servants of God (Rom. 13:1–7).

I started out this chapter by saying that Chapter 9 is one of the
most significant for the message of *The Shack*. I think that the
preceding discussions of wrath and the children of God, of "the
circle of relationship," and of the institution of the church show
how true this statement is.

Final Comments

Paul's chapter concludes with some final, surprising statements. To
Mack's final comments that he can't "imagine any final outcome that
would justify all this," Papa replies: "We're not justifying it. We are
redeeming it" (127). Again, "redeeming" is the standard language
of universalism to describe the meaning of the suffering in hell. God
uses the suffering to "chastise, redeem, correct, and discipline" people
(universalists use all such terms to describe the purpose of the sufferings of hell). Evangelicals never use this terminology.

Papa's final words mean ultimately that there is no final judgment, only redemption. Yet Mack's question begs for an answer.

If God respects human choices, and some choose evil, how are the choices of evil dealt with when love is rejected? Universal reconciliation affirms that by means of the corrective fires of hell God leads those who have rejected him to repent and embrace him after death.

But does not such suffering constitute the coercion of a "bully insisting on his own way" which Papa affirms he/she is not? Does this not suggest that within universal reconciliation God does not honor human freedom or choices?

It is as though Jesus at his death says to one thief: "Today you will be with me in paradise." To the other thief he says: "Tomorrow you will be with me in paradise after I have chastised you enough to force you to repent." This is neither an act of love nor a response of faith. Instead, Jesus describes everyone's destiny as either everlasting life or everlasting suffering and separation from God (Matt. 25:46).

It is an odd irony, and a contemptible one, that universal reconciliation follows Jesus in understanding God's love, but it rejects Jesus for teaching the eternal suffering of those who reject him. But no one can make this separation. To believe Jesus to be the embodiment of love means one must believe him to be the judge at the end of the age (Matt. 25:46). The Jesus of universal reconciliation is not the biblical Jesus. The biblical "ultimate good and most loving outcome" for the wicked who reject Christ is judgment and everlasting separation from God.

Universal reconciliation ends up being the most deterministic of all the positions on hell and the future. From the will of God it arrogantly excludes God's will that humans should be free to exercise their will to choose to reject God, to be free to reject God's will.

· 7 ·

The Meaning of Evil

WHERE IS THE DEVIL? WHAT IS THE MEANING OF SIN?

W e now come to Chapter 9 of *The Shack*, "A Long Time Ago, in a Garden Far, Far Away." Paul Young places Mack in a garden tended by Sarayu. The topics concern the original Garden of Eden and the impact of the events there. It makes little difference if some reject it as an actual garden, Paul Young writes, since "rumors of glory" are often hidden in myths and tales (134). In Sarayu's garden there is an infinitely changing pattern of growth and complexity—a "fractal," as Sarayu terms it. Surprisingly, her garden is chaos in color, a total disregard for certainty (128–129). Mack tires from the work of pruning the garden but is reminded that it is "not the work, but the purpose that makes it special" (131). Science is described as the discovering of what God has hidden (132). In humanity's desire for independence from God it lost freedom, for freedom "involves trust and obedience inside a relationship of love" (132).

Then there ensues a discussion between Mack and Sarayu to discover why eating from the tree of the knowledge of good and evil in Eden was so devastating. In seeking independence from God, humanity divorced the spiritual from the physical (135). Lust for independence, to decide what is good and evil apart from God, is the evil of Eden. Sarayu goes on to explain that evil is simply the absence of the good, it has no "actual existence" (135). This meaning of evil is found in early church fathers.

Young has Sarayu assert that independence brings death because people have separated themselves from God, who is Life. People seek rights only to avoid relationships; if they would give up their rights, enter into relationship with God, and become dependent on him, they would find true freedom (137). At the end of their conversation, Sarayu reveals to Mack that the garden they have been tending is actually his soul, a true fractal with its mess and beauty wrapped together.

This chapter has many positive features, with the predominant emphasis on the surprising work and words of the Holy Spirit. Young projects this person of the Godhead as unpredictable and free. It is a creative idea to have the discussion of the Garden of Eden occur for Mack in another garden, which turns out to be his own soul. To describe Mack's soul as both a mess and beauty wrapped together is an apt description of Mack's condition.

Another helpful feature is to describe the original sin as seeking independence from God. The Bible describes the original sin as primarily pride (note Isa. 14; and Ezek. 28). Later Jewish writers of the period between the Old Testament and the New Testament (in the Apocrypha and Pseudepigrapha) concur in the primacy of pride. And Paul the apostle speaks to the primacy of arrogance and the pride of human reasoning (Rom. 1:21ff.; 1 Cor. 1–2).

Paul Young seems to be looking at the result of pride (independence) rather than dealing with the motive, the evil, that leads to independence. But if one understands pride to be the defining of oneself independent of and distinctive from how God defines one, then Young's idea is not far off.

Also the definition of science as that which discovers what God has hidden in his creation is good. The Apostle Paul declares that "in Christ lie hidden all the treasures of wisdom and knowledge" (Col. 2:3). Thus Scripture is even narrower than Young's statement, for the apostle says that all discoveries in all realms of existence pertain to Jesus Christ. There are no exceptions.

Freedom and Truth in Jesus Christ

Young's discussion of freedom is also quite helpful. Contrary to the natural impulse that many feel, true freedom is found only in relationship with God himself, which comes about by placing faith in the Lord Jesus Christ. To the degree that one is committed to Jesus Christ, to that degree one finds freedom.

From personal experience every Christian can witness to this reality. What the world champions as freedom to indulge in every kind of behavior, belief, thinking, entertainment, and a multitude of other things is actually bondage or captivity by such things. Such things become the master; the person is mastered by his indulgence, his "freedom" to do as he pleases. It is only as one comes to believe the gospel message about Jesus Christ and give personal total allegiance to him does one discover deliverance from such a "freedom" (a.k.a. bondage).

There is a particular encounter that Jesus had with the Jewish leaders as recorded in John 8. Jesus affirmed these great truths regarding freedom, slavery, and the devil. In several great statements from Jesus we find the true essence of freedom. It is anchored to knowledge of Jesus himself and of the truth that Jesus embodies. These affirmations are the following: "If the Son shall make you free, you shall be truly free." Jesus not only saves us from the penalty of our sins, which is death (Rom. 6:23), but also from the power of sin. Contrary to popular opinion, Christians are the freest people in the world. They live to serve God in Jesus Christ.

But these great truths become actualized only in those who believe in Jesus. They are spoken only to those "Judeans who had believed him" (John 8:31). Jesus said: "'If you continue to follow my teaching, you are really my disciples and you will know the truth, and the truth will set you free.' Some protested that they had never been slaves, and Jesus replied: 'I tell you the solemn truth, everyone who practices sin is a slave of sin. The slave does not remain in the family forever, but the son remains forever. So if the Son sets you free, you will be really free'" (John 8:31–36).

Like no one else, Jesus precisely and clearly draws the relationship of truth to freedom. In the upper room discourse (John 14–17), Jesus identified himself with the truth: "I am the way, the truth, and the life. No one comes to the Father except through me" (14:6). Truth is not just abstract or propositional but also moral (in that it is able to set one free from bondage). But it is also supremely personal, embodied in Jesus Christ. Thus to know Jesus personally is to have the "truest" truth, which is true freedom. John 14:6 (just cited) is one of the greatest statements regarding reality and truth in all of literature. To the question asked by Pilate at the trial of Jesus, "What is truth?" Scripture answers, "Jesus Christ."

But in John 14:6 Jesus makes these claims in an exclusive manner. There is no other access to God except through or by means of the Lord Jesus Christ. This distinctive claim runs counter to much of contemporary American religion, even contrary to what some Christians believe. But a person cannot claim to be a Christian, a follower of Jesus Christ, without believing him on this point, along with many others. It is unfortunate that, in a later chapter, *The Shack* does not make this point crystal clear when the opportunity arises to do so.

The Apostle John, near the end of the New Testament era of the first century, brings his first epistle to a close on a similar exclusivist claim regarding Jesus being the truth. He writes: "We know that the Son of God has come and has given us understanding to know him who is true, and we are in him who is true, in his Son Jesus Christ. This one is the true God and eternal life" (1 John 5:20). Earlier he had said (5:11–12): "This is the witness: God has given us eternal life, and this life is in his Son. The one who has the Son has this eternal life; the one who does not have the Son of God does not have this eternal life." The exclusivist claims that the Apostles make concerning Jesus Christ come directly from Jesus Christ himself.

The relationship between bondage to sin and freedom in Christ is also discussed by the Apostle Paul. He deals with sin as both a penalty and as a power that captures and enslaves one. In one of the most powerful texts dealing with sin and freedom from sin Romans 6 makes several declarations:

> We know that our old man was crucified with him
> so that the body of sin would no longer dominate us,
> so that we would no longer be enslaved to sin. . . .
> Thanks be to God that though you were slaves to sin,
> you obeyed from the heart that pattern of teaching you
> were entrusted to, and having been freed from sin, you
> became enslaved to righteousness. (I am speaking in
> human terms because of the weakness of your flesh.)
> For just as you once presented your members as slaves
> to impurity and lawlessness leading to more lawlessness,
> so now present your members as slaves to righteousness
> leading to sanctification (Rom. 6:6, 17–19).

Notice that freedom from sin comes as a result of obeying the truth (v. 17)!

The Unpredictable Spirit?

But Paul Young's discussion in this chapter does raise several concerns. One issue concerns how he depicts the Holy Spirit (his Sarayu) as championing uncertainty. When we look at the Bible, we discover something much different. I will take up this topic in a later chapter. But it seems to me that Paul Young portrays the Holy Spirit more like the fictional character Tinkerbell, flittering here and there and sprinkling star dust, than like the third person of the Trinity. Jesus says that the Spirit is bound to reveal him (John 14:26).

Where's the Devil?

Equally disturbing is Paul Young's discussion of sin and the Fall. Perhaps the most serious question that this chapter gives rise to is this: Why is there no mention of the embodiment of evil, of independence from God, namely Satan, known also as the devil? The Genesis account (Gen. 3) makes this self-exalting angel the direct cause of the temptation of Adam and Eve.

Without acknowledgment of this being's reality, the explanation and understanding of evil in the universe is incomplete. Without acknowledging his involvement, why did Eve and Adam ever commit sin?

This created being, probably the most beautiful of all the angels ever made (see Isa. 14 and Ezek. 28), out of pride rebelled against God and set evil and sin in motion in the universe. His evil works are many. He caused Adam and Eve to sin, thereby plunging the whole human race from then until now into darkness and evil. Because of him, the entire animate and inanimate creation has been plunged into bondage and death. He led Cain to murder Abel. His works are described as opposing God's good angels in their divinely appointed tasks (see Dan. 10). Near the end of the Old Testament, he accuses Israel of the guilt of sin so as to prevent Israel from experiencing God's deliverance that is promised with the coming of the Messiah (identified as God's servant, the Branch; Zech. 3:1–10).

More significantly, the devil has a major place in the New Testament, first in the life of Christ and then in the lives of the apostles and Christians. No one encountered the reality of evil embodied in Satan to the degree that Jesus did. Before he ever started his ministry he had to pass the tests posed by Satan who sought to divert him from his divinely appointed role as Savior and Redeemer. The temptation in the wilderness (Matt 4) exposes Satan under three titles, Satan (the opposer, v. 10), the devil (deceiver, vv. 1, 5, 8, 11), and the tempter (vv. 1, 3). It is significant that the title "deceiver" is the one used most frequently, for each of the three tests represented attempts to turn Jesus from his true identity and calling by offering something enticing yet wrong and evil. Had Jesus yielded to just one of Satan's temptations, Jesus could not have been our Savior and Redeemer. Evil would have conquered the world, and all of us would be in Satan's clutches forever.

No one understood the reality of the devil more clearly and fully than did Jesus. Jesus recognized that those Jews who opposed his mission did so as a result of belonging to their "father, the devil . . . a murderer from the beginning, not holding to the truth, for there is no truth in him. When he lies, he speaks his native language, for he is a liar and the father of lies" (John 8:44). To describe Satan's power, Jesus went so far as to call him the "ruler of this world" (John 14:30). If we are to be Jesus' disciples, can we, should we, think any less about the devil when Jesus thought so much about him? Whom Jesus called the "ruler of this world" Paul Young ignores. Apparently Young considers him far less significant than Jesus did—perhaps as ruler of little or nothing at all?

When we consider the apostles of Christ, the devil is clearly a reality to them as well. In one place Paul the apostle refers to the devil twice as the devil (Eph. 6:11) and as the evil one (v. 16). Indeed, Christians' greatest conflict is not with the physical reality ("flesh and blood") but against "the rulers, against the authorities, against the powers of this dark world and against the spiritual forces of evil in the heavenly realms" (v. 12). Thus the Christian's way to victory is to take on spiritual armor and the Spirit and prayer to combat spiritual forces of evil—fallen angels (vv. 13–20).

It is these very forces of evil that Jesus conquered in his death on the cross (Col. 1:19–20; 2:15). Indeed, the reality of Satan is crucial to understanding why today so many in the world are deceived and why there is so much sin in the world. To practice sin is to belong to the devil. It was also one of the reasons why Jesus Christ died on the cross. He destroyed the one having the "power of death, that is, the devil" (Heb. 2:14).

Finally, Scripture gives a test to distinguish the children of God from the children of the devil. If the devil doesn't exist, then such a test is meaningless.

All of the preceding thoughts derive from the text of 1 John 3:8 and 10:

> The one who practices sin is of the devil, because the devil has been sinning from the beginning. For this purpose the Son of God was revealed: to destroy the works of the devil. . . . By this the children of God and the children of the devil are revealed: Everyone who does not practice righteousness—the one who does not love his fellow Christian—is not of God.

In interviews Paul Young has addressed the omission of the devil and explained that he could not put everything in the novel. But this is unacceptable. This chapter of *The Shack* is devoted to telling what happened in the Garden of Eden, just as it unveils what is in Mack's "garden." It goes to great lengths to elaborate on independence from God and its consequences.

But the story is incomplete and distorted without the devil as the instigator of evil. Why else did Eve and Adam disobey God? There was nothing in them as created in God's image and likeness to cause them to make evil choices. Something or someone had to instigate the rebellion. Genesis 3 makes it Satan, the serpent. Young is culpably negligent here.

Without the presence of the Evil One, Young's understanding of sin (called hamartiology) joins with his distortions of angelology and satanology. He ends up making Adam and Eve more culpable for evil than they deserve. Adam blamed Eve, and Eve blamed the serpent—and she was right. What was the deceit that led them to disobey, if it did not come from the devil? All three (Eve, Adam, Satan) were held culpable, and all three suffered consequences. But the devil suffered the greatest consequence: God would use this great evil hatched by the devil to bring destruction on the devil himself by the woman's seed—Jesus Christ. But Paul Young ignores the devil.

Furthermore, it is characteristic of other religions that there is an insufficient appreciation of a personal being who "embodies" all that is evil, whether the religion be Hinduism, Buddhism, Islam, or Shinto. There is also an omission of Satan or the devil in universalism. Or if he is mentioned, he is presented as one who will finally repent with his fallen angels, escape hell, and enter heaven.

The Devil and Mack and *The Shack*

Why would Young omit this great distinctive feature of Christianity, the basis of the study of Satan (satanology) and angels (angelology) from his treatment of the Fall and the reality of sin and suffering for Mack and this present world? Is it not probable that part of Mack's great "sadness" is due to the work, the deceit, of Satan? Is it not true that part of the explanation for why Mack's Missy is murdered is that it was the work of Satan, the one called a "murderer from the beginning" (John 8:44), the one who "has been sinning from the beginning" (1 John 3:8)?

To fail to mention the devil in an entire chapter devoted to the Fall, and to fail to mention him in a novel devoted to explaining the evil in Mack's life and in the world, is an un-Christian omission. It is being terribly naïve in its attitude toward sin and evil.

Is not part of the reason for Mack's "great sadness" the fact that the devil has deceived Mack about the nature of God? Remember the story of Job and his wife in Chapter 1 above? It was Satan who instigated the trials of Job, one result of which touched his wife. She turned the testing into a temptation and ended up blaming and defying God. The devil took advantage of her difficult circumstances.

So too the devil has taken advantage of Mack's trying circumstances. Why did Mack denounce his seminary training? Why did he stop going to church? Why did he never enter the ministry? Why did he become bitter at God? Is he not like Job's wife? Has he not succumbed to the deceit of the devil? Without having the devil involved, Mack's suffering lacks adequate explanation.

The Bible warns us to be alert to the fact that the devil seeks to deceive God's people. In the Old Testament he gave messages to false prophets (1 Kings 22:21–23). In the New Testament Christians are warned about him by the Apostle Paul (Eph. 4:27; 6:11–16; 1 Thess. 3:5; 1 Tim. 3:6–7; 5:15; 2 Tim. 2:26); by James (4:7—we are to "resist the devil"); and by Peter (1 Pet. 5:8—"the devil as a roaring lion walks about for someone to devour"). Indeed, in this last reference the devil is linked with the sufferings of Christians (5:9). Finally, several verses are devoted to his judgment and everlasting suffering (Rev. 12:9–12; 20:1–10). These are just a few of the many references to the devil.

Could it be that in his first telling of his tale, in his story originally written for his children, Paul Young had no Satan because, at the time he wrote it, he was a committed universalist? And could it be that this omission, characteristic of the creeds of universal reconciliation, persisted in the revision because he had not thought differently about the devil? In other words, if the devil is the author of deceit, and universalism bears witness to being deceived by its omission of reference to the deceiver, has Paul continued to be blinded to his reality?

Consider also the implications for helping scores of readers of *The Shack* to come to know God as first-time Christians, or to come to know God more deeply as growing Christians, if the readers are not alerted to the personification of evil, the great deceiver himself, the devil. How are readers to weigh properly all the competing truth claims if they are unaware that Satan may deceive them and

THE MEANING OF EVIL

how he might do it? Is it not probable that readers will remain continually defeated by an unidentified foe? How will they ever come to know victory if they are unaware of the battle being waged by the devil?

More directly, may they not fail to evaluate the doctrines of *The Shack* if they are unaware of the devil's deceit? Is this one reason why there are so many who favor the book while many teachers and pastors of churches are deeply opposed to it?

The Apostle Paul warned the Corinthians (2 Cor. 4:4) that Satan has the role of blinding people to the gospel. Surely these words apply to universalists and perhaps to some of the readers of *The Shack*. In the context the apostle refers to some who "deceive and distort the word of God" and do not "set forth the truth plainly" (4:2). Later (11:3–15), the Apostle Paul warned the same readers that Satan "disguises himself as an angel of light" who comes in the form of "servants who disguise themselves as apostles of Christ" and as "servants of righteousness." He writes:

> But I am afraid that just as Eve was deceived by the ser-
> pent's cunning, your minds may somehow be led astray
> from your sincere and pure devotion to Christ. For if
> someone comes to you and preaches a Jesus other than
> the Jesus we preached, or if you receive a different spirit
> from the one you received, or a different gospel from
> the one you accepted, you put up with it easily enough.
> . . . For such men are false apostles, deceitful workmen,
> masquerading as apostles of Christ. And no wonder, for
> Satan himself masquerades as an angel of light. It is not
> surprising, then, if his servants masquerade as servants
> of righteousness. Their end will be what their actions
> deserve (1 Cor. 11:3–4, 13–15).

These are sober warnings that Christians should apply to all that they hear and read, including *The Shack*.

A Distorted View of Sin and Evil

In this chapter, as elsewhere, Paul Young regularly avoids using such terms as "sin," "iniquity," "transgression," and "disobedience." Why is he short on his vocabulary for sin? The Bible (both Old Testament and New Testament) uses a variety of terms for evil, probably because of the Bible's view of the enormity of evil in contrast to a holy God.

Does not his omission of the devil accompany his omission of an adequate vocabulary for evil? The great negative tone of the novel flows from the burden that Mack carries, namely his "great sadness" that colors all of his living. His past influenced his present, and the murder of his daughter deepened his sorrow and intensified his anger at God. But is not the "great sadness" actually sin infecting his behavior and his attitudes? Is not his reluctance to use the term of "sin" and various synonyms a reflection of Young's view of the devil—that he is much less inclined to see the fullness of evil as the Bible does?

For Paul Young to fail to mention the devil in telling the story of the Fall is like telling the story of creation without mentioning God, the Creator! It is like telling the story of the cross and the events of Good Friday and the resurrection without mentioning Jesus Christ! One of Jesus' purposes for dying was to destroy the power of a real devil (Heb. 2:14), but Paul Young leaves the devil out of the picture, as though he is unreal.

· 8 ·

Living in Relationships and Roles

DO ROLES DESTROY RELATIONSHIP WITH GOD?

C hapter 10, "Wade in the Water," is, as the title indicates, Mack's opportunity to walk on water. It is a chapter devoted to explaining the meaning of living in relationships, whether with God or with other humans in marriage or other relationships. In many ways it builds upon the topic of relationships introduced in Chapter 8 of *The Shack*.

Mack and Jesus walk across the lake, sinking down only a little, less than their ankles. Jesus exhorts Mack to live in the present and to stop imagining the future, since this leads usually to what harm may lie in the future, usually something fearful and without God. Imagined fears lead people to try to control the future, to have power over it. People fear because they do not believe in, they do not know, the love of God and that he is good. This makes one incapable of finding freedom in God's love (142). When Mack and Jesus reach the other side of the lake, Mack reflects on the beauty of the creation that Jesus has made. Jesus reminds him that it has been given to humans to care for and they have usually plundered it, in part because of war. Because of love, Jesus has never acted in his capacity as "Lord and King" to take control of his world (145).

Young proceeds to describe genuine relationships as marked by submission, as in the Trinity where each is in submission to the other. There is no hierarchy among the Three or among humans where love and respect prevail. Similarly, the Three are in submission to human beings so that a "circle of relationship" might prevail! Jesus says that he does not want "slaves to my will; I want brothers and sisters who will share life with me" (146). When Jesus is one's life, submission in all other relationships, including marriage, will prevail. Relationships are broken because people in Eden sought independence from God. Men express this by seeking fulfillment and identity in their work; women express it by seeking fulfillment in relationships apart from God—in their husbands who aren't up to the task and end up playing God and exercising power and rule over them (147). (Here there is an inherent logical contradiction, for Paul has already rejected the exercise of power within the Godhead! Thus, for universal reconciliation to be consistent, men do not act as God!) Men turned to themselves and to their work; women turned to another relationship. Both need to "re-turn" to God and relationship with him. God does not desire that men and women simply fulfill roles because "filling roles is the opposite of relationship" (148).

God took woman out of man so that he might create a "circle of relationship"—she out of him and then all males birthed through her, and all birthed from God (reflecting 1 Cor. 11:1ff.). This makes possible a being that is fully equal and powerful in the counterpart, the male and the female (148). But independence always leads to a quest for power and the destruction of relationship. The scene concludes with Jesus asserting that his life was not meant to be "an example to copy," to be like him. Rather, one's independence needs "to be killed." One needs to follow Jesus in the sense of letting Jesus live out his life in him/her and let Jesus be expressed in every way.

There is much in this chapter that is commendable. The idea that in true love there is no fear is a biblical truth. First John 4:18 makes the explicit assertion, "There is no fear in love, but perfect love casts out fear, because fear has to do with torment. The one who fears punishment has not been perfected in love."

Also, every reader can applaud the emphasis on building a relationship with God. It is a pursuit every Christian should engage in. It is at the heart of Jesus' last prayer for his disciples before he went to the cross and died. Several times Jesus asked the Father to bring his followers to unity in a deep, reciprocal relationship with himself and with the Father (since he is in the Father and the Father is in him). Note the multiple assertions of this reciprocity in the upper room discourse alone, in John 14:10–11, 17, 20; 15:4–7; 17:11, 21–23, 26. There is nothing on earth that could ever match this reciprocal relationship with God through Jesus his Son. The believer has a heavenly relationship that transcends all other relationships. This relationship is probably most actualized or realized in prayer. And it is certain that whatever the Son asks the Father will be granted. But this relationship is not limited to prayer. There is a daily walking and talking with God that is the privilege of every Christian. But Young's understanding of an intimate relationship with God is seriously lacking.

In Chapter 5 above I have already dealt in large measure with the errors of Young's concept of the "circle of relationship." I pointed out the inadequacies of Paul's portrayal of it. But this chapter raises even more concerns about what Paul says about the relationship modeled after the Trinity. In the summary I've just given several questions arise. Again, I will concentrate on only three.

An Aside on War

But first I wish to write a brief criticism that points to an ongoing attitude on the part of Paul Young. His side remark about how war plunders the earth given to humans in stewardship is true. But this side remark reflects Young's anti-institutional bias against government in general. Such a bias runs directly counter to what both Scripture and history affirm. God has instituted (note the words, "God has instituted"—people have not) government to restrain a greater evil that anarchy brings, and history agrees. Governments can pursue just wars. This understanding is at the heart of the most explicit passage about this—Romans 13:1–7. In turn, this teaching derives from one of the most powerful statements Jesus made to endorse human government. In Matthew 22:15–22, Jesus asserts: "Render to Caesar what is Caesar's; and render to God what is God's." Never before in the history of the world did anyone endorse a legitimate place for a secular state alongside God's rule. Prior to this, all societies, including the Greeks and the Romans, embraced the idea that all rule, whether the king's or the deity's, were divine and required that there be no division between the state and the religion.

Our American republic was the first government in the history of mankind to reflect the significance of Jesus' words. As a result, our system gives unprecedented opportunity for freedom to serve God and our fellow human beings. Yet we properly assert that all our freedoms come from God, not government, the servant of God. People are "endowed by their Creator with certain unalienable rights."

(1) Are God and People in a Circle of Relationship?

Now I turn to my three more weighty concerns of this chapter, which I express as questions. First, as Young continues in this chapter to build on his concept of a "circle of relationship," he makes some sweeping statements about the nature of God. He asserts that in the Trinity there is mutual submission of the Three to each other, that there is no hierarchy, and that this is a pattern for humans to embrace. The goal is a "circle of relationship" in which the Three-in-One and humans all are mutually in submission to one another and there is no hierarchy but only love and respect.

Yet is this a correct representation of the nature of the Trinity? It is not. While I pointed out just above that there is a wonderful reciprocity of the Three-in-One, and of it/them with humans, this reciprocity does not cancel out who God is. There is also subordination within the Trinity represented in their deeds, as dealt with above. The Father and the Son "send" the Spirit, for example. In addition, Jesus says that the Spirit will not speak on his own "authority [literally 'by himself'], but he will speak whatever he hears [from the Father]" (John 16:13–15). These verses make it clear that the Spirit is subordinate to both the Father and the Son.

Subordination in the Godhead

But there is more, and it is obvious to every Christian. The Father is Father, the Son is the Son, and the Spirit is subordinate to the sending and will of both the Father and the Son. These roles are never confused or reversed. Just as humans endorse a particular role for human fathers that differs from the roles of mothers, and parents from children, so there is a difference among the Trinity. When humans endorse a denial of these roles, there is confusion and disruption of society, as when a society endorses civil union or marriage for homosexuals or cross-gender behavior and cross-dressing. To deny subordination within the Godhead is akin to this confusion.

While it cannot be dogmatically affirmed, this subordination in the Godhead seems to be eternally so, backward and forward (see 1 Cor. 15:24–28). The last verse clearly asserts both the subordination of humans to God and subordination within the Godhead: "And when all things are subjected to him [Christ], then the Son himself will be subjected to the one who subjected everything to him, so that God may be all in all" (but see also Rev. 21:22–23; 22:1, 3, where the view of the future places the Father and the Son on an equal par). Certainly for the present era of time, until the "new heavens and new earth" arrive, there is subordination within the Godhead.

Subordination of People to God and Jesus Christ

Furthermore, it is obvious to all that while a deep relationship with God is possible for humans, perhaps even what some call a relationship of "theosis," Christians have never taken this to mean that humans become divine like God is. We may "partake of the divine nature" (2 Pet. 1:4) and become "sons of God" (John 1:12), but we never become deified. It is the idea of becoming as God that was the meaning of Satan's temptation of Eve and Adam at the Fall (in Gen. 3), and is the greatest sin of humankind. It is also the essence of Satan's third temptation of Christ in Matthew 4:1–11. The thought comes from the personification of evil, the devil.

Interestingly, even the myths of non-Christians represent the greatest error (or sin) of trying to become as the gods. This error is common to such stories as the "fisherman and the sea"; and to the tale of Daedelus and Icarus his son (who took wings to escape from their prison). In each story the boast of becoming like the gods is the critical turning point that leads from blessing to cursing and destruction.

In addition, the Bible makes it clear that some will become the "footstool" of Jesus' feet, as Jesus himself and virtually all writers of the New Testament affirm, when they quote Psalm 110:1. This verse says that Jesus Christ has been exalted to the Father's right hand "until his enemies become his footstool"—when the judgment at the end of the age unfolds. This verse shows the subordination of the Son to God the Father (of "my Lord" to the "LORD") and of some people to Jesus Christ. This last idea is not a loving submission but a conquest of resistant people (see Matt. 22:44ff.; Heb. 1:3, 7–8, 13; Rev. 19:11–16; etc.).

Thus Jesus Christ may address his followers as "friends" rather than "servants" (so in John 15:14–15) or as his "brothers" (so in Heb. 2:11–13). Yet there is no record that his followers in the New Testament reciprocated by calling Jesus Christ "friend" and "brother" (although it is not necessarily inappropriate to do so). Instead, the language is reverential: they call him "Teacher and Lord" (for so he was; John 13:13–14), and throughout the New Testament those who were in closest relationship to the risen Christ, as we now know him, called him "Lord," "Christ," "Savior," "Sovereign," and many similar names. All of these recognize a hierarchy of relationship between Christians and their Lord.

Reverential Respect

This last thought of reverence raises another question regarding relationships. Young asserts that people fear because they do not believe in, they do not know, the love of God and that he is good. This fear makes one incapable of finding freedom in God's love (142). Yet is there not a place for fearing God while in intimate relationship with him? The entire thrust of *The Shack* is that because God is a God of love there is no place for fearing God. Yet what of the idea of godly fear or reverence that the Bible speaks about (as in Isa. 6 or Heb. 10:30–31 or Rom. 11:20)?

From the reading of this chapter one gets the impression that there is no such place for a sense of awe of the transcendence and majesty of God that one should have while in intimate relationship with him, in a "circle of relationship." But the Christian is hemmed in by both love and reverential awe.

It seems that *The Shack* and other sources fail to separate the being of God, his Triune nature and essential essence, from his works or deeds—the economic Trinity. While all in the Trinity are of equal essence, they have differing functions or works. To deny subordination in a "circle of relationship" that involves humans is a great distortion. Relationship pertains to God's works, not his essence, or at least to the expression of his essence by acts of will as far as humans are concerned. God is love, and he also loves.

My other concerns about this "circle of relationship" are expressed in the earlier chapter. My thoughts there should be integrated with those of mine here and those that follow.

(2) Filling Roles Is Opposed to Relationship?

The next serious concern is expressed in my second question. Is it true that the filling of roles is antithetical to relationships? Young asserts that "filling roles is the opposite of relationship" (148). Since Young doesn't expand on this, it seems that he is saying that in a "circle of relationship" there cannot be the fulfilling of roles.

But all that I've written just above about relationships within the Trinity and in the relationship between God and people says something else. If Christians have a deep relationship with God, it is with the knowledge that this God is omniscient, omnipotent, and omnipresent. Thus he knows everything about the relationship, whether it is truly open and honest. He is able to sustain and keep the relationship, let us say, against all onslaughts. He is able to be present with everyone everywhere on the face of the earth, all at the same time. Thus it is his filling of his role as God that the relationship can exist at all. And any suspension of his filling of his role as God will end the relationship—not empower it!

It seems that it would be better to assert that followers of Christ can have an intimate relationship with God because of Jesus and his relationship with the Father. Because the Son is in the Father (note the implicit acknowledgment of roles in the terms "Son" and "Father") believers can have an intimate relationship with God the Father. Christ's relationship with the Father is the basis of and key to our relationship with God (2 John 8–11).

On the human level, the Bible gives balance by affirming that all should be "in submission to one another" (Eph. 5:21), and yet it immediately upholds the existence of roles (5:22ff.). Thus fathers are to treat their children with respect for their personhood; husbands are to love their wives; wives are to submit themselves to their husbands; and children are to obey parents (see all of this in Col. 3:18–21). Obviously the biblical writers did not view the filling of roles as opposed to relationships of mutual submission.

Why would Paul Young hold such a view of relationship? Perhaps it is his general opposition to institutions, including the church, that has influenced his view. The Bible presents the institutional church as an organic body, the head of which is Christ and where the deepest of relationships should prevail (see Col. 3:12–17 for one of the clearest exhortations about the body of Christ, the church). Obviously, not only should they prevail but they can prevail; otherwise the Apostle Paul's exhortation is hollow.

The Church

Yet such a body has leaders who fulfill several roles in their capacities of teachers, elders, deacons, pastors, evangelists, apostles, prophets, and other roles (see Eph. 4:11–12; Rom. 12:3–8). And it is only as everyone is exercising his or her gift that Christians come to maturity (Eph. 4:13), that false teaching is exposed, and that purity of the truth is secured.

In Paul Young's "circle of relationship" there can be no ultimate authority (God or Jesus) or even secondary sources of authority (people such as elders, deacons, presidents, mayors, teachers). Thus there is nothing or no one to define what love is or whether the relationship is good or bad. Anything goes, and every belief is acceptable.

So once again it seems that the concept of universal reconciliation lies at the foundation of a "circle of relationship" in which there is no hierarchy, authority, or role-filling. In universal reconciliation it is unkind and unacceptable to judge, to find doctrinal error, to fault another. Why does universalism take this view? Since love trumps all of God's other attributes, love should be supreme also for people and all their capacities and behaviors. If God does not judge sin (as discussed above), then he cannot really judge false teaching to be such, including the denial of the uniquely divine-human being who is Jesus Christ. And if God cannot and does not so judge, then neither should people.

Thus this kind of a "circle of relationship" easily accompanies universalism. It is the consequence of an improper view of love that negates the attributes of holiness, truth, and justice. *The "circle of relationship" is not an innocent word picture but one heavy with unbiblical overtones of universalist thinking and anti-institutional bias.*

The effect of Young's view of opposing the institutional church and his resistance to the "filling of roles" is to breed chaos, dissension, disrespect, dishonor, and the end of relationship. The consequence is just the opposite of what Young says it will be. Pure relationships are a false hope and empty promise. Rather than bringing people into a deeper relationship with one another and, in turn, they with God, the "circle of relationship" is a circle of deception and distortion.

Is Jesus Not Lord and King?

Furthermore, Young's subversion of hierarchy in the Godhead spills over to his thoughts about Jesus in his roles of Lord and King. Young sets forth the example of Jesus as one who never acted in his capacity of "Lord and King" to take control of the world "because of love." Young wants to support his idea of what genuine relationships involve. By implication, Young rules out Jesus' second coming to fulfill these roles since then one could not have a relationship with Christ.

But Young's portrayal of Jesus goes too far. It is true that while he lived Jesus never acted as Lord and King, but he said he would do so someday! He promised to come again as Judge (the topic of the next chapter) (Matt. 19:28; Luke 3:17). The Olivet Discourse (Matt. 24–25) is Jesus' portrayal of the future when he will return in power and glory, and judge all the nations. Jesus also instructs his followers by parables in these same chapters to warn of his coming as King, Judge, and Shepherd to judge the people of the world, sending some to "everlasting torment" and the righteous to "everlasting life" (Matt. 25:31–46). Jesus also affirmed that the Father had appointed him to be the future Judge of all human beings. His being Judge of all was forecast by countless prophecies (Ps. 72:2, 4; 75:2; 96:13; 110:6; Isa. 2:4; 11:3ff.; Mic. 5:1; Mal. 3:2).

Furthermore, the epistles of the New Testament speak of Jesus' returning as the coming King to fulfill the "Day of the Lord," which is a day of judgment (1 Thess. 5:1ff.; 2 Thess. 1:5ff.; cf. Acts 10:42). The Apostle Paul asserts that Christ will exert "his power to subject all things to himself" (Phil. 3:21) and to judge the entire world (Acts 17:31; cf. Rom. 2:16; 14:10; 1 Cor. 4:5; 2 Cor. 5:10; 2 Tim. 4:1), including Paul himself (1 Cor. 4:4; 2 Tim. 4:8). James affirms Christ as Judge (James5:9). Most of the book of Revelation reveals Jesus as the coming King and world conqueror (Rev. 4–22; cf. 2:23).

While Young was not directly speaking of the future, his statement suggests that it is contrary to the character of Jesus and having a relationship with him to present him as "Lord and King." But Jesus is much more than a peaceful Savior; and if we do not recognize his lordship and kingship, we do not know him as friend and have no complete relationship with him.

Young's linking of Jesus' refusal to act as Lord and King "because of love" represents universalist thinking. What seems at first a somewhat innocent remark is upon reflection a serious error. Young is unbiblical by opposing Jesus' lordship and kingship to love as though Jesus would not be acting in love if he acted as Lord and King. But this is a false dichotomy. Jesus, and the entire Trinity, are always love and just and holy and perfectly so. One attribute cannot be opposed to another; it cannot be limited by another; but all of them are perfect and in perfect balance. Lordship and kingship represent authority and suggest subordination of others to God and thus contradict Young's understanding of a "circle of relationship." These roles come from Scripture. It is Young's understanding of the "circle of relationship" that is wrong because of both love and holiness. To deny to Jesus his roles at any time as Lord and King "because of love" reveals the heart of a universalist.

(3) Is Jesus Not an Example to be Copied?

The third and final question to arise in this chapter is this: Is Jesus not an example to be copied? Here Young is making the case for the idea that Jesus is not an example to be copied, that Jesus does not want us to be like him. Instead, people need to follow Jesus in the sense of letting Jesus live out his life in an individual and letting Jesus be expressed in every way.

While the latter is indeed a biblical concept, it need not be put in opposition to the idea of following Jesus as an example to be copied. Others have written about discipleship in similar terms— letting Jesus live out his life in mine as if he were I.[41] Letting Jesus live out his life in me is a truth at the heart of much of what Jesus says to his disciples in the upper room discourse (John 14–17), about which we've said much already.

But Jesus also said that we should follow him (John 13:15), and Paul the apostle exhorted early Christians to follow Christ's example (Phil. 2:5; 1 Thess. 1:6). In so doing they would be doing what the apostle does—following Christ's example (1 Cor. 11:1; Phil. 3:17). Peter also exhorts his readers to follow the example of Christ (1 Pet. 2:21). In addition, there are several texts in which Jesus exhorts his people to follow him. Do not such words mean that we should take him as an example "to be copied" in all that we think, say, and do, in all of our living?

Finally, the Apostle Paul exhorts Christians to let their thoughts be the same kind of thoughts that Jesus had. To the Philippians he writes: "You should have the same attitude toward one another that Christ Jesus had" (Phil. 2:5). These words led the apostle to cite the great example of humility that Jesus Christ showed when he went to the cross (vv. 6–11), which eventually led to Jesus' exaltation.

Thus it seems confusing to say that we should be followers of Christ but not "copy" his example. In some ways we cannot today follow his example, because he lived in another time and place. But in many ways, such as in his attitude, character, speech, deeds, and personhood, we should copy him.

Consider the content of this chapter, "A Wade in the Water." The chapter begins by having Mack do what Jesus did when he walked up to his ankles in the top of the water across the lake. Does this not mean that Mack was copying Jesus' example when he walked with him across the lake?

· 9 ·

God as Judge

DOES MERCY TRIUMPH OVER JUSTICE?

In some ways this chapter is the centerpiece of *The Shack* and thus becomes the centerpiece of its criticism.

God Loves All His Children the Same Forever

Chapter 11, "Here Come Da Judge," is an especially crucial chapter for Young's view of God as judge and the meaning of judgment. He focuses on the issue of God acting as judge of the wicked and denies that there is such judgment. The chapter is at the heart of the book both physically and theologically.

The chapter unfolds in the following way. Across the lake Mack mysteriously penetrates into the rock face of a mountain and enters a pitch black room where he faintly perceives the presence of a judge—a beautiful, tall, Hispanic-looking woman in a flowing robe. The judge questions Mack regarding his love and his judging of his children and others. In this light, Mack (acting as God does) affirms that he loves all his children the same; he just loves them differently. He loves them in spite of their occasional disobedience; they will be his sons and daughters forever. His capacity for knowing them grows and "love simply expands to contain it [the knowledge]" (155). The judge tells Mack that God loves his children in a similar way (156).

Clearly Paul intends that the whole discussion about Mack's love for his children should find its parallel in God's love and his relationship to all humanity. This is the crucial point for Paul's universal reconciliation. As humans care for their children, so God cares for his. There is an assumption that everyone has been reconciled to God and that all enjoy the privilege of being God's children by virtue of this reconciliation. This chapter in *The Shack* lays the foundation for the next one where universal reconciliation is more strongly affirmed.

In an earlier chapter I showed that the New Testament makes it clear that while there is a general sense in which everyone is an offspring of God on the basis of all being the offspring of Adam and Eve who were created by God, there is a much more particular sense in which many are not children of God. Passages throughout the New Testament, including Acts 17:22ff. and John 1:12, show that one becomes a child of God by placing faith in Jesus Christ. This narrower category is what determines one's eternal destiny. Indeed, Jesus said that if one does not believe in him, that person is a child of the devil, while still being the offspring of God and even of Abraham, the father of the Jews. Jesus has an extended discussion of who is a child of the devil and who is a child of God in John 8.

I continue on with this crucial chapter. When Mack challenges the truth of God's love for all his children in light of the death of Missy, Mack thereby fills the role of judging God. The judge asks Mack to assume the role of judge and act like a judge of his own children in the manner that he thinks God judges his children. The judge reminds Mack that he has had much practice in judging others, in acting superior over the ones judged (159). (This is Paul's definition of judging.) There are many who, Mack believes, deserve judgment, such as the greedy, those who sacrifice their young for war, wife beaters, those who abuse children, and murderers of children.

I pause here in the telling of this story to draw attention to the subtle antiwar theme that appears again, as it did in the previous chapter. Such an attitude accompanies Young's general anti-institutional bias that he has against government in general.

The judge asks Mack to choose two of his five children to spend eternity in heaven and to choose three of his children to spend eternity in hell (162). When Mack protests that he could never do such a thing, the judge tells him that this is only doing something that he believes God does. Yet Mack protests that just because his son or daughter had sinned against him he could never send either of them to hell. It wasn't "about their performance; it was about his love for them" (163). Finally, Mack volunteers to go in their place to be tortured for all eternity.

(1) The Distortion of Denying People's Performance

As in the earlier chapters, I want to focus on three questions that deserve exposure and answering. The first one arises here in the progress of this chapter. It is this: What determines one's eternal destiny? In particular, does God arbitrarily choose to send most to hell and the rest to heaven? Is this how people end up in hell or in heaven? Note that in this section there is nothing said regarding faith.

It is popular with Paul Young and his fellow editors of *The Shack* (Wayne Jacobsen, Brad Cummings, and Bobby Downes) and others to make the refrain repeatedly that one's relationship with God is not about one's performance but all about God's love and acceptance. But while this sounds good, it is not an adequate understanding of relationships.

Now it is true that many mistake personal performance, as in keeping the law or the Ten Commandments, for simple trust in God's gracious extension of his love for people—for his people. In the New Testament this keeping of rules and laws is often identi-fied with legalism. The whole book of Galatians was written by Paul the apostle to show that salvation is impossible on the basis of works because no one is able to do everything perfectly without failure. Our failure, our sin, and God's character make it clear that God did all that was absolutely necessary to save us by sending his Son to be the Savior available to the world. All that people need to do is to embrace the work of salvation that Jesus did on the cross. He died to pay the price that our sins demanded in order to have fellowship, relationship, and eternal life with God (Rom. 6:23). In an earlier chapter I cited several texts from 1 John that show that God accomplished the basis for everyone's salvation in the death of Christ on the cross.

We cannot be saved by works. In Ephesians 2:8–9, the apostle writes: "For by means of grace are you saved by means of faith, and it is not by yourselves. It is the gift of God, not by means of works, lest anyone should boast." There is no clearer pronouncement that rejects works or performance as the means of salvation and that specifies that faith is the means of receiving salvation.

It Is Faith All the Way
It is also true that people cannot maintain or keep their salva-tion by works. The Christian's relationship with God begins with faith and continues and grows by faith. Again Paul writes: "I am not ashamed of the gospel of Christ, for it is the power of God unto salvation to everyone who believes, to the Jew first and also to the Greek. For therein is the righteousness of God revealed from faith to faith, as it is written, 'the just shall live by faith'" (Rom. 1:16–17). The best explanation of these words is that the Christian life begins by faith and it continues by faith. The righteousness that God requires comes from God as a gift to the one who believes and continues to believe. The apostle told the Galatians that they began with God on the basis of faith and they could continue with God only by faith (Gal. 3:3–5). We

cannot become holier by performance. We grow in sanctification, in holiness, by faith.

The example of David from the Old Testament illustrates this well. When David, one of God's people by faith, committed his horrible sin with Bathsheba, the prophet Nathan brought to light his sin of adultery and the accompanying murder. The sacrificial ritual instituted at God's command called for a sin offering in order to find forgiveness for those sins committed accidentally or inadvertently. But David's sin was not of this kind (see 2 Sam. 11–12). It was worse. It was deliberate, premeditated sinning. Thus all that David could do was to confess his sin and to plead for the mercy of God. And this is what he did, as recorded in Psalms 32 and 51. It was David's faith that continued God's righteousness apart from works.

The Apostle Paul makes this assessment of the event as recorded in Romans 4:6–8: "David says the same thing when he speaks of the blessedness of the man to whom God credits righteousness apart from works: 'Blessed are they whose transgressions are forgiven, whose sins are covered. Blessed is the man whose sin the Lord will never count against him.'"

Thus far Paul Young is correct to write that our relationship is not "about performance" but about God's love. This message is quite needed for many who are taken up with tendencies of legalism. But as with much of what Young writes, there is distortion here.

Young and others take their denial of performance too far. They use it to condemn contemporary evangelical teaching about the need to go to church, to obey rules and regulations, to seek to obey commandments to please God, to obey institutions. They make a cleavage between obedience and believing and/or loving. But such a cleavage in either case is unbiblical and a distortion of the truth. It is a distortion in two ways.

Two Distortions/Errors

First, when it comes to the destinies of heaven and hell, it is indeed not about performance nor is it even about God's love—for he has shown incomparable love—but it is about exercising faith to respond to God's love. The critical matter is the exercise of faith. Faith is what determines one's destiny, but Young says absolutely nothing in this chapter about believing. But in an earlier chapter I pointed out the essential role of faith (John 3:16: "For God so loved the world that he gave his one and only Son that whosoever believes in him shall not perish but have everlasting life"). Similarly, the Apostle Paul writes of the absolutely essential role of faith in receiving salvation (Rom. 10:9–10). Indeed, the Bible says that "without faith it is impossible to please God" (Heb. 11:6). Without exercising faith, no one ever receives God's righteousness; no one is ever saved.

Second, the cleavage driven between faith and works is unbiblical when it denies the evidentiary role of works to prove one's faith. Works give evidence that our faith is genuine. Remember how the book of James argues that "faith without works is dead" (Jam. 2) and cites the example of Abraham and Rahab who proved their faith by their works. It is an entirely unbiblical view to affirm that one is saved by faith and then can live any way he or she wants. The old adage is true that says: The fact that we are saved by faith alone does not mean that the faith that saves is alone.

In an earlier chapter I showed that Jesus himself identifies love with obedience to God's commandments, and the same can be said of faith and obedience. To have faith is to obey God; to disbelieve is to disobey. This point is made in back-to-back statements in Hebrews (3:18–19; cf. 3:12; 4:11) where "disbelieve" and "disobey" are put in parallel to each other. Even the Apostle Paul himself declared that "the only thing that has any value is faith expressing itself through love" (Gal. 5:6). Faith must be accompanied by works to be considered genuine.

Divine Sovereignty and Human Responsibility

The biblical emphasis on faith illustrates the beautiful balance between divine sovereignty and human accountability or responsibility. These two areas of accountability —the vertical and the horizontal— permeate Scripture. But they must not be confused so as to mean that the work of salvation is accomplished by both God and man. No, it is God's work to bring salvation; our faith is our response to God's work. Faith is not a work, for then it would violate Ephesians 2:8–9 cited above. Faith is the means to appropriate salvation; works are not.

But people are responsible to call on God in order for them to receive salvation: "For whosoever shall call on the name of the Lord shall be saved [by God]" (Rom. 10:13). Works are an absolutely necessary consequence of salvation received by faith. Calvin himself, the great champion of salvation by faith, asserted this. Works are absolutely necessary. They simply are not the means of salvation nor the grounds of it. Faith is the means; and the grounds of salvation is the death of Jesus Christ.

The Doctrine of Election

In light of the foregoing, it is a terrible caricature of divine election (Rom. 8:28ff.; 9–10) to assert that God "sends" people to hell. Those who go to hell are not "sent" there by God in some arbitrary fashion. Those who go to hell do so as the result of their own choice not to believe, a choice for which they are fully accountable (John 3:16–18).

The way that *The Shack* puts it is a horrendous subversion of the love of God, the justice of God, election, and salvation. In writing in this way, the author virtually identifies himself as a champion of universal reconciliation, since it is not about what people do (including, in light of Chapter 13, exercising faith) but about God's love alone. The reader will remember that the matter of faith never comes up in this chapter.

One other reference needs to be put here. Hebrews 5:8–9 says without equivocation that only those who obey Jesus Christ are saved. The text says that "Jesus Christ became perfect or complete as a human being by learning obedience from the things which he suffered" (v. 8). Consequently "he became the source or cause of eternal salvation to all who obey him" (v. 9).

If he the Son of God learned to obey God so should we. It's as simple as that!

We Will Be Judged for Our Works

Works are a necessary accompaniment of a profession of belief for another reason. One day everyone will stand before the judgment seat of Christ to give an accounting for how he or she has lived. Each will be justly and correctly rewarded. Jesus claimed to be the one to act in this future judgment scene (Matt. 25:31–46), and Paul the apostle spoke of it as well (Rom. 14:10–12): "For we will all stand before the judgment seat of God. It is written: 'As surely as I live,' says the Lord, 'Every knee will bow before me; every tongue will confess to God.' So then, each of us will give an account of himself to God." See similar instruction in 1 Corinthians 3:12–15. There is eternal reward coming for those who do works for the kingdom; and loss of reward for those who do not.

(2) The Distortion of Saying, "Mercy Triumphs over Justice Because of Love"

The second critical question that flows from this chapter deals with how Young treats the relationship between the love and justice of God. When Mack volunteers to go to hell in place of his children to be tortured there for all eternity, the judge tells Mack that he is acting like Jesus, that he has judged his children to be worthy of his love, even if it costs him everything (163). Jesus loves "all his children perfectly" (163). The judge tells Mack that Missy died because "it was the work of evil"; it was not part of God's plan (164). The judge tells Mack that God has done all he can do to right the evil. She says he did it "for love. He chose the way of the cross where *mercy triumphs over justice because of love*" (164; italics mine). The judge exhorts Mack to turn from his independence, to turn from his being the judge of God and how he thinks the universe should be run, and to trust God to run his universe. Mack confesses that he wants to trust God and to stop being a judge.

Now it is certainly a proper thing to have the judge correct Mack in his attempt to judge God. The arrogance of people judging the Judge of the universe is rightly corrected. But it is another thing to extend Mack's personal problem, or anyone's for that matter, of rebellion and to build on it universal statements that distort God's judgment. Thereby Young does the very thing that the novel condemns Mack for doing! Paul Young judges God's judging as unacceptable!

The words I have placed in italics above probably form the most all-encompassing statement of the novel to reflect explicitly the errors of universalism or universal reconciliation. The statement, "Mercy triumphs over justice because of love," is the bedrock of all universalist thinking, and it is unbiblical. The words are an explicit affirmation that judgment is unnecessary because Jesus in love has already borne all judgment and "mercy triumphs over justice." There is no future judgment.

The Meaning of James 2:13

While the sentence, "Mercy triumphs over justice because of love" is almost word-for-word from Scripture (James 2:13b), Paul Young makes crucial changes. He has added "because of love" and assumes that *God's* mercy is the alternative to justice, as shown by his next sentence: "Would you prefer he'd chosen justice for everyone?" Yet the context shows that James is not talking about God showing mercy to people at the cross but about believers showing mercy toward the poor. James 2:13 actually says: "mercy triumphs over justice." That's it. The words "because of love" are not in the text.

Paul Young also fails to quote or use the first part of the same verse ("For judgment will be merciless to the one who has shown no mercy"; 2:13a). Thus God's judgment is "without mercy"—just the opposite of the point that Young tries to make in this chapter, that God will not judge sin in the future. These words clearly speak of God's future judgment based on justice that depends on what people do, even though Jesus has already died under judgment for sin. *It means just the opposite of what Paul's universalism affirms—that mercy limits God's justice.* Indeed, by these biblical words there is no mercy to those who show no mercy! The part of the verse that affirms "mercy triumphs over justice" is speaking about what Christians do. The context shows that James is dealing with human partiality and that works of impartiality are a necessary evidence of a Christian's faith.

Even the wording for "triumphs over" in James 2:13 is a bit misleading, for the Greek words are better translated as "boasts against" or "is joyfully confident over." James is referring to believers' needing to show by their works that they are impartial toward the poor. The idea is that in the future believers' mercy (not God's) expressed in good works will deliver them from the judgment coming on those who show partiality. Even if "God" is assumed into the text, the verse is saying nothing of God judging unbelievers. Finally, this verse and the preceding verse make it very clear that God will judge in the future—an idea that universal reconciliation and *The Shack* deny.

The verse is not a discussion of God's nature or actions but a principle of human behavior toward others. It does not say that because of his mercy God after the cross will no longer act to judge and apply the sentence of judgment already placed on those who disbelieve (John 3:16–18). James is dealing with expressions of human mercy.

A Limitation to God's Mercy

While God does extend mercy to all unconditionally, Young neglects all the texts that also assert that God fills the role of Judge past and future (beginning with Gen. 18:25; Heb. 10:30; etc.); that there is a limitation to God's mercy if disobedience and unbelief occur (Rom. 11:22–23; Heb. 4:1–3, 11; 6:3–6; 10:26–31; 12:25–29); and that those who reject Christ in this life will experience judgment afterward (Heb. 9:27). God judges according to a standard (asserted several times in Rom. 2). All the world cries out that the standard be what is right or holy (so Gen. 18:25) as well as loving or merciful. But it is never said to be love alone or limited by love. Above I cited many texts from the Old Testament (beginning with Exod. 34) and from the New Testament that point to the balance of justice and love in the nature of God.

It seems that a more biblical way to relate justice, mercy, and love is to say that God's love was the reason that God sent the Savior to pay the penalty of our sin so that the full requirements of justice, and of the law, might be met (cf. Rom. 3:25–26) and mercy could be extended to all. Mercy does not "trump" justice or "triumph" over it or limit it. Justice is fully served.

Also, this chapter distinctly says nothing about those passages of the Bible that speak of lasting torment or separation of the wicked who refuse to believe Christ. Instead this chapter leads the reader to believe that there is no such suffering in an eternal hell. As I've shown in earlier chapters, the very strongest words in the Bible come not from Paul or John or Peter, but they are those of Jesus who asserts that the wicked will suffer "eternal punishment" just as the righteous will enjoy "eternal life" (Matt. 25:46; Luke 16:23, 24, 25, 28). For Paul Young to ignore totally these words and truths makes his picture of Jesus and God distorted. In his writings from 2004, he dismissed these texts as merely stories and parables without theological import.

There Is Something That Almighty God Cannot Do

Finally, if Hebrews 6:3–6 says that it is impossible for God to renew to repentance those who turn away and reject him, then it is impossible for God to do something that would allow mercy to triumph over justice. That something is to overturn the human choice to disbelieve and disobey the gospel and, according to the claims of universalism, to bring a person through the purifying powers of hell so that the person repents and comes out of hell to God. This verse says that God cannot override a person's unbelief, but universal reconciliation asserts that God's love must do this.

When God Ceases to Be God

It is the greatest distortion to subsume justice under mercy, when the Bible presents God as perfect in all his attributes. This means that one attribute cannot be exalted over another, and the Bible never does this. The Bible says that God is holy (Lev. 19:1), light (1 John 1:5), just (2 Thess. 1:5–6), and that he is love (1 John 4:8, 19). Truth and love are interlocking themes in 1, 2, and 3 John. Note also that Jesus "loves righteousness" (Heb. 1:9; cf. all of Ps. 45, from which the quote is taken).

In addition, the requirement for an Old Testament believer is clearly balanced (Mic. 6:8): "He has showed you, O man, what is good. And what does the LORD require of you? To do justice, and to love mercy, and to walk humbly with your God." Finally, if mercy or love "limits justice" then love becomes the only lasting, eternal attribute of God, and God ceases to be God. And Jesus reflects this same thing when he defines "the more important matters of the law" as "justice, mercy and faithfulness" (Matt. 23:23). There is no disconnect between justice, mercy, and obedience.

Now someone will say: "Didn't God's love override God's justice at the cross?" If this is meant in the sense that love led God to deal justly with our sin by applying his justice to the person of Christ for what we truly deserve, then the answer is yes (see Rom. 3:25ff.; John 3:16). This is not love overriding or displacing justice. Justice was served. But this is not what universal reconciliation asserts. Instead, universalism contends that God cannot fully exact justice on unbelievers who reject Christ because his love restrains or limits him from doing so.

Love and Justice

Note that *The Shack* has Wisdom pitting the choice of love over against the choice of justice. Immediately after the words, "He chose the way of the cross where mercy triumphs over justice because of love," Young has the judge ask: "Would you instead prefer that he'd chosen justice for everyone? Do you want justice, 'Dear Judge'?"

The universalist ministers of Boston announced in 1878 that "justice is limited by God's love." As long as one unbeliever remains in hell God's love has failed and he is unjust. While such a person is there for rejecting Christ, God's love will deliver him/her from there given enough time of "corrective suffering." This is what universal reconciliation teaches.

(3) Is Judgment about Setting Things Right and Not about Destruction?

Near the end of this chapter the scene shifts from what Mack is learning on earth about the future to a scene of what goes on in heaven. Somewhat in reward for the progress that Mack has made in his thinking about judgment, the judge gives Mack the opportunity to see through a waterfall his daughter Missy playing in the presence of Jesus. She is able to perceive her father's presence, even to mouth an "I love you" to him, but she cannot see Mack. The judge affirms that Mack is not to blame for her death; and even if he had been to blame, Mack is told: "Her love is much stronger than your fault could ever be." As the scene of bliss disappears, the judge tells Mack that "judgment is not about destruction, but about setting things right" (169).

This discourse gives rise to the final crucial question: Is Paul Young being biblical when he has the judge tell Mack that "judgment is not about destruction, but about setting things right" (169)?

It may come as a surprise to most readers that these words come right out of universalist thinking. It arose first in the third century from one of the leading biblical scholars of his day, Origen. Origen did much to defend the Christian faith against attackers. But Origen had a serious flaw. He often sought to meet his opponents on the ground of rationalism, of reason, and strayed from the Bible on several matters. One of these matters concerned the future destiny of the wicked.

Christian universalists love to cite Origen as being the first, persuasive spokesman for the view that God's love is such that he cannot allow evil to exist forever into the future and that all the wicked in hell will repent because of the purifying fires of hell. Neither of these arguments finds expression in the Bible; and they both overlook countless texts (many from Jesus) that speak about the eternal judgment in hell of all the wicked who reject God. The arguments that seem so winsome and generous and logical lack biblical support and are contradictory to other teachings of the Bible.

Now I return to the statements of *The Shack* that "judgment is not about destruction but about setting things right." It so happens that the last words are exactly those found in Origen and represent the Greek word *apokatastasis*, "setting things right." The word occurs only once in the New Testament, in Acts 3:21. In this text Peter is preaching to fellow Jews that they needed to repent and believe in Christ so that times of refreshing may come (v. 19). Christ "must remain in heaven until the time comes for God *to restore everything*, as he promised long ago through his holy prophets" (3:21).

In the context Peter is referring to a restoration of blessing for the Jews that would come with the second coming of Christ. The "restoration" of all things refers primarily to renewed blessing for Israel. If it is extended to include the whole world, there is nothing in the text here or elsewhere to lead to the meaning that this must include the repentance of the wicked in hell so that hell is emptied and ceases to exist. Clearly it points to the millennial kingdom Christ will inaugurate when he returns. It may refer to the coming of the new heavens and new earth (in light of the words, "of all things") promised in the Old Testament (Isa. 66) and reiterated in the New Testament (2 Pet. 3:13) when righteousness is all-pervasive. But there is absolutely no basis here for finding respite for the wicked in hell to give them a second chance once they have rejected Christ while alive.

But Paul Young has the judge promise Mack, "Judgment is not about destruction but about setting things right." The last words are the translation of *apokatastasis*.

Interestingly, in recent years, scholars have reexamined Origen's view of the destiny of the wicked and find that he says several apparently contradictory things. So it may well be that Origen is not the champion of universal reconciliation for universalists after all!

But Origen is the first to express his "hope" that the wicked would be rescued from hell and not suffer eternal torment. Universalists have continued to use this "hope" terminology ever since. And the author of *The Shack* has used it in public settings.

Judgment Is about Destruction

The other part of the statement that the judge makes to Mack needs to be critiqued as well. For the judge to say, "Judgment is not about destruction," is patently false. It does reinforce the basic universalism embodied in the complete statement and goes well with the words, "But about setting things right." Yet it contradicts what Jesus and all the apostles say.

Let's take Jesus' words first. In the powerful Sermon on the Mount, Jesus warned that there were two ways, one broad way leading to destruction, and a narrow way leading to life (Matt. 7:13). In the parables he spoke of only two destinies, one that is eternal life, the other that is eternal torment (Matt. 25:46) and eternal fire (25:41). The Apostle Paul writes of "vessels of wrath fitted for destruction" (Rom. 9:22), of the wicked whose "end is destruction" (Phil. 3:19; 1 Thess. 5:3), and who "are punished with everlasting destruction" (2 Thess. 1:9). The Apostle Peter writes that the wicked will experience "swift destruction" (2 Pet. 2:1; 3:16). Future judgment is about destruction.

Even more persuasive is the Old Testament evidence. It is filled with warnings about the destruction of the wicked and of the present order of things. New heavens and a new earth will replace the current ones (see Isa. 66:22-24). It is from this text that Jesus often drew his words concerning the judgment and destruction to come, that is hell "where their worm does not die and the fire is not quenched" (Mark 9:42-48).

In addition, the New Testament speaks of the end of the wicked under other terms, including "perish," "punishment," and "separation" from God. These terms reinforce the idea that the end of the wicked is judgment and destruction. Again John 3:16 says it well: "For God so loved the world that he gave his one and only Son, that whoever believes in him will not perish but have everlasting life." John's words clearly parallel Jesus' warning about the two ways.

The word "destruction" does not mean that something or someone is utterly consumed so as to cease to exist. Rather, the term means that one ceases to exist as he normally does on earth. His living and his activities are totally changed into a form suited for an everlasting state of separation from God that transcends the physical realm. One's earthly life ends; one's everlasting suffering begins.

Universalism Judges God

In light of this biblical evidence, it is a terrible misstatement for Paul Young to have his character say, "Judgment is not about destruction but about setting things right." It is to mouth the universalist line and to oppose the clear statements of Jesus himself and his apostles. One wonders how such blatant distortions ever got into *The Shack*. It seems that the editors were influenced more by contemporary concerns about postmodernity and what is politically correct than by the Bible. It is post biblical.

As I observed above, Young makes such great distortions in this foundational chapter about eternal judgment that he should heed his mythical character's advice to Mack and stop judging God. It is a pattern that represents the fundamental flaw of universalism—

God's character and revelation are put into the service of what people think that God should be and what his word should say. They have exalted human conceptions and rationalism above the self-disclosure of God. It amounts to nothing more than wishful, deceived thinking.

Defining the Church and a Christian

WHAT'S WRONG WITH THE INSTITUTIONAL CHURCH?

Chapter 12, "In the Belly of the Beast," is Young's attempt to deal with such concepts as wisdom, time, and reality and to denounce all institutions, including marriage, as wrong. He also defines who a Christian is. As usual, I begin with a summary of the chief matters of the chapter and then critique it by asking and answering two or three questions.

Mack notices that "The Great Sadness" has gone for good, which had crippled his life ever since Missy's death. He is also told that the judge in the previous chapter is Sophia, wisdom, a personification of Papa's wisdom. He also learns that his other children were present in their dreams when he saw his Missy playing with Jesus. He learns too that Missy was in communion with Jesus before she died and knew his peace. The way for Mack to cope with his loss is to learn to live loved (175), to experience life together with Jesus as friend, in dialogue, and to share his life, wisdom, and love (175). Only then will Mack begin to understand what "it means to be truly human" (177). Heaven is going to be a cleansing of the present universe and look a lot like the present one (177). The description of heaven as pearly gates and gold actually describes Jesus' bride, his church, forming a spiritual city. Jesus tells Mack that his disappointment with the visible church should not deter him, for Jesus did not come to build "the institution, a man-made system" (178). Rather Jesus' church is all about people and relationships, a living "breathing community of all those who love me, not buildings and programs" (178).

This chapter begins with some creative ways to present the realities of heaven and the future. It is commendable that the Great Sadness has finally left Mack once and for all. Also, it is a positive encouragement to say that Mack has to learn to live loved, to appropriate his relationship with Christ as intimate as friend with friend. Indeed, it is only then that one realizes what it truly means to be human.

If we want to know what it really means to be a human being, we do not look around us to find some examples, but we look "away to Jesus, the pioneer and completer of our faith" (Heb. 12:2). While we see all around us the effects of the Fall, we are exhorted to "look to Jesus who was made a little lower than the angels, now crowned with glory and honor because he suffered death" (Heb. 2:9).

I suspect that many Christians cannot relate properly to God because they do not sense that God loves them. Yet it is a truth that pervades the Bible. It is especially communicated in the book of Psalms.

An Example from My History

My mother lost her husband, my dad, when he was forty-two. He was taken from us five kids by the terrible disease of polio during the polio epidemics of the late 1940s and early 1950s. Only the generation that lived through those times realizes how much terror the epidemics spurred at the time.

My mother grew in her relationship with God during the time Dad was in an "iron lung"—about seven or eight months. It was a device shaped like a cylinder, six feet long and about three feet in diameter. It forced air into the patient's lungs so that he could breathe.

Psalm 37

After his death, during the ensuing years back on the farm in Illinois, Mom grew to love the Psalms. She wrote poetry in praise of God, no doubt inspired to do so because of the Psalmist himself. Her favorite was Psalm 37, which is one of my favorites, too. It seems that the Holy Spirit through the Psalmist was thinking of people just like Mom whom he could encourage. Note these words from several of the verses:

> Do not fret because of evil men, or be envious of those who do wrong; For like the grass they will soon wither, like green plants they will soon die away. Trust in the LORD and do good; dwell in the land and enjoy safe pasture; Delight yourself in the LORD and he will give you the desires of your heart. Commit your way to the LORD; trust in him and he will do this: He will make your righteousness shine like the dawn, the justice of your cause like the noonday sun. Be still before the LORD and wait patiently for him; do not fret when men succeed in their ways, when they carry out their wicked schemes. . . . But the meek will inherit the land and enjoy great peace. . . . Better the little that the righteous have than the wealth of many wicked; for the power of the wicked will be broken, but the LORD upholds the righteous. The days of the blameless are known to the LORD, and their inheritance will endure forever. In times of disaster they will not wither; in days of famine they will enjoy plenty. . . . The LORD delights in the way of the man whose steps he has made firm; though he stumble, he will not fall, for the LORD

upholds him with his hand. I was young and now I am old, yet I have never seen the righteous forsaken or their children begging bread. They are always generous and lend freely; their children will be blessed. Turn from evil and do good; then you will always live securely. For the LORD loves the just and will not forsake his faithful ones. They will be protected forever, but the offspring of the wicked will be cut off; the righteous will inherit the land and dwell in it forever. Wait for the LORD and keep his way. He will exalt you to possess the land; when the wicked are cut off, you will see it. The salvation of the righteous comes from the LORD; he is their stronghold in time of trouble. The LORD helps them and delivers them; he delivers them from the wicked and saves them, because they take refuge in him (Ps. 37:1–7, 11, 16–19, 23–29, 34, 39–40).

The promises of this and other Psalms gave strength, hope, and perseverance to my mother in the most difficult of times. It is a pity that there is hardly a word in Young's novel to encourage Mack to lay hold of the great promises of God found in the Bible for his strength and deliverance.

Strangely, the "wicked" are mentioned in this Psalm about fourteen times—more than once every three verses. I wonder why? Is it that this Psalm is so down to earth, so true to our circumstances, that it gives a realistic place to the power of evil that confronts the lives of the righteous?

One of the great biblical encouragements for us children growing up were the words, "When parents forsake me, the Lord will receive me" (Ps. 27:10).

We can all rejoice that a great transformation in Mack has taken place. But I wonder: On what basis did this transformation occur? If it has been on the basis of the many distortions I have already pointed out, has the right kind of transformation occurred? Has

Mack been restored to the God of the Bible or to a redefined God somewhat made in man's image and likeness, in the image of post-modernity and what is politically correct?

(1) Did Not Jesus Create Institutions?

The first question of importance to ask in this chapter is this: Is the institution of the church a God-given entity that is indispensable? I've addressed this matter at length in an earlier chapter, but I return to it again because Young does, with even more extreme statements than those made before. The following will justify my claim.

The words that Young uses to show his opposition to the institutional church are his strongest words yet. It is especially offensive that Young has Jesus tell Mack that he doesn't create institutions—"never have, never will"—whether political, economic, religious, or even marriage (since marriage is said to be a relationship, not an institution) (179). Young even becomes slanderous, I believe, when he has Jesus assert: "'Like I said, I don't create institutions; that's an occupation for those who want to play God. So no, I'm not too big on religion,' Jesus said a little sarcastically, 'and not very fond of politics or economics either'" (179).

Are Institutions a "Trinity of Terrors"?

But there's more. Jesus immediately adds: "And why should I be? They are the man-created trinity of terrors that ravages the earth and deceives those I care about. What mental turmoil and anxiety does any human face that is not related to one of those three?"

Do you realize what Young is asserting here? He virtually equates all mental problems and anxiety to these institutions. Yet the Bible says God created them. As I pointed out in the earlier chapter on institutions, God created these institutions: marriage in Genesis 2, the institution of government in Genesis 10–11 (cf. Rom. 13:1–7); and the Christian church in Acts 2. They are not "man-created." Strangely, Young is oblivious to the fact that without institutions, chaos reigns. It is the work of the devil to breed chaos, to try to destroy every institution, but of course Young doesn't recognize the existence of the devil in his novel. The "trinity of terrors" is the devil's work, not people's. He says these "terrors" deceive people, but it is actually the devil that does. Young's discourse could be hardly any further from the truth.

Jesus (in *The Shack*) continues by saying that "these terrors" (including institutions, structures, and ideologies) "are tools" that humans create to provide some sense of certainty and security where there is none. "It's all false" (179). Jesus asserts that institutions are part of the world system but his people are to be in them but not of them (181). With Jesus they will grow in "the freedom to be inside or outside" any system (181).

To have Jesus tell Mack that he did not come to "build an institution, a man-made system" sounds appealing to all those who have been hurt by the institutional church or for some other reason have come to reject it. But Scripture makes it very clear that the institutional church, with all of its warts and problems, is God's organism and organization (of whatever form) for reaching the world and for building community and relationships. In the chapters above I devoted much space to show how terribly wrong it is to oppose institutions, including the church, the government, marriage, and others.

Young's identification of the "institution" with a "man-made system" is an error. It is God's system for promoting intimacy with him and others and furthering his plan for bringing the good news to the whole world. In fact, all the institutions that are common to civilized, Christianized society derive from God, not people. Left to their own devices, people would soon be duped to give allegiance to the devil and his design of anarchy for all institutions. The devil is the author of chaos, not order or rule (see Col. 1:13; 2:15).

The Shack also makes the institution a part of the "world system" (181). But this is an invalid association. In the New Testament, the world is opposed to Jesus Christ (John 14–17) as that which hates him and his apostles, and is under the rule of Satan (John 14:17–19, 22, 27, 30–31). The world cannot include the church, for Jesus Christ established the church. He loved the church and gave himself for it. The world did not establish the church. In 1 John 2:15–17, the world is viewed as something to be avoided, as something immoral and evil, and affection for it is opposed to love for God and actually puts one outside the realm of God's love for such a person. One cannot love both the world and God.

Young's negative attitude toward the church soon deteriorates into what can properly be described as his determination to subvert the church as an institution. Like the insurgents who reside within a country for the sole purpose of destroying it from within, Young is an insurgent within Christianity to destroy its institutions. Reviewers of *The Shack* have recognized this.

As with other things in the novel, Young's basic anti-institutional beliefs are autobiographical. They reflect his general practice of not attending a local church for many years. His view of the local church ignores such texts as Hebrews 10:25—"not forsaking the assembling of yourselves together." This assembling involves a meeting place where pastors, elders, and deacons exercise some kind of leadership and authority and are to be obeyed.

Authority in the Church of Jesus Christ (Hebrews 13)

The context of Hebrews explicitly exhorts such obedience to leaders (13:7, 17):

> Remember your leaders, who spoke the word of God to you. Consider the outcome of their way of life and imitate their faith. . . . Obey your leaders and submit to their authority. They keep watch over you as men who must give an account. Obey them so that their work will be a joy, not a burden, for that would be of no advantage to you.

One of the reasons for these commands to obey leaders is given in the verses between the two quoted. Verse 9 says: "Do not be carried away by all kinds of strange teachings. . . ." Is it not self-evident that such leaders are necessary to guard the truth and block false, even heretical teaching? It seems that *The Shack* and some literature of the emergent church are doing this very thing—rejecting the evangelical, institutional church and promoting "strange teachings" that should be avoided.

Quite obviously, if people are to be in the relationship of the church, they have to get together, be instructed, worship, and do business (such as finding out about needs, spending funds, choosing leaders, and many other things). The early chapters of the book of Acts record the beginning of the church, and many of these matters find a place there.

Young's view virtually has no place for spiritual gifts, including that of leadership (Rom. 12:8) and their exercise at some place! In addition, the two ordinances of the church (baptism and the Lord's Supper) are the great means of promoting and experiencing relationship with Christ and with one another—matters that Jesus commanded. But these go unmentioned here in *The Shack*.

The verses from Hebrews 13 also call for submission to the authority of the leaders. Young believes that authority is opposed to a "circle of relationship," of intimacy with God and with others. But these verses show that Young's view is false. It is one of the "strange teachings" to be avoided.

The often-heard complaint of many in our day is that there is not a good church in their neighborhood. Some use this argument to attend church on the radio or on TV or by podcast; others use it to meet in their own homes with friends. Yet all of these fail to benefit from the mutual edification possible by the exercise of spiritual gifts, and having duly appointed or elected elders and deacons.

There is no perfect church. All churches are flawed in some way. This is clear from the New Testament itself. The churches of the book of Acts had their problems. Remember Ananias and

Sapphira, who died for lying to the congregation in Acts 5? And of the seven churches of Revelation 2–3, only two (Smyrna and Philadelphia) are commended by Jesus and have no faults cited. The other five are severely criticized: they had lost their first love (Ephesus), were involved in sexual immorality (Pergamum, Thyatira), were spiritually dead (Sardis), and were so spiritually corrupt as about to be vomited by Christ (Laodicea). Jesus commanded these to repent.

The best guide for Christians is to heed the biblical exhortation to keep on assembling together. Get involved, exercise one's spiritual gifts, improve the spiritual life of the church (Col. 3:12–17 specifically addresses how this can be done), and reach out to the neighborhood and the world. There is nothing less at stake than the next generation of Christians in our nation and the world.

(2) Who Is a Christian?

When Jesus tells Mack that the people who know him are "free to live and love without any agenda" (181), Mack asks whether this is what it means to be a Christian (182). Jesus replies that he is not a Christian and doesn't try to make any one such. Rather, from all walks of life and from all religions come people who love him. He is seeking to join people "in their transformation into sons and daughters of my Papa, into my brothers and sisters" (182). When Mack asks whether this means that all roads lead to him, Jesus replies that it does not mean this. "Most roads don't lead anywhere. What it does mean is that I will travel any road to find you" (182).

These words give rise to the final question for this chapter. What does it mean to be a Christian? The final words of the chapter must give pause. While Paul does not say that there are many roads or ways to God, of which Jesus is only one, he does seem to confuse the issue. And later he will say that Jesus is "a path of reconciliation" (222) not "the path."

It is appropriate in some cultures to avoid using the title "Christian." I've traveled twice to Afghanistan, and there I had to learn quickly to avoid using terms such as "missionary" and "Christian." Christians avoid using the term "Christian" to identify themselves because most Muslim Afghans and other Muslims around the world think that every American, even every Westerner, is a Christian. And they mostly know America by the media and the entertainment industry. Thus every American is painted by what comes out of Hollywood and TV and the Internet. They believe that every American is a loose person morally, that sex and scandal and lust for power and money and such things characterize every Christian.

Thus Christians in such places use the words a "follower of Jesus" to identify themselves. Jesus is highly respected in the Qur'an and in the cultures and religious practices of the Muslim world. Jesus is regarded as one of the great prophets, although Muhammad is regarded as greater.

A Story from Afghanistan

I remember well the special occasion of being in rural Afghanistan south of Kabul, the capital, one afternoon in October 2005. I was part of a team of Americans helping a Christian organization assist the beginning of schools for girls. Such education was banned while the Taliban were in control before America and its allies came into the land to quash the Taliban in 2002–2003. While in a home during a session for the forty or so girls in attendance, the mother of the teacher came into the room. She was visiting from Iran. She was impressed by our bringing for these and the other girls gifts of pens, pencils, writing pads, reading books, and a shawl for each one. Through our Muslim translator, we learned that she blessed us in the name of Allah and Isa (the Arabic equivalent for Jesus). When I heard the name Isa, I asked our Muslim translator to ask the woman if she believed in Isa. I knew it wise to avoid asking whether she was a Christian. He replied: "Of course, she believes in Isa, just like she believes in Moses, Abraham, and all the prophets."

I think that our translator was being a bit defensive and did not want a conversation about Isa to take place between us and the Iranian woman. It could be that she was a believer in Isa. It is unfortunate that such schools have since been closed due to renewed incursions and pressure from the Taliban, including the murder of teachers! Later, the Lord gave me the opportunity to discuss at some length my faith with our translator.

I tell this story to validate the fact that there may be good reasons to avoid using the term "Christian" in some situations. But the term "Christian" is a good word. It comes into being first in Antioch (Acts 11:26), where "great numbers of people" were coming to the faith and were being instructed by Paul and Barnabas: "the disciples were first called Christians at Antioch." The word means to be a follower of Christ, and no doubt arose to distinguish the believers who were coming to believe in Christ from those who remained Jews or were in the more broad category of "Godfearers"—non-Jews who feared the God of the Old Testament.

What is a Christian?

The title "Christian" exposes one who wishes to identify with Christ as one's Lord and Savior. The term was proudly claimed by the early martyrs of the faith, such as Polycarp. When challenged to renounce Christ or be burned at the stake, Polycarp replied: "For eighty-six years I have been the servant of Christ, and he has done me no wrong. How can I blaspheme my King who has saved me? I am a Christian." He died in Rome in A.D. 156.[42]

The title Christian finds support in the phrase "in Christ," which the Apostle Paul and others use on multiple occasions as they write to new converts to the gospel (see Ephesians and Colossians). Obviously, Jesus would not identify himself as a Christian, and so Young is correct in having him say that he is not a Christian. He could hardly be a follower of himself!

Clearly, by Jesus' conversation with Mack about the word

"Christian" Young has something else in mind. He wants to impress his readers with the idea that Christian goes with the institutional church, which he opposes. I think that his aversion to the word "Christian" also flows out of his basic universalist tendencies. It is not used in any of the universalist creeds. In Chapter 10, Paul Young had also rejected the idea of Jesus being an example to copy.

So what do we call one who follows and believes in Christ—a "believer"? Yet Paul Young gives little if any mention of this word.

Also, the discussion here gives rise to a related question. Young does not indicate how one is transformed. Isn't it a bit strange to have Jesus say that he "joins people in their transformation into his brothers and sisters" when Scripture speaks of people first coming to Christ who then by the Spirit transforms them? Then the reciprocal relationship begins and develops deeper and deeper (John 14–17).

It seems that Young could have stated here what Jesus emphatically states: "I am the way, the truth, and the life; no one comes to the Father but by me." It is not about many roads but about the Road, and his followers join the Way (he doesn't join their ways). It isn't a matter of plurality but of singleness. Jesus is the only person in the entire universe worthy of our total allegiance, and who will never disappoint. People are called to depart from their false gods, embodied in all kinds of religions and nonreligion, and come to Christ. And we need never fear that our giving total allegiance to him will be betrayed. In a text precious to Christians (Matt. 11:27–30), Jesus said:

> All things have been committed to me by my Father. No one knows the Son except the Father, and no one knows the Father except the Son and those to whom the Son chooses to reveal him. Come to me, all you who are weary and burdened, and I will give you rest. Take my yoke upon you and learn from me, for I am gentle and

humble in heart, and you will find rest for your souls.
For my yoke is easy and my burden is light.

It seems that universal reconciliation has again influenced Young's understanding of what it means to be a Christian. The idea of Jesus' traveling "any road to find you" may reflect universalism's teaching that Jesus may even go a thousand times to hell to bring out the wicked who repent there. Of course, there is no biblical support for such a notion.

I now turn to a discussion of the next chapter. It concerns theological truth that is among the most weighty in the Bible—the meaning of reconciliation and who is involved in being reconciled to God. It is at the heart of the claims of universal reconciliation.

Reconciliation,
Part One

O ne of the most successful Christian books ever written has been *Peace with God* by Billy Graham. I suppose that many younger readers may not realize the significant impact that Billy Graham has made on American Christianity and actually, on Christianity worldwide.

Peace with God means to be reconciled with God. To be reconciled with someone is to be at peace with that person. Obstacles that have brought alienation and hostility have been removed.

Chapter 13, "A Meeting of Hearts," provides Paul Young the opportunity to address the matters of grace, the meaning of Christ's death, and reconciliation. It is one of the most important chapters because of its concentration on the meaning of what it means to be at peace with God, to be reconciled with God. Reconciliation is what Mack desperately needs. Obviously the word "reconciliation" is at the heart of the teaching of "universal reconciliation."

Reconciliation is so important that I devote this chapter and the next to addressing all of its dimensions. The two most important

issues are how reconciliation relates to the love and wrath of God
and how reconciliation relates to faith. Both of these issues are at
the heart of the conversation at the end of this chapter in *The Shack*.
In the present chapter, I concentrate on reconciliation as it relates
to the love and wrath of God. In the next, I take up reconciliation
and the condition of faith.

The Shack Continues

Mack joins Papa on the back porch of the shack and over food
engages in a conversation about grace. Papa makes it clear that he
never causes tragedies but uses them and brings good out of them.
Grace does not depend on suffering to exist, but where suffering
does exist grace can be discovered (185). Papa acknowledges that
people often wrongly associate her/him with being stern and Jesus
with forgiveness.

Papa then deals with the issue of lies, how people hide within
them to find power and safety, to protect themselves, but lies are
unloving. Instead people need to risk being honest, to confess to
others, ask for forgiveness, and let forgiveness heal them (188).

These two matters of grace and lies are important and reinforce
both the depth of God's love and why Jesus died on the cross.
The depth of grace displayed by God at the cross that brought us
forgiveness and spiritual wholeness is beyond comprehension. It
is no wonder that Christians have made "Amazing Grace" the best
known hymn around the world. Young is correct to note the crucial
blessing of grace. That God accomplishes good out of the evil that
befalls us agrees with the precious promises of Romans 8:28: "And
we know that in all things God works for the good of those who
love him, who have been called according to his purpose."

Also, Young's discussion about lying is insightful. Unfortunately,
he omits reference to the deceiver, the "father of lies," the devil,
who makes it his business to deceive people, even to try to deceive
the elect of God. Jesus so identified him in John 8:44: "You belong
to your father, the devil, and you want to carry out your father's

desire. He was a murderer from the beginning, not holding to the truth, for there is no truth in him. When he lies, he speaks his native language, for he is a liar and the father of lies." Jesus could hardly speak more clearly about the source of lies. All lying has its source in the Liar, but Young fails to mention him

The discussion about how love and independence relate is helpful. Papa respects people's freedom to choose independence, to their own destruction, for to deny this freedom destroys "the possibility of love. Love that is forced is no love at all" (190). God purposes what he does as always an expression of love (191). In reply to Mack's question as to what Jesus accomplished by his dying, Papa says that he accomplished everything that love purposed from before the world was made (191). "Creation and history is [*sic*] all about Jesus. He is the very center of our purpose . . ." (192).

A Contradiction?

At this point Young seemingly parts company with those who incline toward universal reconciliation and others, since he acknowledges by the words of Papa that there are those who choose freedom, "to their own destruction." This contradicts what he wrote in an earlier chapter about the idea that the end is not about destruction but about setting everything right—which is universal reconciliation. So here Young is more biblically and theologically sound but in conflict with himself. He understands that love must be free, able to flow from a willing choice to love. The alternative is to act independently of God, not loving him, and suffering the consequences of such a choice.

But even here it is not clear whether Young has totally excluded the possibility of changing one's destiny under the pressure of corrective discipline so that one may repent in hell and get into heaven. Papa affirms that everything God does is an expression of love, and this language sounds like universalist speech again. Why is something not said along the lines that everything that God does is an expression of both love and holiness or justice?

In other words, in light of Young's statements earlier, it is possible that Young is still thinking and writing as a universalist. He simply does not address here whether choices made in this life fix one's everlasting destiny. "Destruction" could be hell itself from which, according to universalist thinking, everyone will repent and hell will then cease to exist. By the end of his chapter, Paul becomes quite confusing about the final end of the wicked.

The Centrality of Jesus Christ

Paul Young's statement that "creation and history are all about Jesus" is one of the highlights of this chapter. It is a clear expression of what early Christians believed, and all Christians ever since have affirmed this truth. It finds its basis in the great Christological passages of the Bible (John 1:1–18; Phil. 2:6–11; Col. 1:15–20; Heb. 1:1–14; and many others). Jesus is the Creator who made all things according to the Father's design. And all history is under God's sovereign control to culminate in the person of Jesus Christ (as the Apostle Paul makes clear in Acts 17:22–31). This should be the conviction of every Christian without exception.

One implication of this focus on Jesus Christ is that Christians should read their Bibles looking for Jesus by prophecy and typology throughout the Old Testament. Unfortunately, Young totally ignores the fact that all the Bible also is about Jesus—and even more clearly so than creation and history. This glaring omission has the effect of robbing every Christian of an incentive to read his or her Bible and the method for doing so—to discover Christ. While it is commendable to cite creation and history as focused on Jesus, it is faulty in the extreme to fail to cite Jesus as the center of Scripture, especially when Jesus commanded his followers so to read Scripture (Luke 24:25-27, 44).

Young makes another grievous error. He immediately follows his great statement with these words: "He is the very center of our purpose and *in* him *we* are now fully human, so our purpose and your destiny are forever linked" (italics Young's). The difficulty comes in Young's words that in Jesus Christ "we are fully human." As I discussed above regarding the crucifixion of Christ, only the Son became incarnate, and only the Son died. To assert that "we" (including all the persons of the Trinity—Father, Son, and Holy Spirit) became human is a distortion of what the New Testament asserts. It confuses the biblical distinctions of the Trinity: the Father planned for the incarnation and the crucifixion, but only Jesus the Son experienced such.

While attempts to understand the full meaning of the Trinity will no doubt escape our ability to do so for all eternity, this ignorance is not license to say whatever may appeal to us or seem clever, especially when it violates what has been revealed. Speculation about the mystery of God is okay when it embarks on areas not revealed, but it remains just that—speculation. For millenia, the church has sought to dispell confusion over how to understand the Trinity, but *The Shack* adds to the confusion.

Making statements about the work of the Trinity and the incarnation and death of Christ are out of bounds when they violate and contradict what has been revealed. And clearly only the Son became incarnate (see 1 John 2:2–3), and only the Son became the Savior by his death (said three times in 4:9–10, 14). God "sent the Son" to be the Savior and the reconciliation for the world. To affirm that the whole Trinity became such is to tread close to the heresy of modalism—that God is singular and simply took different forms to become incarnate and to die. In modalism there is no Triune God. Yet I'm sure that Young would resist being called a modalist just as he denies being a universalist.

This is an example of what Young does throughout his novel. He skates along the edge of the precipice of heresy but denies that he is indulging in it. He even feels offended that people should think of him this way.

We must bring all our thoughts to the touchstone of Scripture and give them up if they violate Scripture. This is not bondage to a creed or even to a text. It is the path to freedom, for Jesus said,

"You shall know the truth and the truth shall make you free" (John 8:32). It is obedience to our Lord. And this is intimacy with the one who said that he is "the way, and the truth, and the life" (John 14:6).

The Shack follows an independence from the norm of Scripture. This is the greatest irony, since Young makes independence from God the greatest evil. Yet he practices the very independence that he condemns in others. The next topic is a clear example of this error.

The Meaning of Reconciliation

This chapter continues on the trajectory of dealing with the meaning of Christ's death. Young introduces a theological term that is part of the discussion that clarifies why Jesus Christ died on the cross and what he accomplished. The term is "reconciliation."

The word "reconciliation" is at the heart of the debate between evangelical Christians and those who embrace universal reconciliation. Obviously the error of universal reconciliation employs the term and adds the word "universal" to indicate that reconciliation is without limits—it includes the entire universe. The person who embraces universal reconciliation gladly embraces this biblical term, but takes it to lengths that Christians throughout the ages have rejected as heresy. The term "reconciliation" is a good, biblical word, as we will see. But how one builds the doctrine of reconciliation upon the term is exceedingly crucial in order to keep true to the Bible.

So what does the term "reconciliation" mean? Let me get to its definition in a moment.

Reconciliation According to *The Shack*: Universalism?

First, I want to show how the term is employed at the end of this chapter of *The Shack*. How Young defines the term and what he says about it is basic to the charge that other reviewers and I have made about whether or not Paul Young adheres to universal reconciliation within this novel.

So let us first return to the encounter given in the closing pages of Chapter 13 (192–193). Papa clarifies in succinct dialogue what Jesus accomplished at the cross and asks Mack to listen carefully. Papa says: ". . . through his death and resurrection, I am now fully reconciled to the world." Mack asks: "The whole world? You mean those who believe in you, right?" Papa replies: "The whole world, Mack. All I am telling you is that reconciliation is a two way street, and I have done my part, totally, completely, finally. It is not the nature of love to force a relationship but it is the nature of love to open the way" (192).

At this Mack confesses that he doesn't really understand reconciliation, and fears emotions. At this the dialogue comes to an end with Papa walking away and uttering that men are "such idiots sometimes."

While Paul Young states truth here he is also involved in great distortion. This will become clear as I take up the word "reconciliation."

The Doctrine of Reconciliation

The doctrine of reconciliation is one of the most important teachings of the New Testament, and one of the most neglected.[43] It is one of the words that explains the meaning of salvation, along with other words such as atonement, justification, redemption, forgiveness, and salvation itself. But reconciliation is the most relational of all the terms. The others are basic and vitally important, but do not emphasize personal relationship as reconciliation does. Because of its emphasis on relationship, reconciliation is one of the easiest terms to understand because everybody knows what reconciliation is, at least on the human level. The word is the least metaphorical of them all.

The biblical teaching of reconciliation is tied to several questions. Some of these are reflected in the dialogue above between Papa and Mack. (1) What does reconciliation mean? (2) Why is reconciliation necessary? (3) Is God already reconciled to the whole world? (4) Who is reconciled to whom? Is God reconciled to people, or are people reconciled to God? Or is it both ways? (5) What role does faith or believing have in the doctrine of reconciliation? It is on the answer to this last question that Paul Young scores an F. (6) How is reconciliation related to the wrath and love of God?

More than any other doctrine, reconciliation goes to the heart of the issue of the wrath of God and the love of God, and how these relate. A correct understanding here shows the shortcomings of *The Shack* as nothing else does.

Challenges to Understanding Reconciliation

These questions arise because the Bible affirms that the world is reconciled to God, as we shall see. But it also says that his anger or wrath is presently being expressed toward the world. Anger is the opposite of reconciliation. In other words, how can the Bible say that God is both at peace with the world and also angry at it? There are other conundrums in the word as well. If Christians are reconciled to God, how is it that Paul the apostle exhorts Christians "to be reconciled to God" (2 Cor. 5:20)? The way one answers these questions betrays whether one believes all that the Bible affirms about God or only part of what it says.

Some other questions are necessary. (7) How is reconciliation related to other doctrines touching on salvation, such as atonement, salvation, redemption, and justification? In a special way the teaching of reconciliation is more important than all the rest. (8) How is reconciliation appropriated? (9) Why is reconciliation so important? (10) Why does Paul the apostle alone use the word? (11) How is it that the teaching of universal reconciliation is neither universal nor reconciliation?

So the teaching of reconciliation is rich with many aspects. I'm devoting two chapters to it because it is at the heart of the Christian understanding of salvation and shows more clearly than any other truth the great chasm between universalism and biblical teaching.

The case for universalism stands or falls on properly understanding this term.

In this chapter, I begin answering the questions listed above. I give special attention to reconciliation as relationship and how the love of God is related to the wrath of God. In the next chapter, I discuss how reconciliation is tied to the matter of faith.

The Terms and Texts of Reconciliation

There are only four Greek terms used in the New Testament that are the source of the English word "reconciliation." These four terms are, however, infrequently used. The verb *katallasso* is used once on the horizontal plane, of a wife being reconciled to her unbelieving husband (1 Cor. 7:11); and five times on the vertical plane, in the Apostle Paul's teaching (Rom. 5:10 [twice]; 2 Cor. 5:18, 19, 20). The verb *apokatallasso*, probably an invention by Paul, is simply an intensive form of the first word, and is used by him only three times (Col. 1:20, 22; Eph. 2:16). The noun *katallage* ("reconciliation") occurs four times (Rom. 5:11; 11:15; 2 Cor. 5:18, 19). The final form, another verb, *diallasso*, occurs in our Lord's words in the Sermon on the Mount (Matt. 5:24) of a person being reconciled to another who has a fault against one. All of these terms mean reconciliation or to make peace. While there are other cognates used in the New Testament, they do not mean to make peace with God or with other people.[44]

The terms cited above occur chiefly in four texts (Rom. 5:1–10; 2 Cor. 5:16–21; Col. 1:19–23; Eph. 2:11–22). Each of these texts is among the most important texts for understanding the work of Christ on the cross and the consequences of it. While these words occur only a total of fourteen times in four passages, the doctrine of reconciliation includes those additional passages where the words "making peace" occur. For example, Romans 5:1 says: "Therefore, being justified by faith we have peace with God." Later in this same text the actual word for reconciliation occurs (three times: vv. 10–11).

The Unique Meaning of Reconciliation in the New Testament

So first of all, what does "reconciliation mean"? It means simply to "make peace" or to "be at peace" with someone. The someone may be a person or it may be God.

The most amazing thing about this word is how it is used in the New Testament. While a couple of the words occur in secular Greek literature prior to the time of Christ and in the Septuagint (known as the LXX, the Greek translation of the Old Testament made from the Hebrew text around 250–150 BC), they never have the meaning of spiritual or religious reconciliation. There reconciliation is always on the horizontal plane.[45] Further, the longer term *apokatallasso* appears to an invention of the Apostle Paul to intensify the basic idea of reconcile. Finally, all these terms with their vertical idea occur only in the Apostle Paul's writings. This raises the intriguing question: Why does only Paul use the term? I will suggest an answer in the pages to come.

So we can already suggest some special findings. These terms are unique to Christianity as far as making peace with God is concerned. No other religion ever conceived of itself as finding peace with God at God's initiative and accomplishment apart from a person making a sacrifice. This point has huge implications.

But there are other distinctives of the terms belonging only to the Bible. I cite them in the category divisions that follow. They help to give us a full-orbed understanding of the word.

1. The Doer or Maker of Reconciliation Is God

Of the fourteen occurrences of "reconciliation," four occur in 2 Corinthians 5 and three occur in Romans 5. These texts and others make it clear that in Christianity, the doer or maker of reconciliation is always God. God reconciled us to himself: "God was reconciling the world to himself" (5:19); "we were reconciled to God by the death of his Son" (Rom. 5:10).

In the New Testament God is never the object of reconciliation.

People do not reconcile themselves to God. Also, God does not reconcile himself to the world, but he reconciles the world to himself.

This distinction is unique to Christian faith. In all other religions, the deity is the object of the reconciling work of men. All other religions put the doing of good first to bring about reconciliation with the deities. People make gifts and offerings to the deity to cause him/her to become reconciled to the worshippers. This is not the pattern in the Bible.

2. Reconciliation by God Precedes All Human Action

Reconciliation is God's unilateral act in Christ. Romans 5:10 says: "For if while we were enemies we were reconciled to God by the death of his Son, much more now that we are reconciled, we will be saved by his life." Reconciliation is the good news that God has already completed reconciliation, which precedes all human action. It is independent of any human action. It remains true whatever one's response is. We, rather, were enemies before God effected the reconciliation. We cannot bring about reconciliation by repentance and confession so that God reacts to us. We were enemies and hostile at the time God reconciled us. Yet, paradoxically, not all are reconciled.

The Greek word in the New Testament differs greatly from the English word "reconcile." The English word communicates the idea that two people mutually make overtures to be reconciled to each other. For example in the sentence, "I was reconciled to my brother over the inheritance," the assumption is that my brother and I came to a mutual understanding of peace. At least we cannot be sure which one took the leadership.

But in the New Testament this is never the idea. It is always God who initiates and completes the reconciliation.

3. The Obstacle to Reconciliation is Sin

The obstacle to reconciliation, the thing that alienated God and us, is sin (Col. 1:21; Eph. 2:1–6). The obstacle is both sin inherited from Adam (Rom. 5) and our daily sins that result from our fallenness. "The wages of sin is death" (Rom. 6:23). God deals with his own wrath against sin and against sinners by removing the obstacle by the death of Christ.

Romans 5 says that we could not initiate reconciliation because of our sin. Instead, we are weak (v. 6), lack merit (are "ungodly," v. 6), lack righteousness (are guilty of "sin," v. 8), and lack peace ("are at enmity with God," v. 10). In taking care of our sin problem, Jesus Christ "became sin for us so that we might be made the righteousness of God in him" (2 Cor. 5:21). Christ suffered all the consequences of the sin of humanity, including its penalty (separation from God), so that all of humanity might participate in all the consequences of Christ's righteousness.

4. The Wrath of God: Who is in Need of Being Reconciled? Who is Angry?

The doctrine of reconciliation assumes that enmity or hostility has been in place but now may be removed. The question arises: Who is at enmity with whom? Is it God who is angry at people? Or are people at enmity toward God? Or are both at enmity toward the other? If reconciliation has been achieved, the attendant question is: How can Scripture say that God does show and will show wrath?

From the Bible it is clear that all humanity, Jews and gentiles, is at enmity or hostile toward God (note Col. 1:21; Eph. 2). But is God hostile toward humanity?

Several texts affirm yes to this question—that God's wrath is presently extended toward humanity (Rom. 1:18–32; Col. 3:6; Eph. 5:6). Other texts show that the consequence of rejecting God's mercy is to stand in the future before God the judge and experience his wrath (Rom. 2: 2–3, 5, 8, 12, 16).

What is meant by the wrath of God? Wrath denotes a "strong and settled opposition" arising out of God's very nature against all that is evil.[46] Wrath is not an attribute of God but is an expression or function of his holiness or righteousness. Unfortunately, the idea that God can be wrathful is virtually rejected in *The Shack*.

There are other ways that demonstrate that God is hostile toward humanity. The use of the terms enemy (*echthros*) and enmity (*echthra*) usually denote reciprocal hostility (Gal. 4:16; Rom. 5:10, 11:28; 1 Cor. 15:25f.; Phil. 3:18f.; James 4:4, 6; Eph. 2:15ff.). Even if one simply acknowledges that God has "made the universe a moral universe in which punishment follows sin," then God cannot be exempted from responsibility when punishment comes.[47] Yet *The Shack* tries to do this very thing by having God say that he doesn't punish sin.

Thus God initiates a two-way process. God is reconciled to people, and people are reconciled to God, and peace is made.[48] But both directions are conditioned on the response of people to the gospel.[49] God remains hostile toward people because they remain hostile toward him by failing to embrace the gospel by faith. It is on this very point that *The Shack* errs so glaringly.

5. Relating the Wrath and the Love of God

How do reconciliation, wrath, and love relate? In reconciliation, has God changed? It cannot be that part of God is love and part is enmity, nor can it be that there is an antithesis between God the Father and Christ the Son, so that the Son has appeased the Father's anger. The Father is the source of reconciliation. God is forever love, even when it is also said that God is angry toward sin as an expression of his holiness. Formerly the world was the object of wrath; now it is the object of his love. But this does not mean that God's anger has been turned into love. God's anger must exist for love to be "the source and ground of reconciliation."[50] God has not "changed his feelings, as if he had somehow to swallow his wrath."[51] This last writer continues:

> Rather in the love which he has always had for the
> world he has given his Son to bear the consequences of

the world's sin and so to remove the barrier caused by sin. God has thus dealt with the sin of the world, and in so doing has rendered his wrath inoperative against those who accept his act of reconciliation.

Thus God remains the same. He both loves the world—when it responds to his offer of love—and expresses wrath toward the world when it rejects his love (cf. John 3:16–18). Wrath is the obverse side of love.[52] But he has removed the barrier—sin—that heretofore made reconciliation impossible.

6. Reconciliation is both Objective and Subjective

Another way to understand reconciliation is to view it as both an objective event and a subjective event. In the former God brought reconciliation for all (Rom. 5:10), but not in all. As enemies we all stand under his wrath. But as enemies we were reconciled to God by the event of the cross (5:8). Thus at the same time God loves his enemies.

Consider the example of a father's love for a child. God waits like a father ready to forgive an erring child. But readiness to forgive is not the same as actual forgiveness. When the father does forgive the penitent child whom he has always loved, his love doesn't change, but his attitude toward the child has changed. Thus in a sense "God has reconciled himself" to all because of the death of his Son.[53]

The subjective aspect to reconciliation is our reception of the divine act of reconciliation accomplished by the cross. The objective aspect of reconciliation does not become efficacious or real for us—fellowship with God is not restored—until we receive the reconciliation offered in the gospel—"be reconciled to God" (2 Cor. 5:20). Faith is the means by which to embrace the divine offer. Inherently, such a reception means that a person's inward attitude is turned from hostility to surrender and obedience.

Any idea that diminishes the severity of God's wrath has

unimaginable consequences. Such a diminishing of the concept is a Greek idea, not a Hebrew or Christian one. Wrath points to a reality in the divine being that "gives point and force to moral sanctions" of people.[54] Without God's standard there remains no standard by which humanity can survive the force of the strongly wicked and seek justice in the earth.

To dilute God's wrath is to dilute God's holiness. Yet *The Shack* does this very thing. It also fails to distinguish different loves in the Bible.[55]

7. Reconciliation Has Been Accomplished for All

The text of 2 Corinthians 5:19 makes it clear that just as Christ is the propitiation for all the world's sins (1 John 2:2), so in Christ God "was reconciling the world to himself." The "us" of verse 18 ("God has reconciled us to himself") is expanded to the "world" in verse 19. The "all" used eight times in Colossians 1:15–20 must include the entire universe of beings, including the fallen angels.

By using "all" three times in 2 Corinthians 5:14-15, Paul the apostle makes it clear that reconciliation has been provided for all; but, in contrast, his use of the words, "they that live" (v. 15) shows that reconciliation is actualized only for some—those who believe.[56]

8. Reconciliation has a Cosmic Dimension

The term *apokatallasso* occurs only in Colossians 1:20, 22 and Ephesians 2:16, and nowhere else in any literature. Yet it basically has the same meaning as *katallasso* discussed above. Colossians 1:19–23 says:

> For in him all the fullness of God was pleased to dwell
> (or, For God was pleased to have all his fullness dwell
> in his Son),[57] and through him to reconcile to himself
> all things, whether on earth or in heaven, having made

peace [through him] by the blood of his cross. And you were at one time strangers and enemies in your minds as expressed through your evil deeds, but now he has reconciled you by his body through death to present you holy, without blemish, and blameless before him—if indeed you remain in the faith. . . .

Three special features stand out from the reconciliation described in Colossians. (1) Christ is the divine one who brings reconciliation. Being without sin, he met the law's requirements; and his death had eternal consequences. (2) Christ, it seems, is the subject, the doer, of reconciliation, as is God the Father (v. 22). (3) Reconciliation has a cosmic dimension. The powers created by Christ (v. 16) have pursued evil and brought a "cosmic catastrophe." The creator of all and the sustainer of all (Col. 1:15–17) has triumphed by the cross over the cosmic forces of evil (cf. 2:15). Therefore, he is the "reconciler of all" (Col. 1:19–20). It is clear that these cosmic forces could not reconcile people to God, for they themselves are in need of reconciliation for their rebelliousness and transgression.[58]

The reconciliation of cosmic forces of evil is not through their conversion or believing. It is a pacification, a conquest, "forcefully brought about by a triumphant victor."[59]

Within this cosmic reconciliation is that of believers (1:21ff.) conditioned by their believing, and the restoration of inanimate creation (Rom. 8). For inanimate creation, believing is not a condition since their bondage was brought about by people's rebellion in the garden (Gen. 3). Christ's death had to be universal, on behalf of all, in order that the inanimate creation might be released from its bondage tied to the fall of humanity. As the creation fell in Adam, it is released from the fall by the reconciliation of all who believe.

9. Reconciliation Creates a New Humanity

In Ephesians, reconciliation is set in the context of the relationship of Jews and gentiles before God. Before Christ came, gentiles were "separated from Christ, alienated from the commonwealth of Israel, and strangers to the covenants of promise, having no hope and without God in the world" (Eph. 2:12). Christ's death has reconciled both gentiles and Jews to God and to each other, making a new humanity. It isn't a restructured Judaism or a reformed paganism, but a third entity, the church. Paul writes (2:14–18):

> For he is our peace, who has made both groups into one, and who destroyed the dividing wall of hostility, by abolishing in his flesh the law of commandments and ordinances, that he might create in himself one new man in place of two, so making peace, and might reconcile them both in one body to God through the cross, thereby bringing the hostility to an end. And he came and preached peace to you who were far off and peace to those who were near, so that through him we both have access in one Spirit to the Father.

Ephesians presents the "one new man" (2:15) who unites Jew and gentile. This reconciliation of Jew and gentile in "one new body" (4:4) is a "microcosm and foretaste" of the reconciliation of all things yet to be realized in God's rule over all.[60] Similarly, Colossians 3:10–11 speaks of "being renewed" to a new image, and in this reality all distinctions cease. The only thing that matters is Christ (v. 11). It is a new third race (cf. Gal. 3:28; 1 Cor. 10:32: Jews, gentiles, the church of God).

The implication is that those who are so reconciled to God need to be reconciled to each other in Christ. The two dimensions of reconciliation (the vertical and horizontal) are inseparable.[61]

10. There Are Three Objects of Reconciliation

In light of the preceding, there are three broad objects of reconciliation. One is the person who believes the gospel (2 Cor. 5:18; Rom. 5:1ff.). Another is the world of humanity, including unbelievers, whether Jew or gentile (Rom. 11:15; 2 Cor. 5:19: "God was in Christ reconciling the world to himself, not counting people's trespasses against them"), and the inanimate creation. The third is the unseen forces of evil, including fallen angels (Col. 1:20; 2:15). Yet there are different kinds, different ways, of reconciliation.

Of what consequence is reconciliation for those who refuse it (part of the second group above)? It seems that the basis for God's judgment and condemnation has essentially changed. Since the death of Christ a person experiences judgment, not because God has failed to provide or because his love has been ineffective, but because one has rejected the reconciliation that God has provided.[62] Peace is imposed on the unseen forces of evil. Their evil designs are often being overruled for good. In principle these beings have been stripped of their power (Col. 2:15) and will be brought into subjection (1 Cor. 15:24–28; cf. Rom. 16:20: "the God of peace will bruise Satan under your feet shortly").[63] Their conquest is *de jure*; it will soon be *de facto*.

Is This Universal Reconciliation?

In the preceding pages I've related reconciliation to the love of God and the wrath of God. The last section above affirms that reconciliation has been accomplished for all. This seems to amount to universal reconciliation. But does it really?

In the next chapter I will show that the other part of Mack's discussion with Papa relates to faith and the condition for universal reconciliation. Indeed, the condition of faith makes universal reconciliation neither universal nor reconciliation.

· 12 ·

Reconciliation, Part Two

THE CONDITION OF FAITH:
HOW DOES FAITH BRING PEACE?

In this chapter, I bring to completion the discussion of the wonderful doctrine of reconciliation. In the previous chapter, I discussed the relationship of reconciliation to the love of God and the wrath of God. We found that the wrath of God is real and not to be qualified or diminished. But God has taken the initiative to remove the cause of alienation between him and all people—the obstacle of sin. He did all that is necessary to bring reconciliation to the entire universe—to people, to fallen angels and the devil, and even to inanimate creation.

Thus far the discussion of reconciliation seems to support the doctrine of universal reconciliation. It certainly seems to support Paul Young's last dialogue of Chapter 13 of *The Shack*, "A Meeting of Hearts." In it God claims to be "now fully reconciled to the whole world," that he has done it "totally, completely, finally" (192).

Yet Mack's question about the role of faith in God, and Papa's reply to it, are pivotal to the whole discussion. Is faith the condition for reconciliation? Does lack of faith consign one to the wrath of God?

The answers to these and other questions will fill out our understanding of reconciliation. In the conclusion I will return to Mack's question and show how the proper answer is devastating to universal reconciliation. I will also suggest why the doctrine of reconciliation appears in the New Testament at all and why it is that only Paul the apostle writes about it. But first it is necessary to sum up some other aspects of reconciliation to increase our appreciation for this great doctrine.

God Has Completed His Work of Reconciliation

On the basis of the work of Christ on the cross, God's work of reconciliation has been finished. All of the main texts mentioning reconciliation make it clear that reconciliation has been achieved by God (Rom. 5:10-11; 2 Cor. 5:14ff.). The completion of reconciliation means that it is a finished gift offered to people.

Supportive of this idea that reconciliation is accomplished is the usage of peace in the New Testament. The translation of the Hebrew *shalom* in the New Testament affirms, among other things, that peace, as Jesus said, comes from God as a gift (John 14:27), that it is associated with Christ's victory over the world (John 16:33) and his work for people (Rom. 8:6). Peace comes from God and describes him (Rom. 16:20). It is nearly identical with salvation (Acts 10:36; cf. Eph. 6:15). These references and others intrinsically associate peace with the work of Christ apart from people's earning it or doing something in response.

Both Christ's death and resurrection bring about reconciliation (Rom. 5:10–11). Like justification, reconciliation rests on justice first being satisfied by Christ's substitutionary atonement (Rom. 3:24–25; 2 Cor. 5:19–20). He became sin for all people; he became the satisfaction for the sins of the whole world (2 Cor. 5:21; 1 John 2:2).

What Are the Results of Reconciliation?

The result of reconciliation is to have peace with God: "Therefore having been justified by faith we have peace with God" (Rom. 5:1). This peace is not subjective (personally felt) but objective, since it flows from justification. It is the removal of God's hostility. It is not a state of mind or feeling but a relationship to God. It is the "outward objective relationship," which may then be followed by the inward peace of heart.[64]

By its association with the other works of God, another result of reconciliation is that every believer is a new creation in Christ (2 Cor. 5:17).[65] We have a new nature and a new destiny—eternal life. Another result is that the Christian has the righteousness of God because Christ became sin for us—he was alienated from God on the cross (2 Cor. 5:21; Matt. 27). Christ became what people are (sinners) in order that they might become what he is (righteous before God).

Another result of reconciliation with God is reconciliation among people. One who has participated in the gift of reconciliation with God can hardly allow estrangement with another human being (Eph. 2). The "ministry of reconciliation" (2 Cor. 5:18) begins with reversing spiritual alienation, but it does not end there. As reconciliation is more and more experienced by the believer, he has a growing relationship with God and with others.[66] The need for human reconciliation (1 Cor. 7:10ff.; Matt. 5:24) is "parabolic of man's need of reconciliation with God."[67] Other results or fruits of reconciliation include assurance of eternal life, the indwelling Spirit of God, and more.

Christ's death was not only substitutionary and representative but also corporate or participationist.[68] Jesus identified with humanity's plight (2 Cor. 5:21), and people by faith identify with him. Christians become united in Christ in his death and resurrection so much so that his experience becomes their history by faith (cf. 5:14: "all died"; cf. Rom. 6:4). This affects our understanding of conversion. There are two times or moments of everyone's conversion: the moment of the event of Christ's crucifixion when in him we died to sin and the moment later in time when we personally exercised faith in Christ.

There is one more important point. The whole purpose of the incarnation is that Christ should die and reconcile mankind. He came into the world to die (Col. 1:19–20; note *allasso* in Heb. 2:14–18; cf. 2:9; Gal. 4:4–5).

The Response of a Person is Necessary for Reconciliation to be Realized

People Must Exercise Faith

This section is the most important of this chapter for understanding the meaning and only limitation of reconciliation. The fact that God reconciles and that people are reconciled does not mean that people are totally passive. While people cannot bring about reconciliation with God by their effort, they can refuse what God offers. When the Apostle Paul commands, "Be reconciled to God" (2 Cor. 5:20), there is an assumption that a person must do something. While God has taken down the barrier on his side, people need to take down the barrier (unbelief, pride, disobedience) on their side. The thrust of Paul's plea is "allow yourselves to be reconciled" or "accept and live in his reconciliation."[69]

Some, including some universalists, take this to mean only that the apostle invites faith in the message that the reconciliation has been brought about. Yet the apostle's 's words are not "believe that you are reconciled" but "be reconciled."[70] The plea for reconciliation parallels pleas from God elsewhere (Ezek. 33:11; Isa. 1:18; Matt. 22:4—the parable of invited guests to the marriage feast of the king's son; Rom. 10:4–11).

People must avail themselves of the provision for reconciliation that God has made. Thus the act of reconciliation is completed only when there is a human response to the command to be reconciled.[71]

Implications for Universalism from the Necessity of Faith

The need for a response has significant implications for the view of universalism and universal reconciliation. None are reconciled to God apart from faith in Jesus Christ. The Bible holds no hope for those who in this life do not believe.[72]

God and people are not equal partners in reconciliation. In the narrow sense of reconciliation, God puts away the wrath caused by the barrier to reconciliation, that is, people's sin. The broad sense means that God enters into a relationship with people on the basis of Christ's death.

Thus there are three stages in the process of reconciliation.[73] (1) The reconciling act of God made possible by Christ's death; (2) the proclamation of reconciliation by the "servants of reconciliation" calling people to respond; and (3) the acceptance of God's message when people believe God's reconciling act based in Christ and put away their animosity toward God. The process of reconciliation is not complete until all three stages are realized. Unless one indicates one's being persuaded of the worth of the gift of reconciliation by taking it, it remains unpossessed and without effect.

Without Faith No One is Reconciled

It is the response of people that is "necessary and demanded."[74] Paul the apostle acts in the interest of Christ, in his stead, as his ambassador, when he pleads: "Be reconciled to God" (2 Cor. 5:20). These words suggest that reconciliation is "incomplete until it is accepted by both sides."[75] The preaching of the gospel is a call to faith so that reconciliation is actualized. This is the "ministry of reconciliation" (2 Cor. 5:20).

This necessary place of faith is made clear in Colossians 1:19–23. After asserting that Christ reconciled the entire universe (1:20), the apostle immediately says that the Colossians were not reconciled (they were hostile to God) until they believed (vv. 20–23).

It is here that evangelical faith parts company with universalism in general. The latter asserts that Christ's work has already accomplished reconciliation whether or not people respond to the gospel in faith. It is also here that evangelical faith parts company with Christian universalism or universal reconciliation. The latter asserts that if people do not respond to the gospel in faith before they die they will respond under the "purifying fires of hell" and there repent and escape. God's love prevents hell from having everlasting existence so that people will not suffer there forever. This is the view of *The Shack*.

Without Faith There is No Reconciliation for the Rest of Creation

It is on the matter of faith that Mack's dialogue with Papa cited at the beginning of the chapter falls apart. It overlooks the fact that different elements in the world are reconciled to God in different ways.

Cosmic forces of evil and the creation in general cannot be reconciled by faith. Satan and his angels cannot repent and believe and be reconciled peaceably. Christ did not come to help angels but only humanity (Heb. 2:16). At his incarnation Christ became a human being, not an angelic being (2:14ff.). His atonement cannot apply to them. Their reconciliation is a conquest. The physical creation did not come into bondage willingly but because of the choice of human beings (Rom. 8). It cannot exercise a will to believe. In a sense, believers mediate reconciliation to the inanimate creation.

Universal reconciliation fails to make these distinctions. It virtually makes faith unnecessary for all three objects of reconciliation (humanity, fallen angels, and inanimate creation). How does it do this? By asserting that in the end the love of God overcomes all obstacles in order to empty hell of the wicked.

Yet Christians are compelled to ask: If the love of God is the ultimate concern, why did God allow unbelievers to go to hell in the first place? Or, a question that precedes this is, why did God allow the Fall ? Why does he allow suffering now?

Reconciliation is the Basis for Assurance

Romans 5:10 affirms that "if while we were enemies we were reconciled to God through the death of his Son, how much more, since we have been reconciled, will we be saved by his life?" The believer's initial reconciliation to God becomes the basis for assurance that this reconciliation will continue on because Christ has risen. The resurrection assures every Christian that reconciliation having been once achieved can never be revoked. Without the resurrection there is no peace with God.

How is Reconciliation Related to Justification?

1. Reconciliation is Dependant upon Justification

Reconciliation is put parallel to the terms, "to be justified" and "righteousness" (Rom. 5:1, 9 and 10; 2 Cor. 5:19 with Rom. 4:3ff). showing that both are related to the death of Christ and indicate the new status of Christians. Justification means that God has declared a person who has believed in Christ to be righteous and thus accepted by him.

Sin, the barrier to reconciliation, has been removed, and reconciliation can occur. People need to be informed of the possibility for peace that is now open to them. Reconciliation and justification are available for the taking—but people must take them.

A person is not reconciled if he or she is not justified; a person who is reconciled is also justified. That is, justification is the necessary presupposition of reconciliation. As the apostle writes, "Therefore, having been justified by faith, we have peace with God through our Lord Jesus Christ" (Rom. 5:1). Reconciliation is the restoration of the justified person to fellowship with God.

Like justification, reconciliation means that divine justice has been executed on mankind, that we have died, "really and definitively," by Jesus Christ taking our place. We have died in and with him.

Faith is clearly demanded of the one who would be justified (Rom. 5:1), and if justification precedes reconciliation, then faith is essential to reconciliation, just as Romans 3:25–26 states. Reconciliation and justification unite in their view of giving real content to the wrath of God. If there is a diminishing of wrath, there is the diminishing of the need for reconciliation, justification, forgiveness, and grace.

These truths directly counter the idea suggested by *The Shack* that reconciliation may occur apart from the response of faith. Mack is rebuked for suggesting that reconciliation has been achieved only for those who believe. In truth, it has been accomplished as a sufficient provision for all but becomes the possession of only those who believe. *The Shack*'s confusing dialogue distorts the gospel and misinforms readers on how to experience justification and reconciliation.

2. Reconciliation Goes beyond Justification

Reconciliation and justification are closely related and inseparable because of the nature of God. Yet they are not identical. Justification suggests the legal scene before the Judge and the declaration that the Judge makes; reconciliation suggests an end to enmity. In justification there may be no personal relationship established, as between a judge and the defendant, but in reconciliation friendship and peace are established. It is more personal and positive. More takes place in reconciliation than the removal of guilt.[76] Reconciliation is stated in contexts emphasizing the love of God (2 Cor. 5:14–20; Rom. 5:1–10). Reconciliation involves a change of one's heart and a restoration of relationship to a former enemy.[77]

Also, reconciliation has a greater scope than does justification. Reconciliation has a cosmic dimension whereby the whole creation, including the spirit world, is included (Col. 1:19–20); justification does not. Thus reconciliation is the "precondition" of salvation and the basis for being a "new creation" in Christ (2 Cor. 5:17ff.).

Again, reconciliation can be commanded to humans since it involves reciprocity ("Be reconciled"; 2 Cor. 5:20); but there is not a command, "be justified." Also, justification is a once-for-all event. People do not keep on being justified. Reconciliation has an ever-expanding depth, unlike justification.

In the objective sense, all have been reconciled by the death of Christ but all have not been justified. Justification is limited to those predestined (Rom. 8:30). Finally, Old Testament saints could be justified (Rom. 4), but it is not said that they could be reconciled—God's wrath had not been averted by Christ's sacrifice. While propitiation is a work objectively toward God, reconciliation is objectively toward people.

The Two Differing Sides of Reconciliation

It is necessary to distinguish what happens on God's side from what happens on people's side.[78] (1) The fault for the breach between God and people lies on people's side. They departed from God by their sin and erected the barrier that separates them from God. (2) On people's side, there must be a complete change. They must repent of sin and turn from it. This has no parallel from God's side. (3) Reconciliation for people comes from outside, from beyond them. But God brought about reconciliation by himself. There was no third party. (4) God's love remained unchanged as he reconciled himself in Christ. Yet the expression of love may not always be the same.

There is a helpful way to illustrate God's unchanging love and anger. A flame of fire may both warm and enlighten, but it may also sear and burn—all without changing its essential nature. When sinful people look at a holy God, all that they can know is the expression of wrath. When they've been reconciled, they know the warmth of his love.

What is the Goal of Reconciliation?

The goal of reconciliation is to build a progressively growing personal relationship with God. It restores a "relationship of mutual, participatory love with God the Father" through Jesus Christ and with the Spirit and with other believers (John 14–17; 1 Cor. 1:9;

2 Cor. 13:14; 1 John 1:3, 6).[79] It means enjoying eternal life, spiritual life, beginning now at the point of conversion and never ceasing. Life "is eternal fellowship with the most fulfilling persons of all—Father, Son, and Holy Spirit."[80] In light of the two great commandments, people cannot begin to fulfill the first love (for God) until they are reconciled to God, and that empowers them also to fulfill the second love (for neighbor).

Conclusions

Some final thoughts about reconciliation will show how crucial and yet life-transforming an understanding of reconciliation can be.

The Importance of Reconciliation

Reconciliation ties much of New Testament doctrine together. Wherever righteousness, redemption, salvation, and justification are mentioned, reconciliation should be assumed as well, as a necessary concomitant. Wherever peace is mentioned, it is reconciliation. Indeed, the whole idea of the kingdom of God is summarized as "righteousness, peace and joy in the Holy Spirit" (Rom. 14:17), a continuation of the Old Testament concerns.

Reconciliation has particular significance for the contemporary world. While other metaphors were perhaps better suited to other times (redemption to the slave markets of the first century, sacrifice to other and earlier cultures, and justification to the concerns of legal status and to the sixteenth century), reconciliation is especially appropriate for what is true in every age: alienation between people and broken relationships (in the home, school, church, government; everywhere). It may well be the "most powerful model for expressing the significance of Christ's death effectively today."[81]

"Be Reconciled to God" As Key to Paul's Understanding of Relationship with God

Why is it that Paul exhorts the Corinthians to "be reconciled to God" (2 Cor. 5:20) when they apparently had already become

Christians? It is probable that the believers at Corinth had become indifferent and callous about the depth of the meaning of the sacrifice of Christ on behalf of their sins. They had failed to grasp all the implications of the gospel. Part of their problem was reflected in their disregard for the Apostle Paul. Their attitude bred a "self-induced alienation" that was just the opposite of reconciliation. Thus Paul exhorts them: "Be reconciled to God" (2 Cor. 5:20).

While they were objectively and subjectively restored to a right relationship with God because of justification, they needed to deepen the subjective aspect of their personal relationship with God. Thus it is not surprising that Paul exhorts the Colossians several times (Col. 1:10–12; 2:7; 3:15–17) to show gratitude for God's work in their salvation—it means to develop more deeply a personal experience of reconciliation.

Why the Apostle Paul Ever and Exclusively Used the Term for Reconciliation

A question remains. Why is it that the Apostle Paul uses the term for reconciliation but no one else ever did? I think the answer lies in Paul's background and in his conversion and calling on the road to Damascus. Paul was the most educated person among the apostles. He was trained in Judaism as no one else in his day or ever since, who then became a believer. At his conversion Paul came to realize that Old Testament Judaism could never bring him or anyone into a personal relationship of reconciliation that was now possible in Christ. After all, for a human being to be fully reconciled with a spirit Being—God—could not really be fully realized.

No Reconciliation in the Old Testament

This is the reason, I believe, why reconciliation with God does not occur in the Old Testament. It was really not possible—for Abraham, Moses, David, Isaiah, or anyone else. Paul had come far, further than anyone else (as he recounts in Phil. 3:8–16), and yet was still far from reconciliation with God. But a person could grow in intimacy and depth with God who has become incarnate as a human being. The "value of knowing Christ was far greater" than his Judaism (v. 8).

But more is needed to explain Paul's passion to know Christ, to be reconciled to God. It is true that Paul's conversion and call lie in the background of his terminology used in 2 Corinthians 5:16–21 (as others have pointed out). But Paul's calling was not only to be an apostle to the Gentiles (see Acts 9:15) but also to suffer much on behalf of the name of Christ as no one else ever would (v. 16). As the first among the apostles, he would suffer the most.

The Growing of Reconciliation in Relationship

Paul's commission to suffering was a call to personal reconciliation. Thus Paul adds that his "aim is to know Christ, to experience the power of his resurrection, to share in his sufferings, and to be like him in his death" (Phil. 3:10). In this text Paul brings together justification (note "righteousness," three times, v. 9), the cross, God's wrath toward sin, and, yes, reconciliation. Reconciliation involves growing more deeply in the knowledge of God, and the main avenue for accomplishing growth is to suffer on behalf of Christ. The apostle writes: "For it has been granted to you on behalf of Christ, not only to believe on him, but also to suffer for him" (Phil. 1:29; cf. 2 Cor. 4:11–18).

Final Thoughts

This lengthy excursion into the beautiful doctrine of reconciliation should bring tremendous joy to every Christian. It is transforming to realize that the living God loved me so much that he averted his wrath by providing the means to remove the obstacle—my sin—to our reconciliation In the greatest act of giving and self-sacrifice ever conceived in the universe and for all eternity, God sent his Son who yielded his life in self-sacrifice to become my Savior. Now I am free from sin and its penalty and able to enter into an ever-deepening relationship with God by knowing Christ.

The unique, Christian distinctive in understanding reconciliation (cited in the previous chapter) mark Christianity as the only genuine, true religion or faith.

Back to *The Shack*

In the dialogue at the end of Chapter 13 of *The Shack*, Paul Young's 's "universal reconciliation" is clearly in the background. Love is viewed as "opening the way" for all to discover their reconciliation. Since there is no judgment or eternal torment, as Young teaches in other chapters (11) and elsewhere, love finds a way for universal reconciliation. Papa as God affirms that he/she has reconciled the whole world already and not just those who believe. Papa virtually rejects the requirement of faith that Mack supposed.

Yet in the passage (Col. 1:19–20) that probably lies in the background of this dialogue, the Apostle Paul speaks of the role of faith in reconciliation. The text affirms that reconciliation is the potential for everyone, and Christ died for the purpose of reconciling everyone (v. 20). But the Colossians were not reconciled until they believed (so vv. 21–23). Instead, they were far from God. Paul Young commits a significant doctrinal error that concerns how God is related to the world of believers and unbelievers. Surprisingly, Mack, who supposes a role for faith, is here more biblical than Papa is!

Suffering by identifying with Christ and his people (note Col. 1:24; Phil. 3:8ff.) is the way to achieve deeper reconciliation—relationship—with God. In *The Shack* suffering in this form goes unmentioned. Thus the relationship espoused therein will remain shallow and unfulfilling. Paul Young's failure to communicate clearly that faith is the means, the key, whereby reconciliation available for all can be appropriated freely by all is a travesty of the word "reconciliation." It is comparable to a scientist holding the only key that will unlock an indestructible box containing the antidote for all the world's diseases. But instead of offering to unlock the box, he destroys the key with a blowtorch so that the antidote cannot ever be used to heal anyone. Thereby he dooms all to die in their illness.

This is what universal reconciliation does.

· 13 ·

The Meaning of Truth and the Role of the Holy Spirit

WHAT IS TRUTH?

In this chapter, I bring together Chapters 14 and 15 of *The Shack*. There is much in these chapters that is laudable, but there are also several conflicts with the Bible. I will limit myself to a couple of questions that arise from the dialogue of the novel and will answer them briefly. My major concerns are centered on what truth is and the role of the Spirit in revealing it.

Chapter 14, "Verbs and Other Freedoms," is Paul Young's presentation of how rules relate to relationship and why the Ten Commandments were given. As Mack paddles off across the lake in the mid-afternoon, Sarayu (as the Holy Spirit) joins him. She promises that she will always be with him and make her presence known. He will hear her thoughts in his own thoughts as their relationship grows (195–196). Emotions are the colors of the soul and are neither bad nor good. Sarayu tells him that *"paradigms power perception and perceptions power emotions"* (italics Young's; 197). What one believes to be true about something leads one to perceive or think of it as true, and this, in turn, forms one's emotions. When Mack complains that living out of relationships is more complicated than living by rules, even the rules of Scripture, Sarayu corrects Mack that the Bible "doesn't teach you to follow the rules. It is a picture of Jesus" (197). She continues that religion is about having the right answers, but she is about the process that takes one to the living answer (Jesus) who is able to change one from the inside (198). She promises to communicate with Mack in unlimited, living, transforming ways, and to be seen in the Bible in fresh ways. Mack is not to look for rules and principles but for relationship with them (her and Jesus).

Paradigms—Perceptions—Emotions?

Let me pause here and raise some concerns about the relationship of paradigms, perceptions, and emotions. First, when one reflects about the statement above that Paul Young put in italics, it reveals why he writes as he does. Virtually everything in the novel emphasizes relationships over truth or doctrine. That is why Young can come to such strange statements about God and about people. I have pointed out many of these in the preceding chapters of this book. And here in Young's own words is the explanation.

As I said at the beginning of this exposé of *The Shack*, Paul Young writes his novel first as theology and only second as a mystery story of suffering, alienation, and reconciliation. In other words, the theology is primary, the story secondary. If this is the case, then Young's theology is paramount. It is what Young believes that influences everything that he writes, and some of it is deeply troubling, even heretical.

Young wants his statement given above in italics to stand out. And it does. It means that what he believes, what he conceives of as truth (his paradigms), has influenced his perceptions about everything, and these in turn have fed his emotions (expressed in relationships).

How the Author of *The Shack* Went Astray

It is my conviction that Paul Young's initial belief in or conviction of universal reconciliation (his paradigm) that he defended in his document of 2004 (described in the Introduction) leads him to the perception that much in evangelical faith is false or distorted and should be questioned. In interviews he asserts that he questions virtually everything. This perception fuels his heavy influence on relationships (emotions) rather than Christian doctrine. In actuality, he puts relationship before doctrine. He derives his doctrine from relationships. Thus he ends up with a paradigm heavily influenced by relationship and distorted doctrine. His faulty belief system leads to faulty perceptions, which lead to faulty emotions.

All universalists place relationship (a.k.a., love) above the revealed Scripture about the destiny of the wicked in hell. Love trumps all of the other attributes of God. This beginning point leads to their perceptions and in turn to their doctrines.

I believe that the Bible puts it differently. Both truth and love are necessary. You cannot sacrifice truth for the sake of love or relationship; and you cannot sacrifice love for the sake of truth. But truth is the determiner of what is to be believed; love is not. Nevertheless, truth, to be convincing, must evidence itself in love.

Faith (affirming the truth) is the means of entering into relationship with God; love is not. We can love only in response to God's loving us first. "We love because he first loved us" (1 John 4:19; cf. v. 10).

As dealt with in the chapters above about reconciliation, God has reconciled the whole world to himself. But for this to be real or true or actual for any individual in the world, that person must respond by faith and trust in Jesus Christ. Faith is absolutely necessary: "For since in the wisdom of God the world through its wisdom did not know him, God was pleased through the foolishness of what was preached to save *those who believe*" (1 Cor. 1:21). This is conclusive.

The Lord's Prayer

Everyone knows what the Lord's Prayer is. Note that it begins with the holiness of God; God's love is not mentioned at all. "Our Father in heaven, hallowed be your name" or "reverenced be your name" (Matt. 6:9). Jesus did not say: "Our Father, may you be loved." Thus in the one prayer that Jesus expressly models for all his followers to pray it is all about God's holiness, not about his love. Why? Because if one is able to reverence God he will also love God. The great doctrinal pillar of Judaism (Deut. 6:4ff.) begins with an affirmation of who God is and is then followed by the call to love him totally.

Christian Holiness

Furthermore, every Christian is called to holiness. The Apostle Paul writes that "God's temple is holy and you are that temple" (1 Cor. 3:16). He exhorts every Christian to keep his body pure "as a temple of the Holy Spirit." Each is to "honor God" with his body (1 Cor. 6:19–20). Indeed, the apostle first exhorts the Thessalonian believers that "it is God's will that you should be holy" (1 Thess. 4:3) before exhorting them to increase their love for other believers (vv. 9–10).

What is Truth?

I think that Paul Young's italicized principle above goes far to explain what *The Shack* is all about. The weekend for Mack, and the book's theme, are all about relationships (102), not truth. This allows Paul Young to do two things: he can "milk" the idea of relationships for all that it is worth; and at several places where he runs up against evangelical doctrine or biblical truth he can respond by saying that the book is not about truth or doctrine, that it is fiction.

Some readers have taken this very approach when confronted with the doctrinal errors of the novel. They simply say that it is a novel; it is fiction. Even Paul Young says this very thing. But on other occasions he says that the book is autobiographical. He cannot have it both ways.

Finally, where one begins (one's paradigms) is very crucial. Paul Young's statement leads to pluralism—everyone's paradigm is just as good as the next person's. Young never says that God's paradigm—his absolute truth—should transcend all other paradigms. In keeping with universalism in general, Young avoids many exclusive claims from the God of the Bible. Such plurality leads to chaos in theology, and Christ's death and resurrection are in the end for nothing.

Truth is what God reveals. It is his word as revealed in the Bible (Ps. 119) and as revealed in the creation around us (Ps. 19). Properly interpreted, the Bible is God's greatest gift of truth to the world. Truth is embodied in the person of the Lord Jesus Christ, who said: "I am the Way, and the Truth, and the Life" (John 14:6).

Rules and Relationships (Again)

The second concern I have involves the statement that Sarayu makes about rules and relationships. We've seen this subject come up before, and I dealt with it then. Is it true that the Bible doesn't tell us to follow the rules, that it's a picture about Jesus?

Yes it is, but wait! While this is the truth, it is not the whole truth. It is the motive for following rules that is the issue, not the rules themselves. Following rules—doing works of the law—can neither save nor sanctify. This is legalism, and strongly condemned by the Apostle Paul in Galatians.

But obedience to Jesus is the necessary evidence or proof of being in fellowship with him. Do you remember what James said in James 2:14–20? "Faith without works is dead." And Jesus laid down some pretty strong rules about loving him and loving one another. "A new commandment I give to you that you love one another" (John 13:33–34). And do you remember what Jesus said to his followers in Matthew 28:18–20? "Go and make disciples of all nations . . . teaching them to obey everything I have commanded you." All followers of Jesus are commanded to make disciples who will obey what Jesus taught.

Finally, Paul Young's basic anti-institutional attitude comes through again in his words that set "religion" in opposition to having a relationship with Jesus. Now it is true that many wrongly believe that they have a relationship with Jesus simply by belonging to a church or belonging to the Christian religion. But coming to God by faith in Jesus Christ does distinguish Christianity from all other religions, and establishes a relationship with him.

Paul's Portrayal of the Holy Spirit is Like Tinkerbell?

We also see here some of Paul Young's very few references to the Bible. Yet one's relationship with God or with the Spirit can only grow as Scripture is read and becomes the basis of relationship with God.

What is the connection of the Spirit with the Bible? The Spirit has the commission from Jesus Christ to lead Christ's followers into the teaching of Christ (John 14:26). Jesus said that the Spirit is the "Spirit of truth, who goes out from the Father, he will testify about me" (John 15:26f). Further, Jesus said that the Spirit does not "speak on his own; he will speak only what he hears, and he will tell you what is yet to come. He will bring glory to me by taking from what is mine and making it known to you. All that belongs to the Father is mine. That is why I said the Spirit will take from what is mine and make it known to you" (John 16:13–15).

Young's teaching about the Holy Spirit (his Sarayu) is distorted because he presents the Spirit as an independent source of revelation and truth, as one "who delights in uncertainty." His portrayal of the Spirit looks more like the storybook Tinkerbell of *Peter Pan* than the Comforter of the Bible.

God as Transcendent

I return to the novel. Over supper, the discussion continues on the line of relationship. The Three tell Mack that he can add nothing to them to make them more fulfilled; they already are fully fulfilled within themselves (201). Papa makes it clear that only Jesus is fully human and fully divine; in her very nature she is not human. She clarifies: "I am truly human, in Jesus, but I am a totally separate *other* in my nature" (italics Paul's, 201).

Here Paul Young apparently affirms the transcendence of God, and the difference between the Father and Jesus Christ. But the discussion in earlier chapters of the Father's being crucified with Jesus (102) contradicts the statements here. Until now Paul Young's total focus has been on God's immanence—his presence. He virtually omits any further reference to God's transcendence.

Yet Scripture balances God's transcendence and immanence. This is beautifully seen in the event of Isaiah the prophet's calling and commissioning. Isaiah 6 portrays God as transcendent, as "seated on a throne, high and exalted," worshipped by seraphs proclaiming, "Holy, holy, holy is the LORD Almighty" (vv. 1–3). But Chapter 7 portrays God's visiting his people in the form of one to be born of a virgin whose name is to be "Immanuel" ("God with us") (7:14). The latter title emphasizes God's immanence or presence. So here both ideas occur back to back.

The Purpose of Rules

When Mack asks what the Three will expect of him once he gets back home, a discourse about "expectation" and the purpose of rules ensues. The Ten Commandments were not given to make it possible to live righteously but to act as a mirror to show just how filthy people are when they live independently of God. Sarayu asks whether one can clean one's face with the same mirror that shows how dirty one is. There is no mercy or grace in trying to keep rules. Jesus fulfilled all the law perfectly so that it no longer has jurisdiction over people and the commands become a promise that God fulfills in his own (202). Jesus is "both the promise and the fulfillment" (203). Followers of Jesus "are not under *any* law. All things are lawful" (italics Young's; 203). Trying to keep the law is a declaration of independence, a way of keeping control over and of judging others and feeling superior to them (203). "Rules cannot bring freedom; they only have the power to accuse" (203).

Dealing this way with the Ten Commandments as a mirror seems to cloud the issue. The law is holy and good (Rom. 7). In addition, the only place in the New Testament that speaks of the law as a mirror speaks of obeying or doing the law in order to be blessed by God, to prove that one's faith is genuine and alive. Works are a necessary evidence of faith (James 1:23–25), as I've said before.

There is also confusion again over the matter of "keeping rules." Since Paul Young and his editors insist that the Christian life is not about performance, they misunderstand the place for rules. It is true that we will fail if we try to keep rules in order to be saved or to be sanctified. These are wrong motives for keeping rules. Yet obeying rules is what Christians do "naturally"—by their new nature as new creations in Christ (2 Cor. 5:17). Because Christ has inaugurated the new covenant by his death (Luke 22:20; 1 Cor. 11:23–25), the Holy Spirit has interiorized God's law in the hearts of believers so that they "obey" him by virtue of their new nature (see Heb. 8:7–13).

Finally, Jesus Christ says just the opposite of Paul Young's Sarayu, that "rules cannot bring freedom." There is truth embodied in rules, and Jesus said: "You will know the truth [Jesus' teaching, v. 31] and the truth will make you free" (John 8:32). This is another example where what Paul Young asserts is incomplete and distorts the truth.

The Christian and the Law

While the exact relationship of the Christian to the law is debated among Christians, it is certainly a mainline view to affirm that Christians are not under any law (so Paul the apostle affirms in Rom. 6:14; 7:6; 8:2; Gal. 5:18). Yet Paul Young gives scant attention to the role of obedience in the Christian's life and thinks of law in opposition to relationship. While the Christian gives loving obedience, it is still obedience to commands (note John 13:33–34; 15:9–17; etc.). And God gave the law so that relationship might be defined.

In other words, there are some relationships that are good and edifying and spiritually profitable. Other relationships may be destructive. The only way to know the difference between the two is to compare the relationships with the definitions that God has set forth, and with his nature and character. But the only way we know God's nature, and whether our experience of it is genuine and godly, is whether it corresponds to the word of God. If we experience a relationship that contradicts the word of God, no matter how pleasant and seemingly satisfying it may be, it should be abandoned.

In his denial of commands to be obeyed, Paul Young, again reflecting his universalism, has Papa virtually deny to God the role of judge. Yet this contradicts the rest of the witness of Scripture. The New Testament identifies God, even after the death of Christ, as the Judge of all, including Christians. James 4:12 says: "There is only one Lawgiver and Judge, the One who is able to save and to destroy." James simply warns that no person take on the role of judge (see also Rom. 3:6).

James' words are similar to Paul the apostle's words in Romans 14:10–13, where the apostle affirms the role of God (or Christ) as the judge of all Christians. In this way everyone will acknowledge— "bow before"—the Lord and give account to him. The apostle applies the Old Testament passage to Christians of the new era. God acts in the role of the Judge of all, including Christians.

The idea of bowing before God (see also Phil. 2:11) does not point to an act of accepting God or Christ as Savior but being brought into submission, to confess and acknowledge God to be what he claims to be—the one worthy to judge people. The passage is not about finding salvation in God or Christ; it is about bringing into forced submission all who are opposed to him.

God is "I Am"

At this point Sarayu launches into a discourse about verbs and nouns, asserting that verbs are to be preferred over nouns because verbs are alive, dynamic, active, and moving. God is a verb. "I am that I am. I will be who I will be," she asserts (204). Nouns pertain to physical reality, and without verbs nouns make the universe dead. It is similar to the difference between grace and law. She illustrates this by pointing out that the nouns responsibility and expectation become alive and dynamic in the verbal forms of respond and expectancy (205). Whereas religion uses law to empower itself, the Spirit, because she is present, infuses people with the ability to respond and to be free to love and to serve. Expectancy is alive and dynamic and undefined, but expectation brings law into a relationship and makes relationships—all relationships—deteriorate into dead things (205). Thus God has no expectations of anyone—he doesn't need any since he knows all that there can be known about one—but God does have expectancy of people in his relationship with them. [I think these claims are baseless].

In addition, Sarayu comments that it is wrong to have priorities, such as to set God first and people second, for priorities suggest a hierarchy and destroy relationship. Instead, God wants all of a person all of the time. Jesus wants to be not at the top of a pyramid of choices but at the center of everything, to be the center of a dynamic mobile (207). The scene closes with Sarayu touching Mack's eyes so that he might see, for a brief time, a bit of what God sees.

THE MEANING OF TRUTH AND THE ROLE OF THE HOLY SPIRIT

God as a Verb?

The preceding discourse is a bit confusing. While many nouns are static, many others are active and bear a verbal dynamic. Love is such a noun.

I think that it should be foundational to any discussion of the importance of theological language involving verbs and nouns that we should be thinking about the original language of the New Testament—Greek—and not English. In Greek many nouns are active in their force—almost any noun that has a verb cognate would be such a noun. Thus while "love" is a noun, its verb "to love" is active; and this suggests that the noun is also an active word. In addition, participial and infinitival forms of nouns (such as "loving" and "to love" respectively) are active and not static, especially in Greek. So the whole discourse about active nouns amounts to little since English does not parallel the structure of the language of the New Testament (Greek).

In addition, the verb "am" is an equative verb expressing a state, and not active, so it seems a bit overstated to refer to God as alive and active on the basis of God's self-disclosure as "I am who I am." To argue about the nature of God based on an English verb seems a bit tenuous. In addition, the "I am" phrase is used by Jesus to make significant claims about himself in the Gospel of John: "I am the door"; "I am the good shepherd"; "I am the way, the truth and the life"; "I am the resurrection and the life"; and so on. These seem to be equally significant in identifying who Jesus is as in making a statement about his being alive or active. Finally, the term "God" is a noun, but God certainly is not physical nor inactive; and he is not dead! Even the Greek would bear witness to this!

A concern arises from what Paul Young says. Does Young reflect biblical teaching regarding the nature of God as a verb? In the great first self-disclosure of God recorded in Exodus 3:14, God reveals himself to Moses by the name (in the Hebrew), "I am who I am." The Greek translation (the LXX) of this has the force, "I am the being." The force of these words is to affirm God as the eternally living one who never changes. It seems to be the basic idea of his name as Yahweh.

Seeing but Not Seeing

Chapter 15, "A Festival of Friends," is the unveiling for Mack of heavenly reality that was initiated at the end of Chapter 14. In the midst of our physical world, it takes special sight to see the heavenly reality, and for a brief time Sarayu treats Mack to such a spectacle. Mack is transported from the shack to the top of a small hill where it is night with the moon and stars overhead. Children and adults, as well as angels, appear as each having a distinct light form (212–213). The light and colors and blaze are unique to each one for each relationship, with children having less color than adults. Each individual personality and emotion has its own unique combination of color and light that is ever changing. It is this that identifies each person and angel. They are all gathered to celebrate the arrival of Jesus.

But one light at the edge of the scene causes commotion and the person cannot contain his emotion. It is Mack's father, who mistreated his son and drove him to run away many years before. Mack rushes forward to his father, embraces him, and by mutual confession and forgiveness both are healed by a love greater than either one (215). Returning to his vantage point on top of the hill, Mack observes the arrival of Jesus clothed in brilliant white and wearing a gold crown. He enters the circle of lights on a carpet of love. Then the beings gather around him, and they, everyone who has a breath, worship him with a song of "unending love and thankfulness." That night, "the universe," Mack observes, "was as it was intended" (216). In the midst of the celebration, Jesus avers his special fondness for Mack. And then all the participants have a personal time with Jesus before departing. Finally, Mack is left alone. He is blind again as his natural sight returns, and he returns with Jesus and Sarayu to the cabin.

Implications

These pages show that angels and people in heaven are still very much alive and fully known, and in a sense present. Each one is identified by his or her unique identity, perhaps as an aura of color and light, and not by physical features. Paul's descriptions reinforce the reality of the future life.

Yet this picture needs to be balanced by the opposite picture of those suffering eternal separation from God in darkness. It is the place of destiny for the murderer of Mack's Missy. Of course, Paul Young would probably never countenance such a picture, but Jesus did. On several occasions he warned that those who reject him would go to a place of torment (Matt. 25:46; Luke 16:19–31); he warns of hell fire (Matt. 5:22, 29, 30), destruction (7:13), darkness, and weeping and gnashing of teeth (Isa. 66:24; Matt. 8:12; 22:13; 25:30); and he warns of eternal fire prepared for the devil (the "murderer from the beginning") and his angels (25:41), and more.

These are the words of Jesus. He spoke of hell four times more frequently than he spoke of heaven. But *The Shack* says nothing about the place and state of unbelievers, including the destiny of the one who murdered Mack's daughter.

Based on the earlier part of the novel, it is clear that Mack murdered his father with poison. This act goes unmentioned in the later chapters of the book. This omission seems quite stark in light of the fact that Mack's father confesses his wrong of abusing Mack. This imbalance seems in keeping with the gospel as Paul Young defines it but not with the Bible. Why does Mack's murderous act get a pass? Is it being judgemental to hold him accountable?

Forgiveness, Forgetting, and Election

DOES GOD FORGIVE AND FORGET ALL?

In this chapter, I take up the last three chapters of *The Shack*. It concerns important issues not before covered, especially the matter of forgiveness. I will address these issues as two or three questions.

Chapter 16, "A Morning of Sorrows," concerns two unfinished items in the remaking of Mack. Mack is awakened by Papa out of his sleep at the end of his second night with the Three. Papa now appears as an older gentleman, not a large black woman, because Mack will need a father today (219). He is able to know God as Father because he had forgiven his father the day before (221). Papa reminds Mack again that he created freedom for people to choose independence if they wish, but it came at great cost—the death of Jesus to provide "a path of reconciliation" (222).

I pause here to draw attention to these last words. It almost slips by the casual reader that Paul Young has identified Jesus Christ as "a path of reconciliation." Elsewhere, Young identifies Jesus as the "best way" to God, not the only way. But Jesus identified himself as the path—"the way"—to God (John 14:6). Young's words are not how the New Testament followers of Jesus thought of him. It has led some critics to charge that Paul Young does not view Jesus Christ as the only way to God. It seems that this is but another hint of the universalism embedded in *The Shack*

I return to the story. To help Mack bring closure to his experience, Papa leads Mack up the trail above the cabin. Yet this experience must involve Mack's forgiving the man who murdered his daughter Missy so that he can be released to God "to allow him to redeem" the murderer since he is also a son of God (224). While Mack struggles over being able to "forgive and forget," Papa reminds him that forgetting is not involved and forgiveness does not in itself "establish relationships" (225). Papa remarks: "In Jesus, I have forgiven all humans for their sins against me, but only some choose relationship" (225). These words deserve special attention below.

Papa goes on to instruct Mack that forgiveness of another does not require one to trust that person, but if a person finally confesses and repents, then reconciliation can begin (226). Papa also tells Mack that he will handle the matter of justice for the murderer (226). Papa also declares that it is all right for Mack to be angry while he forgives the murderer, because "anger is the right response to something that is so wrong" (227). It may be that one day Mack will hand the murderer over to Papa "so that my love will burn from his life every vestige of corruption" (227). These words also deserve special attention in the pages that follow.

Having accomplished one task, the other unfinished task was to find Missy's body. Papa points out to Mack that the murderer has marked his trail with a small red arc to lead to the cave where he left Missy's body. Upon discovering the body, Mack places it in a special bag made by Sarayu and begins carrying it back toward the shack. So ends Chapter 16.

Several Statements That Raise Theological Concerns
There are several smaller issues that I address before taking up the larger issue of forgiveness. First, Papa asserts that he will deal with

the matter of justice (226). While it is refreshing to have Paul Young bring up the matter of justice, it is not clear what this means, especially in light of earlier statements in the novel that God does not judge sins. Is this Paul Young's accommodation to the obvious, that the sin of murder must be judged by someone on the earth?

Second, another point needs to be made. A bit earlier, Paul Young has Papa assert that it is okay for people to be angry toward wrongdoing, such as murder (227). But, I ask, if it is okay for people to feel this way, why is it wrong for God to be angry with those people who reject him? Why does Young take an approach to the wrath of God that basically denies God's anger toward sinners and toward sin, especially unbelief, when many biblical texts affirm God's anger (Rom. 1:18–32; 2:1–16; 2 Thess. 1; Rev. 6; etc.)? Is there any justification for human anger if God is never angry? Must not all human anger of this kind find its basis in God's holiness and justice? Does not Paul Young make God into Santa Claus, who never has a harsh word or deed for anyone?

Third, it is strange that the act of murder is called "corruption" (227), and not called "sin" or "evil," or even a "crime," especially when acting independently of God is described as evil. Also, how is it that love will "burn away corruption"? Readers should know that "burning away" is the language of universalism, that all suffering is corrective, chastening, purgatorial, and redeeming, but not punitive.[82] Love takes the form of the fires of hell so that all—people, fallen angels, and the devil—repent in order to escape hell. Universal reconciliation has no place for justice and punishment, for suffering the consequences, that is, the punishment, of one's evil deeds. Yet there is absolutely no word in Scripture that affirms universalism's view of punishment nor of an opportunity to repent after death.

Also, *The Shack* says nothing about the murderer being held accountable for his evil act, for justice to be served before the state. Does this not reflect Paul Young's opinion that the state is among the "trinity of terrors" that have ravaged the world? Yet Paul the apostle says that laws exist to deal with the lawbreaker and the immoral and others, including murderers, who do evil acts (1 Tim. 1:8–10), and that government has been established by God to punish evil (Rom. 13:1–7). How else is justice to be served on earth? Young's anti-state attitude leaves injustice without a remedy, allowing it to thrive and leading to anarchy (as I pointed out in the preceding pages).

Finally, it seems that Paul Young makes God's act of redeeming another person dependant on our forgiving that person (224). But is God's redemption of another related to our forgiving that person? Does not redemption come to people because God chooses to redeem them and because they believe the gospel? But Young rejects the doctrine of election, as found in John 3:16–18 and Romans 8:28ff.

Rather, God's forgiveness of *us* depends on our forgiving *others*, as Jesus clearly affirms in the Sermon on the Mount (Matt. 6:12, 14–15). These verses say: "Forgive us our debts, as we also have forgiven our debtors. . . . For if you forgive men when they sin against you, your heavenly Father will also forgive you. But if you do not forgive men their sins, your Father will not forgive your sins."

(1) Are All Forgiven?

But the bigger issues in this chapter concern the matters of forgiveness and relationship with God. The novel has brought up these matters before, and I've addressed them earlier. But this chapter gives a new twist to them. I'm concerned with the statement: "In Jesus, I have forgiven all humans for their sins against me, but only some choose relationship" (225). The first big question for this chapter is: Are all forgiven?

If all people are God's children and are forgiven already for their sins, does this not include their lust for independence? Does it not include unbelief? And if these are forgiven, then why are not all people thought of as having just as close a relationship with God as those who actually desire or "choose" it? By this logic it seems that in the end there is none out of relationship with God. It seems then that this is naked, uncovered universalism—what universal reconciliation is all about in the end. All already have a relationship with God apart from believing.

Yet biblical witness and human experience contradict this conclusion. The Bible teaches that one must believe and receive the offered gift of forgiveness (Rom. 6:23; John 3:16) for reconciliation to become effective or operative. This is one of the major points made in earlier chapters.

In addition, all people have a moral sense within (called conscience) that says that there is a difference between Mother Theresa and Adolf Hitler as far as evaluating their morality is concerned. We grant to juries of fallen human beings the ability to discern significantly the difference between right and wrong. Thus there is something more that needs to be involved to classify one as forgiven. It seems that faith and trust are necessary, and without faith people's sins are not forgiven. The forgiveness is not actual for all but only potential for all.

Again, forgiveness for all has been made possible by the death of Christ. But those who reject the forgiveness that comes because of the cross do not receive forgiveness. They cannot have what they reject.

It seems that Paul Young's universalism has blinded him to the reality that the Bible identifies some people as both hating God and under his wrath (Rom. 1:18ff.; Col. 3:5) because they fail to repent and believe/trust Christ. There are those who are in a state of condemnation because they are not in Christ (Rom. 8:1) because they do not believe (John 3:16, 18). They will perish (3:16). What is more, the Bible gives no hope that this destiny can be reversed after having once begun.

(2) Are the Words "Choose Relationship" Biblical?

This discussion brings us to the second large question based in the statement: "In Jesus, I have forgiven all humans for their sins against me, but only some choose relationship" (225). Now Paul Young may protest that his words "choose relationship" are what he defines "believe on Jesus Christ" to mean. But why does Paul Young not use the words "believe" and "faith," which occur over six hundred times in the Bible, while the terms "choose relationship" *never* occur in an English Bible? Of course, the words "choose relationship" focus on what *The Shack* is all about. But there is theological danger here.

As I pointed out in the chapters above, the biblical word for relationship is reconciliation. Reconciliation, as shown above, is initiated by God, not by people; and God removed the obstacle (sin) to relationship. Thus, none can "choose relationship." The one condition for it to become real in a person's life is exercising faith—believing Christ to be who he claimed to be. But Young rejects God's election and views sin in an unbiblical way. Thus there is no substance to Young's idea of relationship.

Elsewhere Paul Young and his editors argue strenuously against Christianity's being about performance. They assert that it is about relationship. But the Bible would place the terms "choose relationship" very close to the doing of a work to be saved, which is condemned: "For by grace are you saved through faith; it is a gift of God, not of works lest anyone should boast" (Eph. 2:8–9). Paul Young and others seem oblivious to the fact that believing excludes all working and demands that something be believed, be accepted as true, be given credence. That something is the core of truths about who Jesus Christ is and what he has done. The words "choose relationship" carry none of this significance. They potentially allow everyone to choose a relationship with God *without* believing and *without* affirming certain necessary facts or truths about him and about our Savior. Colossians 2:6 makes it clear that one must receive or believe the instruction about Christ.

The words "choose relationship" also strike one as an attack against divine election, which Paul Young vigorously rejects as a doctrine of the Bible (in his document of 2004). For him, it is totally a matter of people choosing God but never a matter of God choosing them. Yet why would Young allow people to choose but disallow God to choose? I'll return to the matter of election shortly.

It is clear why *The Shack* uses the terms "choose relationship." They agree with Young's whole concept of knowing God in a "circle of relationship" where there is neither authority nor subordination—all are on a "level playing field." But as I've shown in an earlier chapter, Paul Young has let his anti-authority bias supplant the biblical teaching. Finally, the words "choose relationship" are anthropological or man-centered. They put the stress on what a person does rather than on what God has done in salvation, as found in the word "believe." The biblical way to secure forgiveness of sins is to believe, not "choose relationship." Until faith is exercised, there is no forgiveness, and no relationship.

(3) Does Not Forgiveness Establish Relationship?

A final concern is this: Does not forgiveness establish relationship? *The Shack* asserts that "forgiveness does not establish relationship" (twice on 225). This statement is connected with the statement, "In Jesus, I have forgiven all humans for their sins against me, but only some choose relationship."

Yet the Bible reveals just the opposite of this! Forgiveness is only potential for all; it does not belong to all. And only when one accepts Christ as one's atoning sacrifice—believes this about him and trusts him for salvation—does this forgiveness become effective. As I have shown above in the chapters on reconciliation, a person can have a relationship with God—have reconciliation—only when that one responds to accept, to appropriate, the reconciliation that God offers to all. One then receives forgiveness. This then is the basis for relationship; it does, indeed, establish relationship (contrary to Young). A person is so intimate with Christ that he or she can be said to be *in* Christ because he or she has forgiveness (see Col. 2:6–15; John 17). And Christ is *in* that person ("Christ in you, the hope of glory"; Col. 1:27; cf. 3:4; Rom. 8:10).

BURNING DOWN "THE SHACK"

It seems that Paul Young creates categories about relationship that are in conflict with the Bible. The Bible teaches that confession and the resulting forgiveness do establish relationship with God (cf. 1 John 1:5–9). Young creates a category of forgiveness apart from relationship with God and also a category of relationship with God that is something different from being a Christian (see Young's reluctance to use the title "Christian" in the chapters above). According to the new covenant that was inaugurated by Jesus at his death, relationship with God, knowing God, and having forgiveness all go hand-in-hand: "I will be their God and they will be my people . . . they shall all know me . . . and I will remember their sins no more" (Heb. 8:10–11).

If those in relationship with God are not Christians, what are they? Are they super-Christians? How deep does the relationship have to be? How does one measure whether it is deep enough? The issue is not various degrees of relationship but simply whether one is in relationship, in union, with Christ. And Scripture makes it clear that one enters into relationship with Christ by the act of faith, at conversion. Thus all Christians are in relationship.

It is more biblical to think of this matter as that of firming up the relationship, of strengthening it, of appropriating it more and more, rather than the Christian's entering into it subsequent to becoming a Christian. This understanding seems appropriate to whether we are seeking forgiveness from God or from some other person.

Is There Not Freedom to Be Unforgiven?

There is another difficulty with Young's conception of forgiveness and relationship. In keeping with his theology, God allows people to be independent from him. This means that God does not force himself on them (as asserted in an earlier chapter). If this is so, then why should some not be allowed to exercise their freedom to be unforgiven or to reject forgiveness? For Papa to assert that he has already in actuality forgiven everyone is to force forgiveness on some who don't want forgiveness. It is the evangelical doctrine of freedom for the individual to choose to reject Christ and to go to judgment that best captures biblical theology.

The biblical distinction is not between some children of God who desire relationship with God and others who don't, but between those who have a relationship with God by virtue of their faith in Christ and are his children and those who don't believe and thus don't have a relationship with God (see John 1:12: "But as many as received him, to them he gave authority to become the children of God—to those who believe in his name"). As I've already said, Paul Young's way of putting it makes salvation anthropological—man-centered—rather than God-centered, since the emphasis is on a person's desire or choice.

Election

On the other hand, since Young considers all to be God's children equally loved by God, he is more deterministic than Calvinism. This brings us back to the issue of election. Young obviously rejects the biblical doctrine of election, which means "to pick out, to select, to choose from among others" (as any good dictionary shows), as Jesus (Matt. 22:14; 24:22, 24, 31; John 15:16, 19) and the Apostle Paul make clear (Rom. 8:28–33; 9:11; Eph. 1:3–14). By deduction, some are not chosen, some are not God's children. Paul Young's view makes all people elect or chosen, even those in hell. But then, election, meaning to choose, ceases to exist as a doctrine, for all are chosen.

Just how important is the doctrine of election? Paul the apostle writes that election, predestination, and love are all connected (Eph. 1:4–5): God "chose [i.e., 'elected'] us in Christ . . . in love by predestining us to adoption as his sons." Thus God's choice of us is an expression of his love, and his love is an expression of his choice. This is how God brought about relationship (becoming his sons and daughters) with him. The apostle also writes that predestination (which assumes election) is one of five necessary works that God accomplishes in bringing a person who is a sinner into heaven as a saint (Rom. 8:29–30: "Those whom he foreknew he also predestined to be conformed to the image of his Son . . . ; and those he predestined, he also called; and those he called, he also justified; and those he justified, he also glorified").

One term that the apostle leaves out is "reconciliation," the only term that speaks of relationship (I covered this term in two earlier chapters). But on the basis of Romans 5:1, reconciliation follows justification and precedes glorification. This being the case, since Paul Young rejects election and/or predestination, he has broken the chain of Romans 8:29–30 so that there cannot be a relationship with God that flows from predestination. If there is no predestination, there is no justification and no reconciliation, and thus no relationship with God.

In addition, no one has experienced God's love if he rejects God's election and predestination. By denying election in this way, Young has distorted the meaning of salvation, love, and relationship.

The gospel according to Paul Young is a teaching independent of and apart from Scripture (God's word). Yet by Paul Young's theology even this bad theology must be forgiven!

Again the universalism of Paul Young comes through. Young's denial of election isn't freedom after all. It is coercion, and this opposes our understanding of the nature of God as love, and the nature of human beings as having freedom "to choose relationship." If all are forgiven and all are God's children, how can people "choose" a relationship with God when they already have one? The contradictions in Paul Young's theology are glaring.

The Basis of Forgiveness

It may escape the casual reader of *The Shack* that there is not really a lengthy discussion given to the basis of forgiveness and relationship with God, namely the death of Christ. Of course, in keeping with the universalist bent of the novel, it is assumed to be the love of God. But the cross is the basis of our forgiveness, not the love of God. Love is the "why" of our forgiveness but not the grounds of it.

I think that Oswald Chambers in his *My Utmost for His Highest* touches on this matter of forgiveness with special clarity. Many of my readers will know this most widely read daily devotional guide, which has been read for over eighty years. Allow me to cite a couple of pages.

> Very few of us know anything about conviction of sin; we know the experience of being disturbed because of having done wrong things; but conviction of sin by the Holy Ghost blots out every relationship on earth and leaves one relationship only—"Against Thee, Thee only, have I sinned!" When a man is convicted of sin in this way, he knows with every power of his conscience that God dare not forgive him; if God did forgive him, the man would have a stronger sense of justice than God. God does forgive, but it cost the rending of His heart in the Death of Christ to enable Him to do so. The great miracle of the grace of God is that He forgives sin, and it is the death of Jesus Christ alone that enables the Divine nature to forgive and to remain true to itself in doing so. It is shallow nonsense to say that God forgives us because He is love. When we have been convicted of sin we will never say this again. The love of God means Calvary, and nothing less; the love of God is spelt [*sic*] on the Cross and nowhere else. The only ground on which God can forgive me is through the Cross of my Lord. There, His conscience is satisfied (324).

Again, Chambers writes (325):

> Beware of the pleasant view of the Fatherhood of God—God is so kind and loving that of course He

will forgive us. That sentiment has no place whatever in the New Testament. The only ground on which God can forgive us is the tremendous tragedy of the Cross of Christ; to put forgiveness on any other ground is unconscious *blasphemy* [italics mine]. The only ground on which God can forgive sin and reinstate us in His favour is through the Cross, and in no other way. Forgiveness, which is so easy for us to accept, cost the agony of Calvary. It is possible to take the forgiveness of sin, the gift of the Holy Ghost, and our sanctification with the simplicity of faith, and to forget at what enormous cost to God it was all made ours.

Forgiveness is the divine miracle of grace; it cost God the Cross of Jesus Christ before He could forgive sin and remain a holy God. Never accept a view of the Fatherhood of God if it blots out the Atonement. The revelation of God is that He cannot forgive; He would contradict His nature if He did. The only way we can be forgiven is by being brought back to God by the Atonement. God's forgiveness is only natural in the supernatural domain.

In the conclusion to this book, I quote Chambers a bit more on this matter.

The Garden of the Heart

Chapter 17, "Choices of the Heart," concludes the special adventure that Mack has at the shack. Jesus has carved a special coffin for Missy's body. It is placed in it, and then it is buried in the clearing that Mack made in Sarayu's garden. Upon burying it, Sarayu sings a song that Missy had written just for this occasion. Then she scatters some of Mack's tears collected for this occasion on the ground under which Missy's body slept (233). Flowers instantly burst forth from the places where the tears fell. The garden represents the garden of Mack's heart (234).

Back in the cabin, the Three and Mack partake of wine and bread. The Three offer Mack the choice of staying with them or returning to his other home. He chooses the latter. Sarayu reminds Mack that every time he chooses to forgive or to do an act of kindness, the world changes for the better and God's purposes are advanced (235). Sarayu also gives a gift to Mack to take back to his daughter, Kate, who has blamed herself for Missy's death. It will set her free from her guilt.

While Mack is changing back to the clothes he wore when he came to the shack, the Three leave. Mack then falls asleep. When he awakens because of the cold, he finds himself in the shack as it looked at the first, and winter has returned outside. He is back in the real (or unreal) world. He goes up the trail to his car and drives back to Joseph, Oregon. There, while pulling into an intersection, he is struck by a driver running through a red light. The crash totals the Jeep, and Mack is rendered unconscious, with many broken bones. He is life-flighted back to Portland, Oregon.

The crash, we later discover, actually happens at the beginning of the weekend, not at the end! All that Mack thought he had experienced over a weekend at a shack actually took place in his dreams while in a coma that began on the Friday of the weekend, not on Sunday!

Everyone Will Confess That Jesus is Lord

Chapter 18, "Outbound Ripples," recounts Mack's miraculous awakening after four days and his recovery. He gradually recalls the events of the "weekend." He is able to bring Kate to wholeness so that she no longer blames herself for Missy's death. After a month, Mack, with Willie, Nan, and the deputy sheriff, return to the trail to the shack and go beyond it. Following the red arcs marking the route, they discover Missy's body in the cave. Within weeks the authorities are able to gather enough evidence in the cave to track down and arrest the Little Ladykiller and to locate the other murdered girls.

So this is the story as Willie recounts it. In the "After Words," Willie ends the tale by relating how much the story, whether true or not, has affected his life and that of Mack. Willie wants "*all* of it [the story] to be true" (italics his, 247).

These words may be taken to refer to the fictional story itself, that he wants it to be true or to refer both to the story and also to the theological content. If it is the latter, then it could mean that Paul Young is speaking through Willie to say that he wants to have all the doctrine espoused in the book to be true or correct.

There must not be any confusion about Young's level of certainty here. In light of his statements elsewhere, it is clear that this is not just what the author "wants to be true," but it is doctrine that he strongly believes to be true and affirms it as such. The doctrine has affected the lives of both Willie and Paul Young.

Since Paul Young originally wrote the novel with its universalism for his kids, then he wrote what he believed to be the truth at the time. He wrote to convert his kids to universal reconciliation! No Christian would ever knowingly write a novel to deceive his or her kids with heresy unless he or she signaled this ahead of time. For Paul Young to dismiss the troubling elements of his theology with the claim that the novel is only fiction is unacceptable.

How Will All Finally Confess Christ?

Willie asserts that Mack is hoping for a new revolution of "love and kindness . . . that revolves around Jesus and what he did for us all" (248). Willie affirms that "if anything matters, then everything matters. And one day, when all is revealed, every one of us will bow our knee and confess in the power of Sarayu that Jesus is the Lord of all Creation, to the glory of Papa" (248).

This is Paul's final assertion of his universalism. While the words faithfully reflect such biblical texts as Philippians 2:10–11, Paul puts them in a context of love and kindness and says nothing about the day of judgment when people make this confession—not as a witness to their repentance and faith in Christ, but as their admission that God's ways are right after all. It is a forced confession.

All will confess Christ, but how they do so makes a world of difference. The confession cannot be made by a person in an intimate relationship with God, for by Young's own definition, any authority and subordination (here reflected by confessing Jesus as "Lord") destroy relationship. It is a confession that results from Christ's conquest, not from a person's faith. This does not constitute believing obedience sufficient to bring a person into an eternity with God. Even the "demons believe and tremble" (James 2:19) before "the one Lawgiver and Judge, who is able to save and to destroy" (James 4:12). These are those who are "enemies of God" (James 4:4) and suffer eternal separation and judgment from God.

In this way *The Shack* comes to an end. But just as the novel has an important "after word," so do I. In the conclusion, I state the most obvious reasons why the novel should be rejected as distorted teaching of the Bible. I then follow this conclusion with several appendices that touch upon related, significant matters (why hell must be forever, why universal reconciliation is neither of these; and so on).

The Serious Consequences
of the Errors of the Novel

We have covered much ground together in our search for biblical truth in light of the contents of *The Shack*. I think one way I can describe the great shortcomings of this novel is to list what Christian doctrines Paul Young has redefined on the way to telling his make-believe story. Remember, the novel was birthed for his children in universal reconciliation, and for over a year he and his editors sought to soften this theological foundation to make the novel palatable to uninformed Christians.

As a result of interacting with his document of 2004 and with *The Shack*, I believe that the gospel according to Paul Young carries very serious consequences. Here is my brief enumeration of them. Paul Young improperly redefines the meaning of the Trinity and the special roles of God the Father, Christ the Son, and the Holy Spirit. He distorts the nature of Christ's crucifixion, the nature of sin and punishment, the wrath and judgment of God, and the nature of God's love and having a relationship with him. He has no place for the devil, the enemy of every Christian. He has corrupted the nature of forgiveness, the nature of faith and reconciliation, the nature of salvation, the very meaning of the gospel, who the children of God are, what the Bible is, and the role of the institutions of the church, the state, and marriage. Indeed, he rejects the latter, twice calling them a "trinity of terrors."

Final Insights from Oswald Chambers

Some of the more fitting quotations that I could make regarding the problems of *The Shack* come from Oswald Chambers in *My Utmost for His Highest*. They go to the heart of how Paul Young's novel distorts the love of God. When you read these words, you realize that Chambers also had to confront those who thought improperly of the love of God and the death of Christ. Almost a hundred years ago he confronted universalist thinking in his day when he wrote (326):

> Never build your preaching of forgiveness on the fact that God is our Father and He will forgive us because He loves us. It is untrue to Jesus Christ's revelation of God; it makes the Cross unnecessary, and the Redemption "much ado about nothing." If God does forgive sin, it is because of the Death of Christ. God could forgive men in no other way than by the death of His Son, and Jesus is exalted to be Saviour because of His death. "We see Jesus . . . because of the suffering of death, crowned with glory and honour." The greatest note of triumph that ever sounded in the ears of a startled universe was that sounded on the Cross of Christ—"It is finished." That is the last word in the Redemption of man.
>
> Anything that belittles or obliterates the holiness of God by a false view of the love of God, is untrue to the revelation of God given by Jesus Christ. Never allow the thought that Jesus Christ stands with us against God out of pity and compassion; that He became a curse for us out of sympathy with us. Jesus Christ became a

curse for us by the Divine decree. Our portion of real-
izing the terrific meaning of the curse is conviction of
sin, the gift of shame and penitence is given us—this is
the great mercy of God. Jesus Christ hates the wrong in
man, and Calvary is the estimate of His hatred."

The Shack has been praised by many as capturing the process,
from a counseling perspective, by which people can move from dark
places of tragedy and alienation to a new spirituality. But at what
price does this take place? For *The Shack*, the price is redefining
God and the meaning of the death of Christ. It does not seem
necessary for Paul Young to have done this. After all, the stories
of the Bible do not do so. Should not all our stories and needed
personal transformation be based in the truth revealed in Scripture?
Our supreme, ultimate calling is to glorify God, to exalt his worth,
to lift him up in the truth as he has revealed it.

Paul Young's *The Shack* is a subversive attack on the Bible and
Christian faith. It has the potential to damage Christian theology
for several generations. If it leads Christians to "question everything," then even what good there is in *The Shack* will also be torn
to shreds. And who, other than the Deceiver himself, would be
behind such chaos?

Questions for Mack
(and Paul Young)

I t seems appropriate that there should be a place for continuing the saga of Mack. Perhaps Paul Young will do this. But in the meantime there are several questions that every well-meaning Christian should ask Mack (and Willie, the storyteller, too). If the encounter he has had at the shack took away the "Great Sadness" once and for all, I am curious about the meaning his encounter has for others. Many have testified, as Paul Young has testified, that the shack is a metaphor for the hidden place in our lives where evil things exist that need to be cleaned out.

In other words, I want to address the vehicle, the format, Paul Young used to advocate his theology about the Trinity. As we discover at the end of the book, everything that Mack experienced took place in a dream, in a coma, while recovering from the vehicle accident that occurred while on his way to the shack in northeastern Oregon. Even the reason for his going to northeastern Oregon, the note he received in his home mailbox from "Papa," apparently was something he dreamed or thought while in a brief coma that happened after slipping and hitting his head on ice outside his house.

So, Mack, I have some questions that arise as to the permanency or ongoing reality of your shack experience. I ask you the following questions about your dream. How do you know when to obey your dream and when not to?

I'm sure that you, like the rest of us, have dreams, but we do not "obey" them all. For example, when my wife Patricia was laid up with a broken hip for many weeks, just days before we were to see the doctor about whether she could begin walking again on her left leg, she had a dream. She dreamed that she was to get up and begin walking immediately without her walker. She dreamed also that when we got to the doctor's office, the people there did not know why she was there. There was nothing wrong with her hip.

Now the next morning, Pat did not believe her dream. She did not push her walker aside to get to the bathroom and say, "I don't need you anymore." Why didn't she trust her dream? Something told her that it did not correspond to reality, and she did not have any reason or conviction that God had worked a miracle in her body.

So I ask you, Mack: Why did the dream change your life? What was in the dream that convinced you that it corresponded with reality, that you should believe what you heard the Trinity say to you? Since you had rejected your seminary training in real life, and in your dream Papa led you to believe that much of what you believed about God beforehand from your theology was wrong, doesn't it trouble you at least a bit that perhaps you are on shaky ground to discern the truth—what you should believe and practice? That perhaps you are not the best person to trust your own judgments?

In effect, doesn't your dream reinforce your rebellion against God that led you away from your seminary training? Isn't the entire story simply reinforcing your own rebellion against God?

Here's a second question. By what means do you trust one dream and not another? It is said by missiologists that about 70 percent of all Muslims who come to believe in Christ according to the gospel do so on the basis of a dream or vision. I know a believing Saudi who was led to Christ by two such dreams. So we know that God can lead this way.

But we also know that our dreams can lead us astray. Your dream had a positive effect for restoring you to God, even if by much poor theology. Perhaps this is what many readers of your story are experiencing also: restoration to God in spite of bad theology.

What if one of your sons, Mack, had a dream that he hunted down the murderer of his sister, Missy, met him in a dark alley, and killed him? Should he follow this dream? Why or why not?

Isn't the answer something like this? We take our dreams as authoritative when they agree with the Bible or principles of the Bible, and we don't follow our dreams when they clearly disagree with the Bible. Most of our dreams are not clear cut for us, and so we tend to wait and see.

But you, Mack, were thoroughly convinced by your dream. Why? Because it agreed with your rebellious position already embraced in your life?

So the chief question is this: Are all your dreams authoritative for your living and choices in life? How do you tell the difference?

Here's the third question. What will you do when the next crisis comes? Do you expect there to be another "shack" encounter where the Trinity is molded in new forms to address new, different kinds of problems?

The fourth question is important. What do you tell your children when they experience suffering or trials or disappointments? Do you tell them to expect their own "shack" experience?

The fifth question is this. The tenor of *The Shack* is that you, Mack, question God on a whole host of topics, just as Paul Young in interviews has asserted that he questions virtually everything in his real life. If this is an appropriate and beneficial approach for getting "divine help," do you recommend your readers to follow your example and to question everything?

More to the point, should your readers question everything that you say and that you do and the resolutions that you discover?

The scope of the novel is to question all kinds of presupposi-
tions. Would it not be legitimate to question the presupposition
of questioning all presupposition?

Finally, Mack, I make these observations about your creator.
On his Web sites, Paul Young has sought to deflect criticism of his
novel by saying that criticism tells him more about the criticizer,
where that person is personally, than to give him pause as to what
he has written. But is this not an approach that is self-promoting,
a way of avoiding difficult questions and observations? Is this not
a defense that virtually deflects all criticism, even that which may
have merit?

What if your readers, Mack, took this approach toward every
criticism leveled at them, even when they had fallen into sinful
behavior? What if I took this approach right now in my book
critiquing *The Shack*? I could insist that every criticism that Paul
Young has of me, or that the readers have of what I've written, is
without merit, as telling me something negative about Paul and
them? By this reciprocal type of thinking, no one can evaluate anything in the search for truth—even truth that may be embedded
in *The Shack*. There can never be an advance in knowledge and
understanding.

In the end no one wants to operate by this principle, for then
none of us can advance in understanding and grow and come to
the truth. Only God, or one totally submissive and abiding in God
100 percent of the time (this is Jesus Christ alone), can operate by
this principle. The rest of us are too prone to self-deceit to claim
this principle.

Also, Mack, your creator has said that your story is a "God
thing" because so many people have been affected by it. But isn't
it possible that if the story is actually bad theology it may be an
"evil thing"? Ought not the test for all claims to truth to be the
Bible and not our experience? Otherwise, any experience, even one
critical of yours, could claim to be a "God thing."

APPENDIX 2

My Answers to Readers' Questions

Questions Worth Asking and Answering

Out of respect for Paul Young and his readers it is necessary to ask some questions that others have raised about my criticism of the book, and to answer them.[83]

Isn't It Just Fiction Anyway?

"Since the book is fiction, why do we have to think that Paul Young believes anything, or everything, in the book, whether it is from Papa or Mack or Willie? In a work of fiction does not Young have license to have his characters say anything he may want them to say, with little or no concern for orthodox or biblical truth or doctrine? Some may only be filler, for color, for shock value."

In reply, I say that an author of fiction certainly may have his characters say anything and he does not have to approve or believe any of it to be true for himself. Yet consider that this fiction is professed to be a Christian work; there is an expectation that the characters will speak truth for the most part. This is especially true if young people or children or uninformed Christians take up and read this fiction. Should not a Christian writer be expected to write for us what agrees with Christian truth or doctrine? When Paul has Papa or Jesus or Sarayu saying things, should not they as God speak the truth? This is not saying that a writer cannot speculate about what the future may hold or look like, and take other license. It simply means that we expect a Christian writer to write in accord with truth already revealed and not contradict what is plainly taught in Scripture. And Young does contradict several great truths, such as his denial that God is Judge, that God consigns anyone to endless torment (or separation from him), that God has established several institutions, including the church and the government, and so on. In contrast to such recent works as *The Da Vinci Code*, we expect a Christian to affirm true truth. And the author has not in public appearances and interviews disavowed any of the doctrine asserted in the novel. He could have easily done so.

Can We Not Benefit from the Good Aspects of the Book?

Another fair question is this: "Regardless of whether or not Young's writing is doctrinally sound, are there not many good aspects of it that will profit many people? For example, the emphasis on a relationship with God will help many to search and find such a relationship when before now they had none or a defective one."

Yet while this may be the case, is it truly helpful if someone helps people in one area while simultaneously propounding error in another area and using it to support the helpful material? If the love of God is affirmed but his justice and/or holiness is shortchanged, will this not lead to a distortion of God and one's relationship with God? When the reader finds out that Young's theology is suspect in one area (such as his support for universal reconciliation), will this not lead the reader to question the other areas, including those where he thinks he has been helped? May it not lead a reader to renounce all of the good parts of the fiction as well, or at least to have suspicion of it? May it not lead some to renounce Christians and the Christian faith altogether?

Does Not the Good Outweigh the Bad?

A question related to the preceding one is this: "Can you not appreciate all the good in the book? Does not the good outweigh the bad?"

The answer to this is similar to that just above. One does not use error to teach truth. Jesus is love, but he is also truth. By de-emphasizing or neglecting the justice or holiness of God in the service of propounding a heresy about the love of God, one cheapens the love of God so as to obscure its meaning.

If we don't understand or fully appreciate a particular attribute of God, our understanding of the others is distorted. God is not conflicted in his attributes, but universalism in all its forms would lead us to believe that he is.

Note the Example of Jesus Christ

The New Testament and the Old Testament present a beautiful portrayal of God's attributes. When we read such prophetic texts as Psalm 45 we realize that the author must have had an intimate relationship with God. Here Jesus is described as "loving righteousness" or "uprightness" and "hating lawlessness" as he wields a "righteous scepter."

Similarly, Psalm 85:10 affirms that in God "love and faithfulness meet together; righteousness and peace kiss each other." Surely this means that love and truth are intimately related. Psalm 62:11–12 records: "One thing God has spoken, two things have I heard: that you, O God, are strong, and that you, O LORD, are loving. Surely you will reward each person according to what he has done." Here special and general revelation combine to tell us that God is both strong and loving when he judges the ungodly and the godly.

As the capstone of what the Old Testament identifies as the true believer we have Micah 6:8: "What does the LORD require of

you? To act justly, love mercy, and walk humbly with your God."
This sums up in wonderful balance what should characterize God's
people because they reflect their God—justice and love, and their
human response to him. Yet universal reconciliation virtually rejects
doing justice—what the text puts first! Or it subjects his justice to
his love. And Jesus upheld the same three virtues (Matt. 23:23).

The New Testament sums up what it means to know Jesus.
For one example, John writes that knowing Christ is to obey his
commands to believe [the truth] and to love others (1 John 3:23).
This is the central verse of his entire epistle. And it comes from the
apostle who had the most intimate relationship with Jesus—the
one whom Jesus loved, the beloved disciple. This verse presents
balance and fullness.

John concludes his letter by affirming what it means to know
God and Jesus Christ—to have an intimate relationship with them.
"We know also that the Son of God has come and has given us an
understanding, so that we may know him who is true. And we are
in him who is true—even in his Son Jesus Christ. He is the true
God and eternal life" (1 John 3:23).

Are You Not Being Overly Critical?

Many readers will ask another question. "Are you not being overly
critical, perhaps reading too much between the lines? Paul Young
nowhere affirms universal reconciliation by name in this novel.
Perhaps you have found it when it isn't really present."

My answer is this. Young himself has acknowledged that universal reconciliation has dramatically changed him, affecting him
personally as well as his theology in several areas. We should assume
that these words include his writing of fiction. In evaluating his
work, my goal is to be fair but critical and truthful. The readers of
the book will have to decide whether I have met this goal. But as
a follower of Jesus, as a friend of Paul Young, and as a teacher of
the New Testament for many years, I have an obligation to exalt
God in the person of Jesus Christ above all else, to glorify him. I

will best do this by seeking to uphold the nature and will of God, of Jesus and of the Spirit, as revealed in the Bible, and to expose those errors that diminish his glory and his love.

If someone claims that a new teaching has changed his total perspective on life and his theology in strategic areas (such as salvation and the church), as Paul Young has made all these claims, isn't it logical to think that such a person will find it nigh impossible to go back completely to his old way of thinking, believing—and writing? As the above book has tried to show, Paul Young skirts along the edge of universal reconciliation, debunking the old beliefs but never plunging clearly into the abyss itself.

Are You Being a Bit Harsh?

Some of my readers may continue this objection. They ask: "Aren't you being a bit harsh? Can't we look beyond the theological issues and profit from the reading of this novel? Isn't the main thrust of the book on the idea that everyone should seek a deeper encounter or relationship with God, and isn't this possible in spite of the book's faults? Is it possible that your concern for doctrine keeps you from profiting from this book? The pluses of the book outnumber the minuses."

The heart of my possible answers to the foregoing is this. Yes, I believe that God desires his children to have a deep, intimate, reciprocal relationship with him, and I strive for this myself. But a key concern is this: How can I have a deep relationship with God, or with a human being for that matter, if it is based on lack of understanding, or even misunderstanding, of who the other person is? Does the lack of knowledge of the person of God lead to lack of faith and false or faulty living or practice? Do we not, should we not, live out our faith?

I can only grow in relationship with God, or with anyone for that matter, if I know him or her. The more I truly know God (while acknowledging the imperfection of all human knowledge), the deeper my relationship will be. But if I am in error regarding what I believe God to be, I cannot grow in relationship. Even Paul Young speaks of knowledge as the basis of love.

Indeed, in the pursuit of a deeper relationship with someone, including God, the more intensely one gets to know the other, and the more intimate that relationship develops, the more one discovers the real essence or reality of the other. But if the basic commitment to the other begins on a false premise, then the more distorted the relationship becomes.

Take an analogy. If I fall in love with a person who seems to be loving but is at heart a conniving thief, then the more intimate I become with this person the more deeply my relationship is distorted. It is a dilemma. For how do I renounce the one whom I have grown to love? How do I have confidence about my future choices?

The Illustration from Islam: There is No Intimacy with Allah

Let me illustrate it this way. God is able to love humans because he is a loving God by nature. Long before he ever created us or anything, love was being exercised within the triune God among the persons of the Trinity. This is a significant truth that validates Christianity over, for example, Islam. Islam adheres to a monadic idea of God—he is single in nature, only one being. In contrast to this monadic monotheism, Christians adhere to a triune mono-theism. Now Islam affirms that God (Allah) does loving acts, among others, but it steadfastly refuses to embrace any knowledge of the nature of God as loving. As far as his nature is concerned it is unknowable. It is even blasphemous to reflect on what his nature might be, since every attempt by humans to understand Allah will fall short and misrepresent him.

Islam takes this view to avoid affirmation of the triune nature of God. If God is by nature understood as loving, then he had to have an object to love before he ever created, and this leads to plurality within unity—to the Trinity. And this Islam vehemently rejects. One can be a Muslim only by affirming that God is one (that is, singular) and that Muhammad is his prophet.

Thus what one believes about the nature of God is strategic to having a relationship with him. Muslims cannot profess a "personal relationship" with God as Christians do. They cannot know God; they cannot be "in God" and he in them by virtue of being in Christ, as Jesus Christ spoke of this in the upper room discourse (John 14–17).

Is Not the Stress on Relationship a Good Thing?

Others will say: "But is not the whole emphasis on relationship with God a good thing and needed today when so many have missed it?"

The answer is that this indeed is good and needed today. Yet this can be done without compromising the balance of love and truth. Indeed, it can only rightly and lovingly be done by doing love in the context of truth (this is the theme of 2 and 3 John).

The emphasis on relationship with God has been made through the ages by many pious writers (Jonathan Edwards' *Religious Affections*; John Bunyan's *Pilgrim's Progress*; Oswald Chambers' *My Utmost for His Highest*; and a host of others). They wrote, and some wrote fiction, without compromising Christian truth.

In recent years many (Richard Foster, Dallas Willard, and others) have reinforced the need to practice the Christian disciplines. These include about a dozen or so practices that help Christians to grow in intimacy with God. While in his novel Paul Young touches on many of these (such as worship, confession, stewardship, silence, mutual submission, etc.), he says little or nothing about other practices that many believe are primary, namely Bible reading and study and prayer. Yet Scripture gives much exhortation about practicing these as the primary ways by which God communicates to us and we communicate to God. These should form the basis of the "circle of relationship" about which Paul Young speaks but distorts.

Assessing the Value of This Book

Let me suggest another approach to discovering the value of the book in light of Young's universalism. Young has affirmed that his consideration of universal reconciliation has made him a better person, to have deeper, more loving relationships with people and with God. For the sake of argument, let's suppose that Young is wrong in embracing universal reconciliation. This means, then, that his closer relationship with God is based on and reinforced by a great error. It means that false teaching or doctrine can have a significant impact, even a good impact, on a person's behavior and personality. Love, the central but unbalanced focus of universal reconciliation, has become the center for Paul Young. What should we make of this? Young became a more loving person while (or by) embracing false teaching!

Most readers of this book are Christians. They need to ask the question: "Should (perhaps "will") I discover from this book a greater love for God and people when it is based in the universalism that has transformed Paul Young?" I suggest that if the doctrine is distorted, so is the relationship.

There are other questions. Should we not bring theology to life? Can bad theology produce good living? Could a person become a properly informed Christian by reading this book? Doesn't the thrust of Paul Young's witness mean that for him experience was the determining factor that validated what he should believe? Yet is not experience to be critiqued by the truth as revealed, for Christians, in the Bible?

If people are impressed by reading this book, are they not in danger of imbibing the theology that lies behind it? Can we not discover in the Bible and in good fiction the encouragement toward intimacy with God? These are serious questions that every reader should ask before recommending the book to others.

In addition, there is the issue of an author's being a role model, particularly for young people and immature believers. By his beliefs and by his way of "doing church," he does not commend the gospel as revealed in the New Testament.[84]

Did Paul Intend to Skirt Important Doctrines?

Another question concerns Paul Young's intent. "Is it not possible that Young did not intend to skirt or diminish certain doctrines?" To put it another way: "Must we demand that Young write equally about all the doctrines of Scripture? Since Paul Young has created a certain plot and certain characters struggling with particular needs, why should we expect Paul Young to weave into his story all the other doctrines of Scripture?"

The answer, of course, is that no writer has to do this. But the matter is different if a writer brings attention to some of the most basic truths or doctrines and then rejects or distorts them explicitly or implicitly. Paul Young gives sustained attention to very crucial doctrines.

To deal with an author's intention is a difficult matter. As I noted at the beginning of this book, Paul Young embraced universal reconciliation before he wrote the novel, and he and his editors carefully weighed everything in the novel with the intent of removing the universalism. In light of this it is legitimate to assert that Paul Young intends to teach theology by his fiction.

But regardless of his intent, he certainly does influence the reader with theology. Thus he should be faulted when he has his characters, the Triune God, deny or reject certain doctrines that the majority in the church has embraced from the Bible for almost two thousand years; and he should be faulted when he has his characters propound beliefs such as universal reconciliation that the same church has pronounced heresy. These words are not meant to exalt the traditions of the church, but to insist that where the church has made its decisions on the basis of the authority of Scripture this tradition is to be embraced.

There is another thought that flows from this question. It is entirely possible that Paul Young himself doesn't realize just how deeply universal reconciliation has infected and changed his theology.

Why the Theology of *The Shack* Is Finally Destructive

The number one error of *The Shack*, its Achilles' heel, is that Paul Young commits the great evil that he faults the human race for committing from the beginning onward. Paul Young makes the number one evil in the world, the evil basic to all the rest, to be the independence from God that Adam and Eve exercised in the Garden of Eden and the independence that all people have subsequently embraced. Yet Paul Young himself indulges the great sin of independence. By embracing the basics of universal reconciliation, Young creates his own view of how love and holiness or justice relate but does not reflect all those texts that talk about the judgment of God on the unbelievers who reject him. At least Young subjects God's virtue of justice to his virtue of love (remember: "mercy triumphs over justice because of love" taken out of context), and creates an imbalance in portraying the character of God. *The Shack* represents a hut of deception awaiting the uninformed reader. It is a place of theological entrapment that is constructed from a failure to represent all Scripture that presents a fuller, complete view of the nature of God, of people, of salvation, of relationship, and of the future and its judgment.

Like many other shacks found in the forest, *The Shack* rests not on a concrete foundation but on wooden pillars that are rotted and insect-infested and in time will fail. One might paraphrase Matthew 4:4 as follows: "Man does not live by [love] alone but by every word that comes from the mouth of God." Jesus said also that every house built on sand will collapse (Matt. 7:24–27); so will every shack in the woods.

The Final Question

No doubt the most practical question that the reader of this book would ask me is this: "Do you advocate the reading of this book?"

My answer is both a tentative yes and no. For those who have a good grounding in the total teaching of Scripture and theology, there is profit in reading *The Shack*. To read it is to understand where liberal theology is going. Yet its benefits represent half truths, half of the picture. Thus for those without maturity, the book is deceptive. It can easily ensnare the reader in false doctrine and an unhealthy, unchristian understanding of the nature of God, the death of Christ, and institutions and church practices.

Thus I do not recommend this book because of the theological error in it. As other reviewers have pointed out, Paul Young is subversive. He is subversive to the truth and to the institutions of the church, the state, and the home. The book hinders rather than helps genuine spiritual growth and understanding. One might think of Paul Young as a theological insurgent, as a doctrinal terrorist, within the Christian church. The effect is chaos and anarchy.

Universalism is the theological torrent that runs behind the shack throughout the story. While the countryside through which this river runs is serene, beautiful, even captivating, the river itself is polluted, carrying poison that threatens the health and productivity of the countryside. It has the potential to drown those without a life vest. The unprepared should avoid this torrent and stay far back from its banks. Once in the river, it is quite difficult to climb up the slippery bank. All who drift down this torrent are in danger of being lost.

It is fitting to close this appendix with the words of C. S. Lewis relating to universalism. He remarked (in *The Great Divorce*): "There are only two kinds of people in the end: those who say to God, 'Thy will be done,' and those to whom God says, in the end, 'thy will be done.'"[85]

The Creeds of
Universalism

The Creed of 1790

The first creed was that agreed on by universalists at their Philadelphia Convention of 1790 and polished by Benjamin Rush. Since the Trinity was under debate at the time, reference to such is not explicit. Note how the attributes of God are subsumed to his love, that there is implicit rejection of judgment and eternal hell, and that there is universal salvation. There is no devil.

Sect. I. Of the Holy Scriptures.

We believe the scriptures of the Old and New Testament to contain a revelation of the perfections and will of God and the rule of faith and practice.

Sect. II. Of the Supreme Being.

We believe in one God, infinite in all his perfections; and that these perfections are all modifications of infinite, adorable, incomprehensible, and unchangeable love.

Sect. III. Of the Mediator.

We believe that there is one Mediator between God and man, the man, Christ Jesus, in whom dwelleth all the fullness of the Godhead bodily; who, by giving himself a ransom for all, hath redeemed them to God by his blood; and who, by the merit of his death and the efficacy of his spirit, will finally restore the whole human race to happiness.

Sect. IV. Of the Holy Ghost.

We believe in the Holy Ghost, whose office it is to make known to sinners the truth of their salvation, through the medium of the holy scriptures, and to reconcile the hearts of the children of men to God, and thereby to dispose them to genuine holiness.

Sect. V. Of Good Works.

We believe in the obligation of the moral law, as the rule of life; and we hold that the love of God, manifested to man in a Redeemer, is the best means of producing obedience to that law, and promoting a holy, active, and useful life.

There were also recommendations passed by the same convention. They concerned war, going to law, opposition to slavery, oaths, and submission to government.[86]

The Winchester Profession of 1803

It is a short declaration and is repeated here in full. It is as revealing for what it does not affirm as for what it does affirm. It reaffirms the essentials of universalism as in the creed of 1790. It was drafted, among some debate with those who opposed any creed at all, by Walter Ferriss.[87] He probably used the Philadelphia articles of faith as a guide:

Article I. We believe that the Holy Scriptures of the Old and New Testament contain a revelation of the character of God, and of the duty, interest, and final destination of mankind.

Article II. We believe that there is one God, whose nature is Love, revealed in one Lord Jesus Christ, by one Holy Spirit of Grace, who will finally restore the whole family of mankind to holiness and happiness.

Article III. We believe that holiness and true happiness are inseparably connected, and that believers ought to be careful to maintain order and practice good works; for these things are good and profitable unto men.

The Creed of 1899

By the end of the nineteenth century, the beliefs of universalists had become so liberal by accommodation to higher criticism, evolution, and the social gospel that a new statement was needed to account for the new views of the Bible, which denied its literal interpretation. Thus the "conditions of fellowship" adopted in 1899 in Boston were stated so generally that Cassara calls it "a masterpiece of theological dexterity."[88] They are as follows:

1. The acceptance of the essential principles of the Universalist Faith, to wit: the Universal Fatherhood of God; 2. The spiritual authority and leadership of His Son, Jesus Christ; 3. The trustworthiness of the Bible as containing a revelation from God; 4. The certainty of just retribution for sin; 5. The final harmony of all souls with God.

The Winchester Profession is commended as containing these principles, but neither this nor any other precise form of words is required as a condition of fellowship, provided always that the principles above stated be professed.

The acknowledgment of the authority of the General Convention and assent to its laws.

The 1935 Bond of Fellowship

In 1935 universalists adopted the Bond of Fellowship. It reveals how far universalists had embraced the social gospel of the day. There is no explicit statement regarding a distinctive belief in universal salvation.[89] It reads:

> The bond of fellowship in this Convention shall be a common purpose to do the will of God as Jesus revealed it and to co-operate in establishing the Kingdom for which he lived and died.
>
> To that end we avow our faith in God as Eternal and All-Conquering Love, in the spiritual leadership of Jesus, in the supreme worth of every human personality, in the authority of truth known or to be known, and in the power of men of goodwill and sacrificial spirit to overcome all evil and progressively establish the Kingdom of God. Neither this nor any other statement shall be imposed as a creedal test, provided that the faith thus indicated be professed.

Summary of the Beliefs of Universal Reconciliation

The following summarizes the beliefs of universalism as found in their creeds. In strategic ways universal reconciliation differs from evangelical beliefs.[90]

1. God wills all his creatures, people, and angels to be saved and to acknowledge Jesus as Lord; and (this

is important) God's will cannot be thwarted (Col. 1:19–20; 1 Tim. 2:4).

2. God's attribute of love limits his attribute of justice. It is unjust for a loving God to send people who have lived a short life to an eternal (everlasting) hell.

3. God has already reconciled all creatures—all humanity and all angels—to himself by the atonement of Jesus Christ at the cross.

4. This reconciliation will be applied to all people either before death or after death, and to all the fallen angels, including the devil.

5. Faith is necessary to appropriate reconciliation in this life; God's love delivers unbelievers (and fallen angels and the devil) from hell in the next life.

6. The sufferings of hell and the lake of fire are not punitive, penal, or everlasting, but corrective, restorative, purifying, cleansing, and limited in duration.

7. God has acted as the Judge of all at the cross; there is not a future judgment for anyone.

8. Universalism is the teaching of the Bible. It is the teaching of Jesus.

9. Universalism was the majority belief of the Christian church for the first five centuries.

10. The evangelical church is an obstacle to universalism. All institutions, including the church and the government, are systems of hierarchy that use power to control people.

The Necessity of
Belief in Hell

In the book that I'm writing on universalism in general, I show that there are two logical and biblical reasons why universalism or universal reconciliation should not be embraced. These reasons take the form of the following subcategories.

1. The Safest Course of Action

To keep to the traditional understanding of the everlasting duration of hell is the safest course of action. To embrace universalism's teaching that hell is not forever, that the wicked and the fallen angels and the devil will repent and escape hell to get into heaven, is not the safest option. Here is why I say this.

The Devil's Work

The proponents of universalism are playing to the devil himself. Compare the differing consequences that attend the two options of evangelical faith or universalism.

If evangelical faith is correct and preaches a place of everlasting separation from God, and people respond and are saved, then some will go to heaven. The rest will go to hell and be lost everlastingly.

If evangelical faith is wrong and universalism is correct, and evangelical faith preaches the usual way, and people respond and are saved, then some will go to heaven. The rest will go to hell but later will repent and get to heaven anyway. No real harm is ultimately done.

If universalism is correct and preaches a second chance after death, and some respond now, then some go to heaven, and others who go to hell now will later repent and get to heaven anyway.

But if universalism is wrong and preaches a second chance after death, and some respond now, then some go to heaven. But the rest will go to hell and never get to heaven. They will be given a false hope of a second chance and that false hope deceives them and dooms them forever. Eternal harm is done.

So which is the greater evil, and which plays the devil's hand? Clearly, the greater consequence follows on the preaching of universalism if it is wrong in its doctrine than the consequence that follows on the preaching of evangelical faith if it is wrong in its doctrine. The devil would rather dupe people with the error of universalism than with the error of evangelicalism.

2. Why Hell Must Be Everlasting
Otherwise, Heaven Is Scary and Unsafe and God's Universe Is Threatened.

The following is a rational discourse on why hell (and heaven) must be eternal (everlasting).

If one doesn't want to take Scripture's teaching on the everlasting nature of hell, let's consider logic and rational thinking.

Now according to universalism, hell is not permanent because its fires are therapeutic, not punitive, and all people and the devil and his angels will repent and will escape it. Yet wait a minute. If the fires of hell are only therapeutic, and limited in their length, would not the unrighteous and the devil in particular only have to wait long enough and the fires would cease? Yet the universalist would say: "The devil doesn't know this." But the devil would know this. He knows biblical teaching. If universalism is correct, he knows that the torments in hell are limited in their duration. Yet, the universalist would answer: "Well, the fires go on as long as anyone or any angel refuses to repent." But the devil could reason: "God is so loving that he could not 'correct' me with the ultimate fires of hell; he could not destroy me if I hold out. Eventually God's love will overwhelm the sense of doing justice, and he will relent." The universalist might reply: "But this is not so with the devil and the most wicked." Yet this is precisely what universalism argues. If God's love trumps his justice at the end, why may it not trump it along the way before the end? Why wait till the very end of the fires and allow them to get so intense?

The devil could appeal to the incident of the rebellion at the giving of the Ten Commandments when God relented out of faithfulness to keep his promise to Abraham and out of his compassion for the people. He did not destroy them all, only a few.

So the only thing that makes hell's fires threatening enough is to know that they are unending. It is only the weight of this reality that is strong enough to bring the unrighteous and the devil to repentance. For they would know and understand the Bible's teaching to this effect. But if it takes the teaching that the fires are everlasting to cause repentance, then it is necessary that the unrighteous and the devil must be there permanently. For why should there be everlasting fires if there is no one there everlastingly?

This argument also means that there cannot be a reversal of destinies for anyone after one dies. If the destiny of one can be changed, then the destiny of all (in light of God's love and justice) can and must be changed.

Another More Scary Consequence

There is another, more alarming consequence if hell is not everlasting. Let's say, for the moment, that the devil and the wickedest of creatures do repent and get to heaven. But note what this means. If the devil can change his mind and repent once, what is to keep him from rebelling again against God in heaven, as he did the first time? With greater knowledge than he had in the first rebellion, his pride could arise again and lead him to think he would be successful a second time. So he rebels again. And again God has to defeat him. But what does God use this time? There cannot be another incarnation of Christ and his triumph on another cross, since the incarnation and death could happen only once in all time and eternity. Christ remains today the triumphant God man. Another rebellion of Satan, the devil, makes his triumph on the cross a failure.

So Satan could rebel again, and God could perhaps conquer him in some other way. Satan's cycle of rebellion—repentance—rebellion could go on for eternity. Yet this is impossible, for it makes the Almighty God impotent and nullifies Christ's triumph on the cross.

Thus there can only be one rebellion and one divine conquest, and there cannot be the devil's repentance without nullifying Christ's triumph and God's omnipotence. Evangelical theology came to this conclusion long ago by affirming the doctrine of the confirmation of the devil and his angels in their evil choice. He and the fallen angels, and so also those wicked who have joined his side, cannot change their minds to get out of hell and into heaven. Otherwise the consequences are unthinkable.

Some universalists, committed to their perverse understanding of the love of God, have anticipated this line of reasoning. They simply argue that the devil, when he once repents, is then confirmed in his good choice. But why should this be the case? Why should there be confirmation in one case but not the other?

Other universalists would exempt human beings from the above scenario and have it apply only to the devil and his angels. People would be able to repent in hell because Christ died for their sins, but not the devil's and the fallen angels'. But this will not do. Universalists build their whole case on the breadth of God's love, that it is unlimited and triumphs over justice. They are compelled to be consistent. Thus the devil and his angels must be able to repent. This reasoning also shows how universal reconciliation ultimately destroys the need for the death of Christ and his triumph, since his redeeming work was not done for angels (Heb. 2:16).

Heaven Must Be Everlasting

The permanency of hell also demands that heaven be everlasting (this is a more precise word than "eternal," since "eternal" leads some to think both backwards and forwards, but only God is "eternal"). If the believer is in Christ and he can never be severed from this standing (cf. Rom. 8:28–39), as even universalists would claim, then there must be a permanent place to accommodate the righteous whose standing can never be altered. Also, this observation argues that, in parallel to heaven, hell must abide permanently. There must exist a haven for the unrighteous. If heaven is permanent, then hell is (see Matt. 25:46).

The permanency of hell also gives strength to the argument that "all" is limited in meaning. The permanency of hell argues that the statements that God has reconciled all (Col. 1:19–20), redeemed and forgiven and atoned for all (1 John 2:2), mean that these great accomplishments of the cross are only potential for all but never realized for all. There is no such thing as *universal* reconciliation.

For if hell is indeed everlasting, as I have just argued, then some must be there permanently, and the expressions that say that all are reconciled, redeemed, forgiven, and so on, are not meant to mean that these matters are actual or realized for many. As long as there is a single individual being (including the devil by the reckoning of universalism) still experiencing suffering, then hell continues to exist and not everyone is reconciled, redeemed, atoned for, and so on. The "all" is not "all." There is not universal *reconciliation*.

Thus we come to this conclusion. *Universal reconciliation is neither universal nor is it reconciliation.*

Shame to Evangelical Pastors and Institutions That Endorse the Book

W hy would pastors and schools invite Paul Young to share his testimony and promote his novel when he is one of the most outspoken people against the institutional church? Does this not witness to their basic ignorance of Scripture, of evangelical theology and history, and of the heresy of universal reconciliation?

Remember that Paul Young is the one who makes demonic the three institutions of the church, the government, and marriage, and twice calls them a "trinity of terrors" that are responsible for most of the evil in the world. Young faults these institutions rather than the devil himself, who goes unmentioned in the novel. Yet pastors routinely invite him to their institutions. It seems as though they are committing institutional suicide. It seems that they care more for the popular, the attractive voice, rather than the truth and love for their people.

Does the antipathy that Paul Young has against the institutional church as found in his novel reflect his real life? The answer is yes. Take just one interview with Paul Young that shows his ongoing antipathy for the institutional church.

In an issue of *Faith Today* (Nov.–Dec., 2008, 20–24) even Paul Young himself expresses surprise at how well he has been received in churches (20). But he refuses to acknowledge that he goes to a church. He claims (24):

> The church as a religious institution is an easy target. Religion hurts people. It damages them. It distances them from God. It sets up a value system based on performance. It separates gender and positions of power. But structure is no rival to God. God will use anything we build to accomplish his purpose. The Church is a great place to drive people to helplessness.

Young goes on. In answer to the question, "But we need Christian community, right?" Young says: "The Church is always people. Always and only people." The church as "systems will move toward dehumanization. . . . To me the Church is people. You either are or you aren't" (24). When asked again: "So you have a Christian community you are a part of?" Young answers: "I've got a few of them."

Clearly Young is obfuscating—hiding the fact that he does not attend or belong to a local church, and hasn't for many years. By his views he has also influenced people to bring about church splits near his home town. And how could he belong to a local church? It would violate what he believes—that the church as an institution is diabolical and part of a "trinity of terrors" (with the state and marriage) that have ravaged the world (see *The Shack*, 124, 178–181). Consistent with his rejection of authority in the Trinity, he rejects the idea of authority that elders and deacons would exercise, going so far as to call a gathering he attends a "fellowship" rather than a "church."

It seems to me that pastors who invite Paul Young to their churches are showing a tremendous naïveté. In addition, they are exposing their people to distortion of the nature of God and a relationship with him that will be hard to correct, since so many are emotionally attached to the novel. These pastors are voiding their calling as "shepherds of the flock of God." Shame on them.

Discussion Guide to
Burning Down "The Shack"

HOW THE "CHRISTIAN" BESTSELLER IS
DECEIVING MILLIONS

Introduction: The Story behind the Story. How *The Shack* Was Built.

1. What statements from *The Shack* raise doctrinal questions, as cited by James De Young at the beginning of his introduction to *Burning Down The Shack*?

2. What relationship did the author of *Burning Down The Shack* have with Paul Young?

3. How does this relationship bring new insight into the errors embedded in *The Shack*? How does James De Young bring credibility to his book?

4. What is the difference between general or pagan universalism and universal (or Christian) reconciliation?

5. What are some examples of the teaching of universal reconciliation that Paul Young embraced in 2004?

6. What plausibility is there that Paul Young still believes in basic universalist teaching?

7. Why did James De Young write his book?

8. What texts of the Bible show that universal reconciliation is unbiblical and un-Christian?

Chapter 1: Exposing the Foundation of *The Shack*. What Is It All About?

1. What is Mack's problem, as related by the first several chapters of the book?
2. What biblical stories does James De Young cite that parallel Mack's story?
3. How do the people in these biblical stories resolve their problems in a way that differs from how Paul Young resolves Mack's problem?
4. Can you think of other biblical stories in addition to the ones that De Young cites?

Chapter 2: The Nature of God and the Death of Christ: What Is God Like? Why Did Jesus Christ Die?

1. Does the portrayal of God as a black African woman violate the Second Commandment? Why?
2. What does the doctrine of the incarnation of Christ mean? Did Jesus ever draw on his deity during his time on earth? What one instance must be acknowledged?
3. Was God the Father crucified with Jesus, as *The Shack* affirms? Did God the Father ever leave his Son, Jesus Christ? If so, why?
4. How does the author of *The Shack* relate the love of God to his holiness? How does this author shirk the holiness of God?
5. Cite some biblical examples that reinforce the holiness and judgment of God. What several parables from Jesus specially support the judgment of those who reject Jesus Christ?

Chapter 3: God Is Holy and Love: How Does the Holiness of God Relate to His Love?

1. In the relationship that Christians have with God, how do authority and power relate? What is the message of *The Shack* regarding these matters?
2. What biblical truths about God show that power and authority are not opposed to relationship within the Trinity?

3. What is lacking in the affirmation of Paul Young that "love is holy"?

4. Why is it necessary that all of God's attributes be complete and fully balanced?

Chapter 4: The Judgment of God and the Children of God: Does God Punish Sin?

1. What is the wrath of God? Against whom is it exercised?

2. What Old Testament text speaks so clearly about the character or nature of God? What attributes are mentioned in this text?

3. How does the pattern of grace and judgment become an interpretative grid for the Bible? Where is it seen?

4. How are divine sovereignty and human responsibility related in the Bible? Why?

5. How does John 3:16-18 impact the topics of this chapter?

6. Who are the children of God? What two senses can "children of God" have? What texts support this two-fold sense?

7. What is sin? What terms occur in the Bible to show its variety? Why are there so many?

8. Does God punish sin, or is sin "its own punishment"? Cite a text from Romans where the latter is taught. Cite other texts where the former—that God punishes sin—is taught.

9. What warnings does Jesus give concerning future judgment?

10. Will God judge his own people? What texts affirm this?

11. What does "I am not who you think I am" mean?

Chapter 5: Relationship and Obedience: How Does a Person Relate to God?

1. What is wrong with the "circle of relationship" as presented in *The Shack*?

2. How is hierarchy within the Trinity taught in Scripture?

3. How does obedience to commands relate to knowing God intimately? What texts are important here?

4. What is the role of the local church in finding relationship with God and with others?

Chapter 6: The Essential Place of Institutions: Are Institutions from God or from the Devil?

1. What view of institutions does *The Shack* present? What terminology is employed? Why does this view exist in *The Shack*?

2. What three institutions are singled out as diabolical?

3. What biblical support is there for each of these institutions being from God and not from the devil?

4. How do institutions benefit society? What does their removal bring to culture?

5. How do institutions promote freedom?

6. What happens if one chooses "pure relationship" over institutions, as advocated in *The Shack*?

7. Which is more important and more basic, the institution of marriage or that of the church?

8. What example does James De Young cite as an institution that loves?

Chapter 7: The Meaning of Evil: Where Is the devil? What Is the Meaning of Sin?

1. How does Jesus weave the connection between freedom and truth and the devil?

2. How does the author of *The Shack* wrongly portray the Holy Spirit?

3. What consequences come from omitting mention of the devil in the novel's discussion of the Fall?

4. How is the devil's omission related to the great evil of independence shown in the Garden of Eden?

5. Who in the New Testament gave the most place to the reality of the devil, Satan? What examples can you give?

6. How does failure to mention the devil at all in *The Shack* affect the understanding of sin?

7. How does failure to mention the devil affect understanding Mack's great sadness? How might we counsel him?

8. How may the failure to mention the devil affect the readers of *The Shack*? What chief work does the devil engage in?

9. What place does the devil have in the teaching of universal reconciliation? What does the Bible say about this?

Chapter 8: Living in Relationships and Roles. Do Roles Destroy Relationship with God?

1. Why is it not surprising to find in *The Shack* an aside against war? How does war fit within the institution of government? What texts support this?

2. Are God and people in a "circle of relationship" where there is no authority and subordination? Is the Trinity to be characterized the same way? Why not?

3. What is wrong with such a "circle of relationship"?

4. How is it that fulfilling roles is not opposed to relationship?

5. What role does the church play in pursuing relationships? How is this opposed in *The Shack*?

6. How does the concept of a "circle of relationship" spring from a commitment to universal reconciliation?

7. How does Jesus as our "Lord and King" fit into such a circle?

8. What is the biblical support for the idea that Jesus is an example to be copied, contrary to *The Shack*? How does *The Shack* itself send out a contradictory message about this?

Chapter 9: God as Judge: Does Mercy Triumph over Justice?

1. How is it not true that God loves all of his children the same?

2. Does God arbitrarily send most people to hell and the rest to heaven, as *The Shack* suggests? What is wrong with this caricature?

3. What is wrong with the idea that one's relationship is not based on performance but upon God's love?
4. What is it that determines our eternal destiny?
5. How are faith and works related? How does this relationship illustrate divine sovereignty and human responsibility?
6. Why is it a distortion of the Bible to say that "mercy triumphs over justice because of love"? What does James 2:13 mean?
7. In what way is there a limitation to God's mercy?
8. How is it a distortion to say that judgment is not about destruction but about setting things right? How does this reflect universal reconciliation?
9. What biblical texts contradict this distortion?

Chapter 10: Defining the Church and a Christian: What's Wrong with the Institutional Church?

1. How does Psalm 37 help Christians to know that God loves them?
2. What biblical proof is there that God and Jesus Christ created institutions, contrary to what *The Shack* says?
3. What biblical support is there for having authority exercised in the local church?
4. Who is a Christian? Is it a good term? Where should it not be used at times?
5. What is a Christian? What does "a believer" mean?

Chapter 11: Reconciliation (Part One): How Does the Love of God Relate to His Wrath?

1. What does reconciliation mean? What role does it have in the teaching of universal reconciliation?
2. How do the words of *The Shack*, that people "choose freedom to their own destruction," contradict what has come in earlier chapters?

3. What is the significance of saying that Jesus is the focus of creation and history, but failing to say that he is the focus of the Bible?

4. What is the fault of saying that God is reconciled to the whole world but not validating the fact that faith is the way that this is accomplished?

5. What are three distinctives of the biblical view of reconciliation in comparison to that found in other religions?

6. Where is the doctrine of reconciliation found in the New Testament? Why is it not found in the Old Testament?

7. List some distinctions of the doctrine of reconciliation found in the New Testament.

8. What is the obstacle to reconciliation?

9. Who is angry at whom? Are people hostile toward God? Is God angry at people? Or, is there mutual hostility?

10. How can God be both angry at people and loving toward them at the same time?

11. Distinguish objective reconciliation from subjective reconciliation. Why is it important to know the difference?

12. What are the three objects of reconciliation?

13. In what different ways are all in the universe reconciled to God?

14. Is there universal reconciliation? Why is the answer both "yes" and "no"?

Chapter 12: Reconciliation (Part Two): How Does Faith Bring Peace?

1. What is the condition of reconciliation?

2. Where does the Bible teach that faith must be exercised in order to be reconciled to God?

3. Is exercising faith a work? What is its role in appropriating reconciliation?

4. For what reasons cannot cosmic forces of evil be reconciled to God as believers can be? What does reconciliation mean for them?

5. How is the inanimate creation reconciled to God? Where is this taught in the Bible?

6. How is reconciliation related to justification? What does the latter term mean?

7. Which comes first, reconciliation or justification? Where does the Bible teach this?

8. If faith is the condition for justification, how is it necessary then for faith to be the condition for reconciliation (cf. Rom. 5:1)?

9. How does reconciliation go beyond justification? How does the former differ from the latter?

10. How do the two sides (God's and people's) of reconciliation differ?

11. What is the goal of reconciliation? How does this illustrate that the work of reconciliation has an ongoing aspect?

12. How important is the doctrine of reconciliation?

13. Why is the Apostle Paul the only one who uses the Greek terms for it in the New Testament? How is his conversion and calling basic to his reconciliation?

14. How is suffering related to growing in relationship/reconciliation with God? How does the Apostle Paul illustrate this?

15. What is so wrong about how Paul Young presents reconciliation at the end of Chapter 12 of *The Shack*?

Chapter 13: The Meaning of Truth and the Role of the Holy Spirit: What Is Truth?

1. What does the saying of *The Shack*, "paradigms power perceptions and perceptions power emotions" (ch. 14), mean? How does it explain how the author has gone astray?

2. How does the Lord's Prayer illustrate the significance of holiness in the plan of God?

3. How does *The Shack* portray the Holy Spirit with respect to keeping rules?

4. How are rules related to relationships? How is motive involved?

5. How is the Holy Spirit related to the revealing of truth? Is this person of the Trinity an independent source? What texts of the Bible are involved here?

6. How is the Christian related to the law?

7. What is the problem of viewing God as a verb?

8. What is missing from Young's portrayal of the future state of humanity (ch. 15)?

Chapter 14: Forgiveness, Forgetting, and Election: Does God Forgive and Forget All?

1. What is the error in Young's saying that Jesus is "a path of reconciliation" (ch. 16, p. 222)? Compare John 14:6.

2. If there is a place for people to be angry, why would Young omit that there is a place for God to be angry?

3. What is wrong in asserting that God's redemption of a person is dependent on our forgiving that person (p. 224)?

4. Why is murder called "corruption" (p. 227) in light of universal reconciliation?

5. Is all humanity forgiven (p. 225)?

6. Who is in relationship with God? How is this related to forgiveness?

7. Does not forgiveness establish relationship? What biblical texts can be cited?

8. How does *The Shack* inherently reject the role of election?

9. How will all finally confess Christ (note Phil. 2:10-11)? What different ways are involved?

Conclusion: The Serious Consequences of the Errors of the Novel

1. What are the major doctrines erroneously taught in *The Shack*? What are the consequences of doing this?
2. How would you summarize what Oswald Chambers says about preaching about the forgiveness and the love of God?

Appendices

1. What questions are pertinent to ask Mack about his experience at the shack?
2. How does James De Young answer questions that critics would ask of his book?
3. What matters and doctrines are left out of the various creeds of universalism through the ages? What is a brief summary of the beliefs of universal reconciliation?
4. a. Why is belief in everlasting judgment for those who reject faith in God necessary as far as its being the safest course of action? What would the devil's work be?
   b. Why must hell and heaven be everlasting?
5. Why should pastors of churches and institutions be ashamed for their endorsing *The Shack*?

ENDNOTES

1. I make no judgment as to Paul Young's salvation. As John Piper writes about those who espouse false doctrine, it is important "to hold out hope that men's hearts are often better than their heads" (*The Future of Justification: A Response to N. T. Wright* [Wheaton: Crossway, 2007], 25, n. 30).

2. My paper was titled, "Universalism: A Response," and was dated Spring 2004. The page numbers in parentheses refer to my paper. It is available, now revised and lengthened, from me.

3. But this is a distortion of church history. I've taught the apostolic fathers of the first one hundred years after the time of Christ, and not a single one deviates from the doctrine of eternal judgment for denying Jesus Christ (8).

4. All of these details are admitted on the Web site of Wayne Jacobsen and Brad Cummings as they seek to explain the charge of universalism often leveled at the book.

5. See theshackreview.com.

6. This is the identical remark that the church father, Origen, made in the third century. He is the first church father to openly embrace universal reconciliation. It is his work that was condemned as heresy in the sixth century.

7. Further details from my reviews may be found on my Web site at theshack-review.com. I had initiated this meeting in my home in order to respond to Paul's sense of hurt at my sharing his paper with the church school where he had lost his part time position (in 2004). I had done this because universal reconciliation violated the doctrinal standard there. At the time I thought that Paul was proud to be known as a follower of universal reconciliation. For three years he had not requested that I not circulate his paper.

8. This ambiguity and obfuscation fits into the frame of mind that often characterizes universalists in general. See Appendix 3 where I cite all the creeds of universalism embraced in America since the late 1700s. Universalism proudly boasts in its creeds that it has no creeds! Universalists do not want to be pinned down. According to one history of universalism (Cassara's *History of Universalism*), a universalist of the 1920s was once asked: "Where do universalists stand?" He replied: "The only true answer to give to this question is that we do not stand at all, we move."

9. Timothy Beal, "Theology for Everyone," *The Chronicle Review*, Jan. 15, 2010, B16-B17, praises the novel for its "non-biblical metaphorical models of God," its non-hierarchical view of the Trinity, and its "theology of universal salvation." On the other hand, Katherine Jeffrey, "I Am Not Who You Think I Am," *Books & Culture* (Jan/Feb, 2010), 33-34, denounces it and its comparison to *Pilgrim's Progress* and Milton's *Paradise Lost*. Both reviewers agree that it attacks evangelical faith.

10. I use "universalism" and "universal reconciliation" interchangeably.

11. Roger Olson, *Finding God in the Shack* (Downers Grove, IL: IVP, 2009).

> One reading of *The Shack* would conclude that *everyone* goes to heaven. That's called universalism, which some of the church fathers believed and taught. But it has generally been considered a heresy among orthodox Christians of all denominations. . . . So it would seem that everyone has a ticket into heaven just because Christ died for them. But it's hard to think the author of *The Shack* wants us to believe everyone will be in heaven. If he does, he doesn't explicitly say so and he would be biblically and theologically wrong. I choose to think he's more biblically and theologically correct than that" (100–101).

So because he does not know Paul's past, Olson makes statements wide of the mark. Although Olson identifies this and other major doctrinal errors, such as Young's having the whole Trinity become incarnate and his having the whole Trinity die on the cross, these are not serious enough for Olson to condemn the book. In his view the book "rings true" to human experience. But, I ask, what about "ringing true" to the Bible? Although he "quibbles" (this is his word) with some details, and finds some things that "might lead to heresy," Olson finds that there are "amazing truths" in the book and these make the book beneficial (17).

12. See Olson, 10–16.

13. Some dislike negative interaction with a book, and only want positive interaction. They don't want to read how others may be wrong. Yet Jesus himself is polemical in defense of his exclusive claims; and so is the New Testament, almost from the beginning to the end.

14. The Apostle Paul affirms that every teacher of the gospel is an "aroma of Christ to God among those who are being saved and among those who are perishing, to one a fragrance from death to death, to the other a fragrance from life to life" (2 Cor. 2:15-16).

15. See "The Healing," *Guideposts* (August 2009): 74–78.

16. Matthew Hale Smith, *Universalism Not of God: An Examination of the System of Universalism* (American Tract Society, 1825), warned of such. After preaching universalism for a dozen years, Smith was converted and

wrote his book to warn readers to "beware of universalist books in disguise," including children's story books and books of "poetry and fiction" (254–255). Similarly, the Baptist champion of freedom of religion and conscience, Isaac Backus, wrote against the evil of universalism in 1773. Beal ("Theology"), B16-B17, says that he hopes *The Shack*'s "alternate theology" will lead people into even "more-recent radical" theology. He cites at least six features of its universalism! Jeffrey ("I Am Not Who You Think I Am") finds it deliberately "post-biblical" and a "repudiation" of all the doctrine assumed in Bunyan's work.

17. In an interview with Matt Slick, July 9, 2008, on "Faith and Reason," KSPD Radio, 790 AM, Boise, Idaho, Christian Apologetics Research Ministry (web site: carm.org).

18. On a radio pod cast, from St. Louis, MO., Spring, 2009. Penal substitution is the view that Jesus Christ became in his death the substitute for sinners who deserved to die and took on himself the penalty that sin demanded. Other views of the atonement (example theory, moral influence theory, governmental view, ransom theory, Christ the Victor view, etc.), fall short of explaining the fullness of Christ's death as the payment to satisfy the wrath of God toward sin so that God could be just (righteous) when he justifies us—declares us to be righteous (see Rom. 3:23-26; 6:23). Apparently Young would embrace a combination of these other views.

19. See *Faith Today* (November–December, 2008): 20–24.

20. Historically the broader universalism has progressively humanized Jesus. See Frank S. Mead, *Handbook of Denominations in the United States*, 2nd rev. ed. (New York: Abingdon, 1961), 212–213.

21. While Paul Young seeks to deny that God is "one god with three attitudes," and affirms: "I am one God and I am three persons, and each of the three is fully and entirely the one," (101), he confuses how the Trinity was involved in the crucifixion.

22. This assertion of co-crucifixion also blurs the distinctiveness of persons within the Trinity. Again, in American history, universalists eventually came to team up with the Unitarians and deny the Trinity. See Mead, *Handbook of Denominations*; and Sydney E. Ahlstrom, ed., *Theology in America* (Indianapolis, IN: Bobbs-Merrill, 1980), 37–41.

23. See James B. De Young, "The Terms for Sin and Sin Offering in the Old Testament," (B.D. thesis: La Mirada: Talbot Theological Seminary, 1968). My Th.M. thesis dealt with the Greek terms for sin in the New Testament.

24. See Leon Morris, *The Apostolic Preaching of the Cross*, 3rd ed. (Grand Rapids, MI: Eerdmans, 1965), 224ff., for an excellent discussion of reconciliation and the wrath of God.

25. Ibid.

26. See Brian D. McLaren, *The Last Word and the Word After That: A Tale of Faith, Doubt, and a New Kind of Christianity* (San Francisco: Jossey-Bass, 2005), and many other books about the emergent church.

27. David Blankenhorn, *The Future of Marriage* (New York: Encounter Books, 2007).

28. Ibid., 60.

29. Ibid.

30. Ibid., 61.

31. Ibid.

32. Ibid.

33. See pp. 57ff.

34. Blankenhorn, *Marriage*, 91, defines marriage thus: "Marriage is socially approved sexual intercourse between a woman and a man, conceived both as a personal relationship and as an institution, primarily such that any children resulting from the union are—and are understood by society to be—emotionally, morally, practically, and legally affiliated with both of the parents." He discusses at length each of the elements of this definition.

35. Ibid., 97.

36. Ibid.

37. Ibid., 98.

38. Ibid. While Blankenhorn uses these words to explain what happens when the institution of marriage is opposed, they are appropriate to all social institutions.

39. Ibid., 168.

40. Ibid., 168–169.

41. See Dallas Willard, *The Divine Conspiracy* (San Francisco: Harper, 1998).

42. I have sought to rekindle the memory of the earliest martyrs by marketing a line of shirts and hats that capture the nine Greek words they created by which to call themselves. Each begins with the name of God in Greek (*theos*),such as "God's Runner," "Taught by God," "Loved by God," "God bearing," "God fearing," "Blessed by God," "God's Ambassador," etc. Polycarp was "Loved by God" (see them all at Thetathreads.com).

43. See my fuller discussion of reconciliation in my paper, "Reconciliation and Wrath Reconsidered in Light of Their Reconstruction in *The Shack* and Emergent Fiction; with Implications for the Metaphors of the Death of Christ and for the New Perspectives on Paul," a paper presented to the Evangelical Theological Society, New Orleans, LA, November 18, 2009.

44. These terms mean to free (Heb. 2:15) or release (Luke 12:58; Acts 19:12); exchange (Rom. 1:25, 26); alter (Acts 6:14; Gal. 4:20; Heb. 1:12; Rom. 1:23; 1 Cor. 15:51f.); and ransom money (Mark 8:37; Matt. 16:26). All of the terms derive from the root, *allasso* meaning to change or alter.

45. There are a few instances of people seeking reconciliation with God (in 2 Macc. 1:5; 7:33; 8:29). These references use only the word *katallasso*.

46. Morris, *Preaching*, 180.
47. Ibid., 224. See pages 219–225. See similar discussions in Gordon R. Lewis and Bruce A. Demarest, *Integrative Theology* (Grand Rapids: Zondervan, 1994), 3:154; and I. Howard Marshall, "The Meaning of Reconciliation," *Unity and Diversity in New Testament Theology*, ed. Robert A. Guelich (Grand Rapids, MI: Eerdmans, 1978), 123.
48. See Benjamin B. Warfield, "Atonement," *The New Schaff-Herzog Encyclopedia of Religious Knowledge* (New York: Funk & Wagnalls, 1908), 1:354.
49. How can it be that believers are loved from the foundation of the world and yet be objects of God's anger till they believe? John Calvin, *Institutes of the Christian Religion*, trans. Henry Beveridge (Grand Rapids, MI: Eerdmans, rep. 1970), 1:437, helps us to understand by citing Augustine who, after citing Romans 5:8, writes in part: "Accordingly, in a manner wondrous and divine, he loved even when he hated us. For he hated us when we were such as he had not made us, and yet because our iniquity had not destroyed his work in every respect, he knew in regard to each one of us, both to hate what we had made, and love what he had made."
50. George Eldon Ladd, *A Theology of the New Testament*, rev. by Donald A. Hagner (Grand Rapids, MI: Eerdmans, 1974), 493.
51. Marshall, "Reconciliation," 130.
52. Morris, *Preaching*, 224.
53. Ladd, *Theology*, 495–496. Morris, *Preaching*, 225–228, 230, speaks of this objective and subjective distinction.
54. Morris, *Preaching*, 212.
55. D. A. Carson, *The Difficult Doctrine of the Love of God* (Wheaton, IL: Crossway, 2000), 67. He points out that in Scripture God can direct both his love and his wrath at the same people at the same time. "God in his perfections must be wrathful toward his rebel image-bearers . . . God in his perfections must be loving toward his rebel image-bearers, for he is that kind of God" (69). In this work Carson identifies five kinds of God's love: for the world providentially, and savingly, for the elect, within the Trinity, and for believers (conditioned by obedience). God both loves the people of the world (John 3:16) and yet has wrath toward them because they reject His son (see John 16–17).
56. See the discussion in John F. Walvoord, "Reconciliation," *Bibliotheca Sacra* 120, no. 477 (January–March 1963), 10.
57. See the NET translation. The differing translations result from taking "all the fullness" as the subject or as the object of the verb. Either is possible since the neuter form is identical in the nominative and accusative cases.
58. Marshall, "Reconciliation," 126; Buchsel, "*allasso*," *TDNT* 1:259, opposes finding the reconciliation of cosmic forces here, citing the terms, "having made peace" and arguing that the meaning of reconcile in v. 20

and v. 22 must be the same. Yet the use of "all" throughout 1:15–20 must be the same: as God in Christ created all so he has reconciled all. See the extensive work in H.-G. Link and C. Brown, "Reconciliation, Restoration, Propitiation, Atonement," *The New International Dictionary of New Testament Theology* (Grand Rapids, MI: Zondervan, 1978), 3:145–176. Their bibliography lists over 130 English, German, and French sources dealing with these terms.

59. See David E. Garland, *The NIV Application Commentary: Colossians and Philemon* (Grand Rapids, MI: Zondervan, 1998), 94; and other commentaries on Colossians by P. O'Brien, M. Harris, F. F. Bruce, M. Thompson (see her discussion on the identity of the hostile forces), Bratcher and Nida, Lightfoot, and others.

60. Ralph P. Martin, "Reconciliation and Unity in Ephesians," *Review and Expositor* 93 (1996) 232.

61. Victor Paul Furnish, "The Ministry of Reconciliation," *Currents in Theology and Mission* 4, no. 4 (August 1977), 217.

62. Walvoord, "Reconciliation," 11.

63. William Hendriksen, *New Testament Commentary: Exposition of Colossians and Philemon* (Grand Rapids, MI: Baker, 1964), 82.

64. Ladd, *Theology*, 497–498. He cites in support Barrett's commentary on Romans (102), Morris, *Apostolic Preaching*, 216, and Foerster in *TDNT* (2:415).

65. See Walvoord, "Reconciliation," 12, for an elaboration of these results; and Osadolor Imasogie, "Biblical Theology of Reconciliation," *Ogbomoso Journal of Theology* 3, no. d (1988): 8–9, who calls them "fruits."

66. Allan M. Parrent, "The Sermon on the Mount, International Politics, and a Theology of Reconciliation," *Sewanee Theological Review* 42, no. 2 (1999): 176–190, has an excellent essay on how Christians can be agents of reconciliation in politics, with the caution that they are not gods; they cannot "become the Reconciler" (188). Also helpful is Dale Aukerman, "The Biblical and Theological Basis of Reconciliation," *Brethren Life and Thought* 41, nos. 2–3 (Spring/Summer 1996): 10–18.

67. Klyne R. Snodgrass, "Reconciliation: God Being God with Special Reference to 2 Corinthians 5:11–6:4," *Covenant Quarterly* 60, no. 2 (May 2002): 11. See also W. Hulitt Gloer, "2 Corinthians 5:14–21," *Review and Expositor* 86 (1989): 398; Furnish, "Reconciliation," 213.

68. Marshall, "Reconciliation," 128.

69. Snodgrass, "Reconciliation," 15.

70. See the discussion in Margaret Thrall, "Salvation Proclaimed: V. 2 Corinthians 5:18–21: Reconciliation with God," *The Expository Times* 93, no. 8 (May, 1982): 228.

71. Marshall, "Reconciliation," 122.

72. See Peter O'Brien, "Col. 1:20 and the Reconciliation of All things," *Reformed Theological Review* 33 (1974): 45–53. See also commentaries on Colossians by Harris, O'Brien, Lightfoot, Bruce, Thompson, et al.

73. Marshall, "Reconciliation," 128.

74. Lewis and Demarest, *Theology*, 169.

75. Ibid., 170.

76. See the discussion in Thrall, "Salvation Proclaimed," 228–229.

77. Lewis and Demarest, *Theology*, 153.

78. Morris, *Preaching*, 246–249.

79. Lewis and Demarest, *Theology*, 156.

80. Ibid.

81. Gloer, "2 Corinthians 5:14–21," 400.

82. Some will think here of the Roman Catholic teaching of purgatory. Yet purgatory is never meant to correct unbelievers, to give them a second chance to go to heaven after they die, but to chastise believers.

83. See a fuller form of these answers on my web site, theshackreview.com.

84. As Timothy Keller, *The Reason for God: Unbelief in an Age of Skepticism* (New York: Dutton, 2008), notes, repentance and faith, the two essentials for becoming a Christian, must have both an individual and corporate aspect. After becoming a Christian one needs to "publicly identify with Christ by becoming part of the church" (235). Christians "should confirm and seal that personal commitment through public, communal action in baptism and becoming part of the church" (236).

85. This is from Lewis and Demarest, *Theology*, 498.

86. Ernest Cassara, *Universalism in America* (Boston: Beacon Press, 1971), 181–182.

87. David Robinson, *The Unitarians and the Universalists* (Westport, Conn.: Greenwood Press, 1947), 56, 58; Cassara, *Universalism*, 110.

88. Cassara, *Universalism*, 243.

89. Ibid., 257–258.

90. Not all advocates of universal reconciliation would embrace all of these statements, nor the exact wording that I have used. But many do.

n air of esteem hovers around Oprah Winfrey, growing her influence even in the spiritual realm.

But are her beliefs biblically sound?

two young women debate in this fascinating tale of friendship and faith by Josh McDowell and
e Sterrett. The characters are fictional. But as with many Oprah fans, the questions they grapple
with remain profoundly real—just like the consequences of misleading teachings.

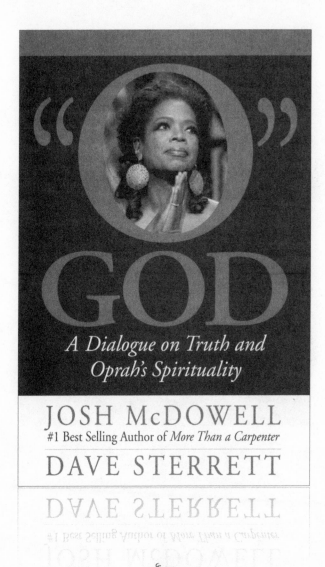

WND Books • A WorldNetDaily Company • Washington, DC • www.wndbooks.com

If there is no thirst for God, there will be no search for truth.

But bestselling author Ray Comfort excels at suggesting spiritual thirst—and how best to quench

With humor and grace, Comfort awakens serious soul-searching (even among those reject the
existence of the soul), and invites all to experience the everlasting refreshment of the Living Wa

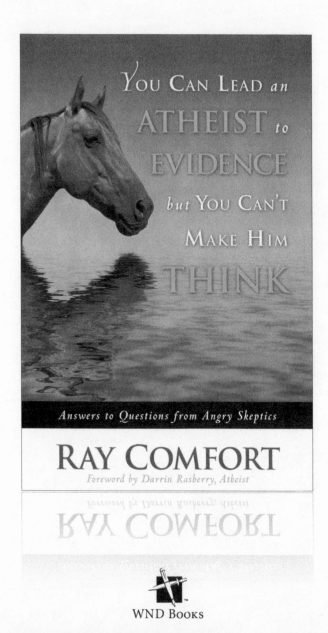

WND BOOKS

WND Books • A WorldNetDaily Company • Washington, DC • www.wndbooks.com

Not fit enough to survive.

That's what best-selling author Ray Comfort exposes after putting the evidence for evolution under the microscope.

If they dare to challenge their own hypothesis, even the most faithful of atheists will find the absent "missing link" a heavy cross to bear, and hunger for real Truth before meeting their Maker.

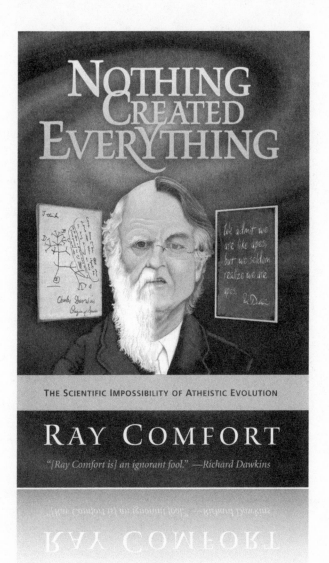

trigue cloaks the identity of the Antichrist, sparking copious interpretations of the prophecies —and some consensus.

Richardson shatters that consensus by illustrating a connection between the Biblical Antichrist and a mysterious Islamic messiah figure called the Mahdi.

ismatic, deceptive and rising up in the promise of peace, myriad eerie similarities exist between Christian end-time prophesy and Islamic expectations of world domination.

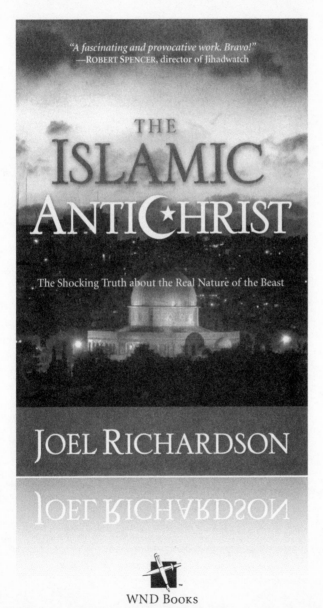

"*A fascinating and provocative work. Bravo!*"
—ROBERT SPENCER, director of Jihadwatch

THE

ISLAMIC
ANTI☾CHRIST

The Shocking Truth about the Real Nature of the Beast

JOEL RICHARDSON

WND BOOKS

WND Books • A WorldNetDaily Company • Washington, DC • www.wndbooks.com

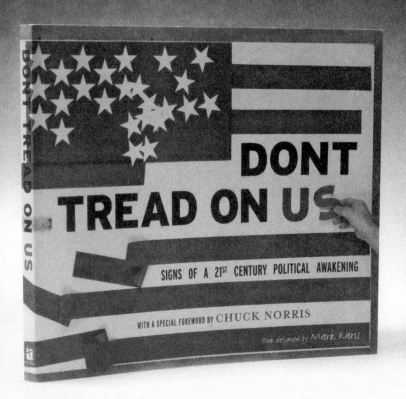

They come from the fields, and towns, and cities.

Sophisticates and the common.

They come to the power centers, exactly like their ancestors two centuries ago.

When American intuition tells the citizens that government by the people for the people is being threatened... they come to make their voices heard!

In this tribute to that spirit of America, *Don't Tread on US!* offers a pictorial record e new tea parties and their participants: classic signs that communicate most effectively with our brethren all across the land who oppose what's going on in Washington today. With a radical health-care agenda being marched across open territory, se citizens — tens of millions of them — are rallying, and will make their voices heard.

The colonial heart still beats today, and the people have spoken: ***Don't Tread on US!***

WND Books

WND Books • A WorldNetDaily Company • Washington, DC • www.DontTreadOnUS.com